THE MIND OF BUGANDA

The Mind of Buganda

DOCUMENTS OF THE MODERN HISTORY
OF AN AFRICAN KINGDOM

D. A. LOW
Professor of History
School of African and Asian Studies
University of Sussex

HEINEMANN
LONDON IBADAN NAIROBI

Heinemann Educational Books Ltd
48 Charles Street, London WIX 8AH
PMB 5205 Ibadan · POB 25080 Nairobi
EDINBURGH   MELBOURNE   TORONTO
NEW DELHI   AUCKLAND   HONG KONG   SINGAPORE

ISBN 0 435 32545 0 (cased)
ISBN 0 435 32546 9 (limp)

Set in Monotype Fournier
and printed by Cox & Wyman Ltd,
London, Fakenham and Reading

For
Penny, Babirye,
and Adam, Kato

CONTENTS

PREFACE

The purpose of this book is to make readily available a series of documents relating to the history of the kingdom of Buganda from just after the middle of the nineteenth to just after the middle of the twentieth century. Like any such collection it is highly selective: inevitably, indeed, idiosyncratic; the choice is ultimately one person's own. It is still, moreover, early days in the study of East African history, so that any such collection is heavily dependent upon what happens so far to have come to light. In due course the present emphases in the available material may well be changed; and, as perspectives lengthen, it may be expected that there will be substantial changes of view. I hope, however, that the present collection may serve to indicate the sharpness and sophistication of one very substantial African political tradition. It would be possible to discourse upon its nature and its content at some length. It has seemed best, however, to let it express itself for the most part in its own words.

The final selection has been made from a somewhat larger collection of items which were originally picked out either because they appeared to have some intrinsic interest to them, or because they seemed to have been of some seminal importance. It was only when this larger collection had been put together that the themes running through them, which are discussed in the Introduction which follows and which now dominate this book, came to be sharply apparent.

Quiller-Couch used to say 'Murder your darlings'. For the most part his advice has been heeded. But not unequivocally so. Some documents which are somewhat incidental to the main themes which have emerged are nevertheless included, either because they seem to be of some considerable general importance, or because they help to block out the arenas within which the main themes operated. Thus there is published here – for the first time – Sir Philip Mitchell's memorandum on the administration of Buganda of 1939. [No. 35] Until 1969 this was a quite secret document: in the Entebbe Secretariat there were numbered copies of it. It was patently, however, a key document affecting Buganda's political history over a period of twenty years, and ought now to be more widely known than it is.

It is about some of the items which have not been reproduced here that rather more than one word of explanation is perhaps warranted. If Mitchell's Memorandum is included, it may seem perverse not to print the whole of the vital Uganda Agreement of 1900 as well – only extracts appear here – or, for that matter, the Buganda Agreement of 1955. The 1900 Agreement has, however, been reprinted on several occasions already,*

* e.g. D. A. Low and R. C. Pratt, *Buganda and British Overrule* London, 1960, Appendix II.

and to most of those interested its full text should be readily available. To have included the text of the 1955 Agreement would quickly have burst the seams of this volume – and to no particularly good purpose either: the other documents from the 1950s both seem more pertinent and more digestible.

There are a number of items that might have been culled from the books of such early European visitors as Speke or Stanley, or from the books about the missionary Mackay. There are several items, moreover, in Dame Margery Perham's and Mrs Mary Bull's edition of *The Diaries of Lord Lugard*, Vols 1–3, London 1959, which might have figured here. But since all these volumes are fairly readily available, it seemed superfluous to seek to reprint items from them here.

More importantly next to nothing has been included from the increasing number of biographies and autobiographies of prominent Baganda that are becoming available. These are a great mine of information, and it is to be hoped that where they are still only available in manuscript or typescript they may yet be published in a more durable form; and that where they lend themselves to annotated editions, these may soon be forthcoming as well. Given, however, that for the purposes of this book there were plenty of shorter items to choose from, there did not seem much point in picking out extracts from these longer works in what could only have been in a very random way.

One further principle of exclusion has operated – for the most part at all events. It would be possible to put together an intriguing volume of the 'I Was There' variety. During the past century Buganda has attracted a succession of notable foreign visitors with sharp eyes and ready pens – from Speke and Stanley in the 1860s and 1870s, to Winston Churchill in 1907, and the two Huxleys, Julian in the 1920s, and Elspeth in the 1940s. There was also in the 1920s the American visitor Buell; and more recently a host of others. But to have put together impressions from their writings would have meant compiling an altogether different book.

Yet to have eschewed visitors' accounts altogether would have meant omitting the Reverend E. C. Gordon's contemporaneous account of the revolutions of 1888; the nub of that has been included here not only because there seems to be nothing quite like it on those vital events, but because it reports deeds which relate to the words with which this book is mainly concerned. To have excluded others has sometimes been very difficult indeed. There are, for example, those remarkably perceptive letters from Sir Douglas Newbold, Civil Secretary (i.e. the senior British political officer) in the Sudan, who visited Uganda immediately prior to the torrent of events which overtook it from the end of the Second World War onwards.

'The general impression [he wrote to J. W. Robertson on 23 June

1944] that I've formed so far admittedly from very cursory observation in a week – about Uganda – is that it's a nice orderly, green Happy Valley with no political or racial or economic problems commensurate with Kenya, Palestine, Sudan, etc., but that this "smoothness" tho' fortunate, is itself a danger as it leads to "ticking over", and vague purposeless benevolence ... "What I most missed was a sense of urgency. I had a feeling that the British were quietly ambling along, very just, very humane, very patient – when they ought to have been impatient and in the dickens of a hurry." There seems no sense of urgency here, re economic or political advance, and I think rural local government is backward (probably again due to native kingdom treaties).'*

And so on. To obey Quiller-Couch when confronted by this kind of passage has been hard indeed.

The headlines designating each item constitute an editorial gloss. The italicized descriptions specify each item as precisely as possible. Whenever it has seemed necessary to give details about the whereabouts of the original, full references have been appended. On several items some unavoidable explanatory notes have been added as well.

I have many debts. Professor Terence Ranger, Professor Allan Ogot and Mr John Nottingham originally prompted the project. Mrs Kate Springford, Mr R. A. Snoxall, Professor W. H. Whiteley, Dr Phares Mutibwa, the Reverend F. B. Welbourn, Mr F. K. Kamoga, Mr S. B. K. Musoke, Mr J. Kabango and Professor Lloyd Fallers have all most generously helped me to secure the translations which were needed. The Reverend F. B. Welbourn, Professor Geoffrey Engholm, Dr Fay Carter, Mr Brian Bowles, Mr Donald Simpson, Mr Essop Pahad, Mrs Anne King, Dr Michael Twaddle, Dr Kenneth King, Professor Crawford Young, Dr Ian Hancock, Professor Lloyd Fallers, Professor David Apter, Mr E. M. K. Mulira, and Dr Phares Mutibwa have all been extremely kind in helping me to procure the texts of one or more of the documents reprinted here. Jenny Connell helped me track down and check a considerable number of items. Yvonne Wood nobly turned a host of varied items into one single format, checked a great many, and kept order where disorder would have reigned. I am also indebted to Dr Audrey Richards. And, of course, to a great many Baganda – to five in particular who taught me more than they will recall: Amos Sempa, Paulo Kavuma, Eridadi Mulira, Samson Sekabanja, Apolo Kironde. To Nalongo my debts are legion.

I have to thank as well, for permission to reproduce items of which they hold the copyright: Her Majesty's Stationery Office, *The Uganda Journal,*

* K. D. D. Henderson, *The Making of the Modern Sudan, The Life and Letters of Sir Douglas Newbold*, London 1953, p. 380. Robertson was later Sir James Robertson, Civil Secretary of the Sudan and Governor-General of Nigeria.

the *Uganda Argus*, *The People*, Geoffrey Chapman Ltd., SCM Press, The Fabian Bureau, the *Morning Star*, Messrs. Frank Cass, Mouton and Co., and Professor P. C. W. Gutkind.

D. A. Low

INTRODUCTION

The documents which form the core of this book relate to the history of one East African kingdom during a period of over a century. A good deal has already been written about the history of the kingdom of Buganda during the past century or so.* More, however, can be expected since the material available upon it is unusually rich, and the themes and episodes in it which are still awaiting inquiry already look to have a wider significance than might appear at first sight. This book can only be concerned with some of them.

It is to be hoped that the documents it reproduces will very largely speak for themselves. It may be of some assistance, however, if a word or two is said about the circumstances to which they relate, and if suggestions are made about the themes which they appear to express.

In the mid-nineteenth century Buganda was one of forty or fifty kingdoms of greater or lesser size which stretched from the southern shore of Lake Kyoga in the north, westwards to the eastern shore of Lake Albert, and then southwards across the Equator, and down through the gap between Lake Victoria and Lakes Edward and George to the northernmost tip of Lake Tanganyika. Along with Rwanda to the south, it was now one of the most substantial of these.

For our present purposes four features of its history up till the middle of the nineteenth century need to be emphasized. First by contrast with most other such kingdoms in Bantu-speaking Africa – but along with several of its neighbours – its history stretched back largely unbroken for four hundred years and more. By the nineteenth century, there was, that is, a very substantial depth to its continuous historical experience. For the present it is well-nigh impossible to adduce detailed evidence of the way in which the political and cultural wisdom which it accumulated over this period took the shape which it did; but that by the nineteenth century there existed a notable substance and precision at its core, the evidence of this book will, it is suggested, fully demonstrate. Filtered through some twenty generations' of experience it had largely freed itself of the dross which seems to be the inevitable accompaniment of a political ideology in the first stages of creation. In its well-tempered forms its gleam was patent for all to see.

In the second place, a key feature of Buganda's historical experience over these earlier centuries seems to have been that whereas it almost certainly began as a small kingdom which was much overshadowed by its neighbours, it only grew to its later size and substance by successfully

* See the bibliographies in the *Oxford History of East Africa*, Vols. I–III. 1963.

overcoming a great many odds, including more especially its initially very much more considerable neighbour Bunyoro-Kitara. It may be mere coincidence that the frame of mind displayed in the documents which follow seems to relate to the dualism inherent in this process. It bears all the marks, however, of having been fashioned in the double-sided experience of a striving for a larger future at a period when the continued independent existence of the kingdom was by no means assured. The dualism, moreover, displayed in the approaches to the problems of seeking to remain uppermost during the century covered by the documents reproduced in this book seems to be in essence a direct continuation upon this.

Then thirdly, it seems clear that by the nineteenth century the kingdom of Buganda was dominated to a marked degree by its ruler, the Kabaka, and his immediate entourage. This has been most extensively revealed in, and explained by, some structural analyses of the polity of Buganda at this time, and for all the qualifications that might well be made in any more detailed account, the dominance of the kingdom by the Kabaka and his court looks to have been both conspicuous and extensive. Certainly the Kabaka figures very prominently in the pages which follow. Fourthly, attention needs to be drawn to the fact that while the territorial chiefs in Buganda had by the nineteenth century almost all become direct appointees of the Kabaka, all Baganda were at the same time members of one or other of its dispersed totemic clans. In their various echelons, these had their own clan heads under the Kabaka. Associated with this double linkage in the authority system of the country were under-currents of opposition to appointed chiefs.

By the opening of the nineteenth century scarcely a hint had reached Buganda of the wider worlds of Asia, Europe and America, or even, for that matter, of much of the rest of Africa. Accordingly the most extensive experience to which the documents presented here relate was the sudden, tumultuous, experience of the encounter with the vast new world outside. It is at this point that the string of considerations we have considered above need to be linked together. For it was in facing the new and very profound forces which now pressed upon it from outside that Buganda brought to bear a mind that had been fashioned not only over several centuries of time, but in a very particular historical experience – that of a small kingdom growing against the odds: and that on the one hand obtained much of its leadership from its ruler, the Kabaka, and found as well its internal cleavages being profoundly affected. This mind, it may be emphasized, was not simply fashioned in response to the alien visitations when they came. It seems to have predated them, as it has certainly outlived their most serious original manifestations (as the last few documents in this book will serve to demonstrate). There was a continuity here which we must explore in more detail in a moment. For the present the point to stress is that it was with an outlook already much elaborated that Buganda came to face the explosive experiences of the past century or so. It is that mind, in encounter with novel forces, which this volume primarily seeks to reveal.

It should be made clear that it is not the mind *of the Baganda* which is set forth here. That is a very much larger task which has already been intriguingly essayed by others. It is *the mind of Buganda* – Buganda the polity – which it is hoped to reveal here. This has been primarily expressed (naturally enough one may say) by those Baganda who have been concerned with its politics, external as well as internal. It must be immediately emphasized, however, that for all that may be true elsewhere, politics in Buganda have not often been politics for politics' sake alone. Despite such appearances as they may periodically have presented politics in Buganda have regularly been concerned as well with what one can only term the cultural destiny of Baganda society. The concern of Buganda's most important figures for the cultural destiny no less than the immediate political future of their society is central to what is here termed 'the mind of Buganda'.

The term is, of course, only used metaphorically. There is no thought of reification, or of any systematic exposition of the political philosophy of Buganda's leaders. The central purpose is at once more modest and more ambitious. The extracts which follow are designed to be illustrative rather than explicatory; but in order that the reader may gain some insight of his own into the attitudes of mind which the Baganda have displayed on issues of major importance to them, the views of some of their leading figures are presented in words of their own. Whether it is possible to discern persistencies and consistencies here which indicate the presence of a sophisticated tradition of political response the reader must judge for himself from the documents which follow. Some suggestions about this are nevertheless offered below. We may affirm, however, that what is meant here by the mind of Buganda has first and foremost the sense we give to that word when we say that a man has a mind of his own, has revealed his mind, or has spoken his mind. Amid the plethora of writing about the African past, there is now a clamant need for some people from it to give expression to these things themselves.

The first contacts which Buganda had with the outside world came with the arrival of the first 'Arab' traders from Zanzibar in the late 1840s. Though their activities were always carefully controlled, they were not denied entrance, and over the next half century they developed a flourishing trading connection with Buganda. They even saw considerable numbers of the Kabaka's courtiers (for a decade and more with his full concurrence) adopting their religion, Islam. The first Europeans, Speke and Grant, came in 1862. They were not, however, followed until the 1870s by any others. But several Europeans then came from the north, and the explorer H. M. Stanley and his party from the south. These visits were marked *inter alia* by earnest questionings by the Kabaka about the conceptions which these aliens possessed of the place of man in society and of man in the universe. [1, 2]*

When this second series of European visitors was followed in 1877 and 1879 by European Christian missionaries, some of them Anglicans and some of them Roman Catholics, who came to stay, some of the young men about the Kabaka's court soon began to take to Christianity as others before them had taken to Islam. [4] The Kabaka, Mutesa I, periodically expressed a keen interest in the missionaries teaching. He was worried, however, lest its adoption should undermine the political economy of his court. [5]

During the 1870s and 1880s, he was concerned as well with the threat which the Egyptian penetration up the Nile represented to his kingdom. He hoped to turn this to his own advantage *vis-à-vis* the neighbouring kingdom of Bunyoro, or at all events to blunt its edge, by appealing to the religious ideology of the European, Colonel Gordon, who stood at its head. [3] Bankruptcy in Egypt, however, and the outbreak of the Mahdiya in the Sudan brought this threat to an end before anything seriously untoward had eventuated.

It was soon followed, from the mid 1880s onwards, by the very much greater threat of the advance from the east of both British and German imperialists. In 1884 Kabaka Mutesa I died to be succeeded by his young son, Mwanga. In the two or three years that followed Mwanga, uncertain of his position *vis-à-vis* the threats piled upon him both from abroad, and now as it happened from at home as well, ordered the murder of the Anglican Bishop Hannington, and sent a number of young Christians at his court to death at the stake. So strong, however, had their attachment to their new religion become that numbers of them resolutely refused to recant. [6] In 1888 when Mwanga threatened to put to death those who survived, they, with some of the Muslims at court, joined hands to eject him from his throne, and effect both an oligarchical and a 'religious' revolution. [7]

Thereupon the situation in Buganda became quite unbelievably complex. Muslims began to fight Christians, and in due course Protestants fought Catholics. At the same time the first British imperialist agents advanced towards Buganda. Kabaka Mwanga (who, astonishingly enough, had succeeded in manoeuvring himself back on to his throne) did not attempt – as he had with Bishop Hannington – to exclude them from his kingdom altogether. He showed himself keenly anxious, however, that they should only come as visitors. [8, 9] The leader of the Protestants in his kingdom was on the other hand much less concerned about this, though he was scarcely less circumspect in his dealings with them. He was much more concerned to establish the dominance of Protestantism, the Protestant ethos, and the Protestant faction in Buganda, and towards these

* The numbers in square brackets refer to the numbers under which the documents which follow appear in this book.

The First European Visitors: Speke and Grant being received by Mutesa I,
Kabaka of Buganda, 1862

Uganda's Independence Day 1962. Kabaka Mutesa II and the Duke and
Duchess of Kent. The Prime Minister of Uganda, The Hon. Milton Obote,
is on the left below the dais.

*Oligarchs of the 1900's: Sir Apolo Kagwa, Yakobo Musajjalumbwa and
Prince Mbogo.*

Daudi Chwa, Kabaka of Buganda, 1897-1939.

The Political Crisis of the 1950's

Sir Andrew Cohen, Governor of Uganda 1952-1957, addressing the Lukiko of Buganda.

Sir Andrew Cohen addressing the Legislative Council of Uganda.

ends was anxious to secure favourable external assistance. [9] Two years of grievous uncertainty, and some open conflict, resulted. In the end, however, the British established their political predominance over the Kabaka, and the Protestants secured the chief place in Buganda. [10] This settlement was more than once ratified in the years that immediately followed, [11] and on the side of Buganda's now victorious Protestant leaders it expressed itself in some effusive expressions of friendship for the British, more especially perhaps to the key figure Captain Lugard. [12] There was even so, beginning in 1897, an open mutiny of the Sudanese troops, whom the British employed as mercenaries, which became linked with a revolt of Kabaka Mwanga himself against the Christian and oligarchical revolution which the British presence was now buttressing in the country.

Both uprisings, however, were repressed; and in the aftermath the Baganda leaders entered into a crucial set of negotiations with a British 'Special Commissioner', [13] which eventually resulted in the very substantial Uganda Agreement of 1900. [14] This not only governed relations between Britain and Buganda for the next fifty-five years. It set forth new developments in the internal political structure of Buganda itself.

So satisfactory did these arrangements prove to be for the British to begin with that it soon began to be their fixed policy to develop the now very much more extensive Uganda Protectorate, of which Buganda only constituted the core, 'through the native governments'. [15, 23] Here the contrast with developments in the adjacent British East Africa Protectorate – the later Kenya – were explicit and substantial. By the second decade of the twentieth century the 1900 Agreement turned out, however, from the British point of view – because its *ipsissima verba* were held to so vehemently by the Baganda leaders as the charter of their special position within the British Empire – to be inadequately flexible, with the result that developments in governmental activity which were not covered by the terms of the Agreement tended to be conducted by the British administration without reference to the Buganda Government. [18]

There were five matters now at issue. First, attempts by the Christian oligarchy that had come to power in the 1880s and 1890s to entrench their position – in 1912 by proposing the addition of an aristocratic chamber to the chiefly Lukiko, Buganda's Parliament [16] – won decreasing sympathy from the British administration, [17] and eventually culminated in a fateful clash between the British and Sir Apolo Kagwa, throughout this time the foremost of the Christian oligarchs. This not only led to his resignation in 1926: it marked the passing of the oligarchical generation of the 1890s. [25]

Secondly, and to some degree in association with this, there was considerable political activity, more particularly after the end of the First World War, by small but influential groups of young mission-school-educated men of the next generation – more especially in the singularly interesting though short-lived Young Baganda Association. [20] Following Kagwa's resignation many of those who had been involved in this found their way into the chiefly bureaucracy in association with some who had been Kagwa's closest associates. A new oligarchical generation was thus installed in power. Some of those who found themselves excluded from this resettlement tried their hands at fashioning a non-oligarchical constitution for Buganda, but in the immediate event were quite unsuccessful in having it adopted. [27, 29]

As a result there was a failure here to establish an effectual nexus between the governing élite in Buganda and the other elements in its society who were now increasingly aggrieved with its progress. Here was the third theme. In the 1920s, there was much ado about the necessity to revise the land settlement embodied in the 1900 Agreement and in particular to return the clan burial grounds to the clan leaders. [24] This had little result. There was, however, one step forward upon this front in the passing of a rent restriction act, the Busulu and Nvujo Law of 1928. In due course this freed most land-occupying tenants from economic exploitation by chiefly landowners and by those who had inherited or bought land from them. But other problems remained, and over the possibility of serious alienation of land, an undercurrent of concern steadily gathered force. [36]

Fourthly, from 1922 to 1932 there was continuing concern in Buganda at a whole series of British initiatives towards the creation of an East African Federation. To Buganda's leaders this could only mean their subjection to the domiciled European settler community in Kenya. They argued that there was – and should continue to be – a world of difference between Kenya and Uganda. They pointed to the sacrosanctity of their 1900 Agreement. They asserted their claim to be accorded the status and privileges of a long-established African kingdom. And they propounded their faith in the mix of Christianity and Civilization which they and their forefathers had first imbibed before the turn of the century. Mwanga's successor, Kabaka Daudi Chwa, led Buganda's campaign against Federation. [26] It was given brilliant expression by the foremost of the new generation of chiefs, Serwano Kulubya, before the British Parliament' Joint Select Committee on Closer Union in East Africa in 1931. [29] Eventually their efforts, coupled with those of a liberal lobby in Britain, and of Sir Donald Cameron, the Governor of Tanganyika, successfully destroyed the Federation idea, at least for the time being.

Finally, there was continuing debate throughout this time over the place of the Asian immigrants in the country. [21] The attitude towards them was not always hostile. [19, 30, 32] It fluctuated in ways which we shall see later on to have been typical. In the end, however, it steadily hardened, [39] and by the 1950s was becoming very uncompromising indeed. [51]

During the 1930s there was concern about educational progress, [30] and, as before, over the further intentions in Buganda of the British colonial administration. [22, 28, 33, 34] There was on the one hand, in the relative calm which prevailed at this time, an explicit formulation in 1935 by Kabaka Daudi Chwa himself of the mind of Buganda in its various reaches which emerges as the quintessential document of this book. [33] It was followed on the other by tension, not to say conflict, between Kabaka Daudi Chwa and the British administration [for an earlier example see 22]. By 1939 the Governor, Sir Philip Mitchell, had compiled a secret *aide-mémoire* setting out in a notably authoritative manner the lines along which the British administration was to conduct its relations with Buganda. [35] At the same time, however, he formulated the doctrine, which, to the delight of many Baganda, his successor was to pronounce as official in 1944, by the terms of which Buganda was to be treated much more formally as a quasi-autonomous 'native state'. [37]

It had already proved to be economically a very fortunate one. Back in the 1900s cotton had turned out to be an unusually viable crop in Buganda conditions. The soil had the right nutrients. There was land to spare on which to grow it, and under chiefly direction the Baganda peasantry took to cotton growing for the world market upon a considerable scale (later they added coffee). Cotton production reached its peak in 1939.

Even so, by the 1940s there was political unrest in Buganda. It first came to the surface over the marriage of a commoner to the widow of Daudi Chwa, who had died in 1939. It expressed itself in a complex upheaval at the premier protestant secondary school, King's College, Budo, in 1942. By 1945 it had become substantial. There was a serious conjunction of acute intra-chiefly factionalism; considerable generational conflict amongst the élite; renewed clan-head agitation; and substantial economic discontent amongst the peasantry. All this now erupted in riots. There were more in 1949. In the years which intervened so much seemed at odds that issues seemed to tumble over each other in quite bewildering profusion. [36, 38, 45] There were renewed worries about the possibility – in the creation of the East African High Commission – of an imposed, and European settler dominated, East African Federation. [40] There was great discontent at the manner in which the cotton crop was being handled once the African grower had grown it and picked it; [41] the price paid to him seemed quite inadequate, and the grip of Asian entrepreneurs upon its processing and marketing was now deeply resented. At the same time there was rising animosity towards the chiefs in power, [36, 40] and a growing demand for the democratization of Buganda's political assembly the Lukiko. All this was vented in a petition to the new Kabaka, the young Mutesa II, at the height of the riots in 1949. [42] Some measure of the extent to which the times were by then out of joint is provided by the pugnacity of the terms in which the spokesman of the most alienated sections,

Semukula Mulumba, couched his telegrams to all and sundry, not least when placed alongside the British administration's promulgation at this time of a 'Red scare'. [43]

Troops were called out, and the rioting was curbed. [44] When Sir Andrew Cohen came out from the Colonial Office in London as Governor of Uganda in 1952 he set to work to mend the fences. The processing of the cotton, and coffee, crops was not nationalized as it was rumoured it might be, but steps were taken to institute a policy by which it should pass into the hands of African co-operatives. Steps were also taken towards the democratization of the Lukiko. [46]

Two developments, however, muddied the waters. A serious contretemps erupted in 1953 when a British Colonial Secretary in London appeared to suggest, in a much-publicized speech, that consideration might be given yet again to the creation of an East African Federation. Since there were all too many signs that the entrenchment of domiciled European predominance all over East Africa – including even over Uganda and Buganda at its core – was still a lively possibility, the slightest further hint of a move towards East African Federation was enough to set off a larger crisis.

This, in any event, was in the making, for Cohen was already looking ahead towards self-government for Uganda. He was convinced that even while due deference must be paid to the particularities of Buganda and its immediately neighbouring kingdoms, Uganda as a whole, which spread substantially beyond these, was still too small to be anything but a unitary state. With a view to steering things in this direction he set about reforming the Uganda Legislative Council, so as to make it very much more of an African forum – indeed the central, and centralizing African forum for the whole country. Some Baganda saw opportunity here. Many others, however, sensed a threat to the quasi-autonomy which Buganda had wrestled hard to secure, and, at worst, the submergence of their centuries-old kingdom in an otherwise largely undifferentiated Uganda. True to part at all events of his hereditary responsibilities, these concerns were translated into counter-proposals by Kabaka Mutesa II. Amid the furore over the 1953 Federation scare he pressed his own solutions very vehemently upon the Governor; and when in the end he pressed them uncompromisingly, Cohen took the fateful decision to deport him to London, and withdraw recognition from him as 'Native Ruler of the Kingdom of Buganda' under the terms of the Uganda Agreement of 1900. [47]

It was a traumatic moment. A committee of Baganda elected by the Lukiko met under an independent chairman, Professor Sir Keith Hancock, to try to sort out the problems. [48] They reached agreement with the Governor on a settlement which, while opening the way for Mutesa II's restoration, gave promise of some substantial security for Buganda's quasi-autonomy, while providing as well for its participation in the central institutions of Uganda. At the same time they finally put paid to the possibility, not just of a European-dominated Federation in East Africa, but of domiciled European and Asian pre-eminence in Uganda. [49]

Henceforward there were no issues of substance between the British and Buganda. Nationalist political parties were formed, but in Baganda hands they were rather tepid affairs. [50] There was some radical-young-man feeling, but against the traditional forces in Buganda rather than the British; [53] and in 1958–9 the long-standing anti-Asian feeling reached its climax with a highly successful boycott of Asian traders. [55]

But the main issue which now prevailed concerned Buganda's relations with its non-Buganda neighbours within the larger aggregation that was the country of Uganda. Here fear predominated. Fear that Buganda would in the end be totally submerged beneath a union of its more numerous neighbours. Fear that some of the new generation of self-styled nationalist politicians would be faithless to the integrity of the Buganda polity – a question which came to be symbolized as a matter of loyalty to the throne. Various ingredients sprang to the surface: the frustration of the *soi-disant* nationalist élite; the longstanding opposition to élitism, which now looked to the throne to be the bulwark against the machinations of 'disloyal' new politicians; the rallying to the throne of many of those in the suspect category who, with the Kabaka himself, were fearful of Buganda's future in a self-governing Uganda; the articulate opposition of leading Roman Catholics in the country to the elevation of the loyalty issue to be the sole touchstone of solidarity, when from their point of view this seemed all too evidently a way of maintaining the unwarranted but long-standing Protestant ascendency in the country; and so on. 'When the fear lest Buganda would continue to enjoy its quasi-autonomy reached its peak, . . .' When the fear lest Buganda would continue to enjoy its quasi-autonomy reached its peak, the Lukiko in 1960 issued a declaration of independence. [52, 54, 55, 56, 58, 59]

It was very soon apparent, however, that it counted for nothing. So, most characteristically, the alternative tack was chosen. [57] *Kabaka Yekka*, the 'loyalist' party, made a *mariage de convenance* with its previous arch-opponent the non-Buganda Uganda Peoples Congress. Their alliance took effect in the coalition government which brought Uganda to independence in 1962. A year later it appeared to be sealed when Mutesa II (already well entrenched as Kabaka of Buganda) became President of Uganda, by which time leading politicians of the Buganda-first *Kabaka Yekka* party were beginning to talk openly of merging with the larger UPC. [60]

It did not prove so easy. Amid another plethora of asymmetrical conflicts President Mutesa and Prime Minister Obote quarrelled increasingly with each other. In February 1966 Obote suspended the Constitution and the President with it. Mutesa appealed to U Thant, the Secretary-General of the United Nations, to support him against what he saw as the autocratic intentions of Obote, [61] but in May 1966 found himself shot out from his palace, with most of his worst fears proved correct.

The aftermath ran true to type. Amongst forward-looking Baganda who were actively engaged with the detailed administration of the country there was little nostalgia; it was the new circumstances, not the old, which engaged their concern, [62] as their compatriot detractors had all along expected. It looked before long as if the kingdom was no more.

This all-too-cursory review must be filled out from the documents themselves. In two of them in particular Baganda themselves relate parts of this history in words of their own. [23, 45] What remains to be discussed are some of the patterns which they reveal.

The various 'British' documents serve to set the context within which the main drama was played out. [e.g. 7, 11, 15, 18, 35, 37, 46] That it constituted a drama, even a great drama, is difficult to gainsay. For the central point of extract after extract is of Buganda's leaders wrestling with the destiny of their kingdom – in the narrow sense in political terms, in the larger sense in cultural terms. Whether it be Mutesa I talking to Linant de Bellefonds, [2] or to the Anglican missionary O'Flaherty, [5] or writing through his amanuensis Dallington Mafutah to Colonel Gordon; [3] or his successor, Mwanga, or Apolo Kagwa, writing to the Europeans at Zanzibar; [9] or the Regents pleading with Johnston in 1900, [13] or Kagwa standing on his own defence in 1926 [25] – not to mention Daudi Chwa in 1935, [33] or the rioters in the next decade, [42] or Mutesa II in 1953, [47] or Bishop Kiwanuka in 1954, [48] or the Lukiko in 1960, [56] or Mutesa again in 1966: [61] on each occasion the central concern that is clearly expressed is for the destiny of Buganda as seen by its prime representatives. These men were no neophytes, but highly responsible political figures speaking in the language of a very long nurtured political and cultural tradition.

The vital fact is that it had two facets. It was not rigidly exclusionist, nor was it uncriticically absorptive. It rested on a fine, indeed fascinating, balance between a determination to hold to that which it already held, and a no less substantial determination not to forgo any creative opportunities that lay within its reach. One can see the agonizing over the precise balance to be reached – in Mutesa I's conversations with O'Flaherty in 1883, [5] or in Mutesa II's advice to the Lukiko in 1962, [57] among a great many others. [e.g. 55]

One can see as well that on occasions the balance was sharply tilted one way or the other. Mutesa speaking to Linant de Bellefonds in 1875, [2] or the Christians writing to Captain Lugard in the 1890s, [12] or the manifesto of the Progressive Party in 1956, [50] all express the persistence of the adventurous proclivities in the minds of the Baganda. On the other hand the Regents' letter to Johnston, [13] Daudi Chwa's letter about Federation, [26] the pamphlet *Buganda Nyafe*, [36] Mutesa II's letters to Sir Andrew Cohen, [47] the unilateral declaration of independence in 1960, [56] all express their defensive posture.

Sometimes both were vehemently expressed contemporaneously. The contrast between the adventurous emphasis in Apolo Kagwa's letter to Zanzibar in 1890 and the defensive emphasis in Mwanga's the very next day is dramatic. [9] This duality was replicated, however, three-quarters of a century later – witness the pamphlet *Buganda Nyafe* and Hamu Mukasa's letter, both dating from 1944–45; [36, 38] or the pamphlet of the *Kabaka Yekka* leaders about amalgamating with the UPC in 1963, [60] and the Kabaka's appeal to U Thant just three years later. [61]

It must be emphasized that this dualism was not institutionalized, in, for example, the distinctive beliefs of two different parties in Buganda. The very same people could at one time be vigorously adventurous, and at others vehemently defensive – see the differences between Kagwa's letters in the 1890s, [9, 12] and the letters he signed as a Regent in 1900, and in 1914, [13, 17] not to mention his fierce personal defence in 1926. [25] See also Bishop Kiwanuka's statement in 1954, and his Archiepiscopal Pastoral Letter of just seven years later. [48, 58] Equally, compare the *Kabaka Yekka* manifesto of 1962 and the pamphlet of 1963. [59, 60] And let us recall that the Mutesa II who in 1953 asked for the separation of Buganda from the rest of Uganda was to become the first President of Uganda a decade later. If, however, there was thus no consistency in the adherence to one side or the other of the balance – it was its very dualism indeed which proved to be its saving and its strength – it does look as if its two facets had by the end become very largely routinized.

Moreover, on occasion – somewhat rare occasion perhaps – both have been expressed by the same person, almost in the same breath, for example by Sir Apolo Kagwa to Gandhi's friend Charlie Andrews in 1919. [19] The two classic occasions which are presented here are first the evidence of Serwano Kulubya to the Joint Select Committee in 1931, and secondly Daudi Chwa's pamphlet of 1935. The first was a brilliant exposition of the mind of Buganda in all its totality upon a seminal occasion expressed with the utmost calmness and confidence and courtesy. [29] The second provides an invaluably pithy summation of the mind of Buganda, not least in the words of its title – *Education, Civilization and Foreignisation*. The text, and particularly the last paragraph, set out in simple form the conditional desire for the first two – Education and Civilization – and the hostility to the last – Foreignisation – in a way that expresses as no other statement has the 'mind of Buganda' in all its fullness. [33] Its poignancy is surpassed only by the recriminations of a despairing 'moderate', [55] and by the last document in this book, which in the quite new, and, some would think, disastrous circumstances that ensued upon President Obote's attack upon the palace of the Kabaka of Buganda in 1966, displays yet again the dual facets which seem so deeply etched in the mind of its leaders, generation by generation. [62] To adapt Clifford Geertz's terminology, politics in this society was a cultural tradition throughout.

This would seem very plain once the top layer of meaning is lifted from the documents which follow. The contrasts to be found in the letters of

Kagwa and of Mwanga in 1890 [9] and between the UPC pamphlet of 1963 [60] and Mutesa's appeal of 1966 are extraordinarily close, [61] as are the similarities of viewpoint both of the first items in each case and of the second. So often one hears the same note recurring. Hamu Mukasa in 1944 refers explicitly to Mutesa I, [38] but in his tones too. [1] Mutesa I's worries [5] in 1883 are little more than rephrased by his grandson in 1935. [33] Kagwa's line of protest in 1926 [25] is reiterated in 1954; [48] the Regents' caution in 1900 [13] similarly; [49] while Abu Mayanja in 1958 [53] seems very much a 'young Muganda' [20] of a generation later. There are good historical memories here. But a persistent political tradition as well.

How was it passed down? This is obviously a complex matter, too complicated for review here. Some suggestions, however, emerge from this quotation from the manuscript autobiography of Eridadi Mulira, the son of a minor chief in Buganda who himself became politically very active in the 1940s, which he has kindly allowed me to quote:

> After moving to Gayaza near Masaka father got many visitors and callers of all sorts, missionaries, clergy, chiefs, educated young men, etc., and all discussed with him the topics of the day. It might be whether there should be a cross in Namirembe Cathedral, or not; which was a better Cathedral Namirembe or Rubaga; should Europeans be allowed to lease land or not; the Malakite Sect; Sir Apollo Kagwa and the Abataka; the resignation of Stanislas Mugwanya; the Luganda orthography; Closer Union; Makerere College; whether students should go to Budo or not; the question of Akasanvu (forced labour). Sometimes they would be discussing personalities such as Sir Apollo Kagwa, Sekibobo (whom they regarded as the cleverest of the lot), Kate Mugema, Nasanairi Mukwenda; Semei Bene Lwakirenzi Kakungulu, Kulubya etc. These topics interested me immensely. I would sit there listening to them and wondering how they knew all these things, without realizing that in this way I was being initiated into politics.

There was, as this indicates, something of a hereditary political élite in Buganda. Its values, and its pragmatic wisdom, were passed down because, very literally, the younger generation sat at the feet of its elders when they discussed great matters of state. Sons would be present when their fathers entertained. More extensively young men who went to 'serve' – their 'apprenticeship' as an Englishman would put it – with the senior chiefs were introduced similarly to the ways of the politics of Buganda at its apex.

There were of course a great many outside their pale. Only infrequently were their voices recorded. There are echoes which date from the 1920s and 1930s. [24, 32, 34] By 1949, however, their sound is becoming clear, [36, 39, 42], while a decade later even the nuances are plain. [48, 54] The striking facts are, however, that here too there is a strong emphasis on protecting the integrity of the kingdom, together with an explicit concern to establish 'the proper foundation upon which you will build your nation. . .'. The suggestion, that is, is not that the nation is already established; a still greater future is eagerly sought for it. It is this combination which is so central to the thinking of Buganda's leaders. And it is striking that it should be present not just in documents emanating from the élite, but even in such an anti-élitist document as the Wankulukuku letter. This contains, moreover, it may be noted, as vivid an expression of the doctrine of 'the general will' as any but the most disillusioned Rousseauite could wish for.

There are, it is true, discontinuities in the pages which follow. One such was the Christian revolution, and it can be no coincidence that it expressed itself in some of the most passionate statements of belief which are to be found here. [6] Its effect upon individuals can be very directly imagined from the Acts of the Apostles quality of the account of the death of perhaps the greatest of the Christian converts, Canon Apolo Kivebulaya, [31] while its continuing influence upon the politics of Buganda can be gauged from Archbishop Kiwanuka's Pastoral Letter of 1961. [58]

Several other considerations remain. It is worth noting that the series of documents in which opinions are expressed about the position of the Asians in Buganda reveal a similar series of viewpoints to those which have appeared upon the other matters which have been presented here. There are favourable statements [32] and hostile ones; [21, 39] balancing statements [19] and conditional ones. [51] As a series they form a counterpoint to the others printed here and have been included accordingly.

Among the other documents, several relate to the history of the parliament of Buganda, the Lukiko. This was first given a fully institutionalized form by the 1900 Agreement. [14] Various modifications were subsequently proposed, [16, 27, 29, 34, 42] but not until 1953 did it secure a democratically elected majority. [46] Thereafter it became the major repository of Buganda's political opinions, [56] to which even Mutesa II in his prime had to be careful to accord attention. [57] There are also several documents illustrating the fluctuating fortunes of the Kabaka's role – from the changes in his powers around 1888, [7] to the uncertainties of his position under the British. [22] They include several which give expression to the vehement opinions upon it which appeared in the 1950s and 1960s. [48, 49, 52, 53, 58, 59]

Nothing, however, is more striking about the documents which have come to hand than the degree to which statements by successive Kabakas seem to figure in them. It might perhaps be expected that statements by the ruler would have more chance of being preserved than those of lesser men. Even, however, allowing for this, there remains the striking fact of the extent to which personal statements by Kabakas regularly revealed their personal sense of concern with, and sense of responsibility for, the progress of the kingdom. For all the perception of many of the other expressions of viewpoint represented here, this quality seems to imbue only the rulers of the kingdom – and quite explicitly here in each one of the four Kabakas with whom we are concerned. [5, 9, 33, 47] Much play has been made – it needs to be made – with the oligarchical revolution in Buganda in the last decades of the nineteenth century. Despite, however, its immediate political importance, it did not, in the succeeding three quarters of a century, engross the whole of the political heritage of Buganda. In the hands of its designated custodians the monarchical tradition did not atrophy quickly. For those of us indeed who would be inclined to discount that it ever possessed much content, the evidence of some of the pages which follow should give us reason to pause. They not only indicate the prime position in the structure of the Buganda polity which was held by its ruler. They give evidence of the extent to which the funnelling of the total societal concerns of a monarchically dominated society upon a single specified individual could evoke in him a most profound awareness of them, apparently regardless of the particular attributes of the person who at any one time filled the office. One does not have to be a supporter of monarchy in its pristine form to give cognizance to its historic role.

Beyond this it is easy and tempting to affirm that the evidence presented here indicates that during most of the period under consideration Buganda's leaders were chiefly remarkable as arch-collaborators of their imperial overlords the British ('Quislings' such people are called in Europe). [9, 12, 19, 23, 28, 38] But it must be suggested as well that taken on its own such a view is at best *simpliste*. It is patent to begin with that angling for external assistance was rarely thought of in Buganda as being illegitimate. Mutesa I asked for outside help from Colonel Gordon: [3] Mutesa II from Secretary-General U Thant. [61] Mwanga sought it from the Imperial British East Africa Company: [8] while the young Abu Mayanja looked for it from the British Protectorate Government, paradoxically enough in one of his more radical moments. [53] At a quite different level both Kalemba himself and his father expected 'truth' to be brought to them by strangers from outside. [4] Seen in this context the effusions of the Christian oligarchs, [12] or of Kabaka Daudi Chwa, [28] or of others later on, emerge as variations upon some quite legitimate themes, rather than – to put them at their worst – the prattlings of betrayers. What is more, if one may judge from a good deal of the evidence which follows, far from being crude collaborators, Buganda's leaders were amongst the most formidable of anti-colonial resisters. The greatest of their efforts were directed towards defending the autonomy – that is the African character – of their centuries' old kingdom; and time and again they withstood their colonial adversaries very successfully. [13, 17, 29, 47] Indeed of all the African voices raised in their own defence – in these parts of Africa and far away to the south as well – not one was more successful in getting itself listened to by the invading Europeans than Buganda's. There was a sublety, and a strength, and a skill to the expostulations of its leaders, which, for long years, not only brought it unequalled success, [14, 15, 37 49] but made it the envy of a great many Africans, in Kenya and Tanganyika as well as in Uganda, and the model for their often desperate efforts to escape the colonialist stranglehold.

1. RECEPTION OF THE FIRST ALIENS
1840s–1860s

Apolo Kagwa and Henry Wright Duta Kitakule, 'How Religion came to Uganda'.

During the reign of Suna* (the king who preceded Mutesa) he was visited by some Arabs: Medi Abraham,* and Kyera, and Amulain, and Mina, and Katukula Mungazija, and Zigeya Mubulusi.

Of these he liked Medi Abraham best, and gave him a great many presents, ivory, women and slaves.

Later on Medi Abraham told Suna, when he saw him killing people, that, although he killed them with so little thought, yet there was a God who created them, and from Him he had obtained his kingdom, and the people he governed, and that he himself was created by Him.

This Suna did not believe, for he said he knew his Lubare gods and they had given him his kingdom, but Medi Abraham repeated his words every time he was called to see him.

Some time afterwards Suna asked Medi, 'Where is there a God greater than I?' And Medi told him that there is a God who will raise up all who believe in Him, and they will go to Paradise.

When Suna understood this, he agreed that Medi should read to him, but only now and then, and he got through the first four chapters of the Koran.

When he had got hold of these, more or less by word of mouth, Medi returned to the coast and did not come again to Uganda, and soon after this Suna died and Mutesa succeeded him, and made his capital at Banda, half-way between Mengo and Ngogwe. He also encouraged Arabs to visit him. Katukula Hali and his friends, and Hamuli Musirimu, and Makwega, a Swahili. Mutesa made friends of these and gave them many things just as his father Suna did before him.

King Mutesa asked Katukula what it was his 'father used to talk to them about, when they visited him', and he told him, 'we used to tell him about God, and King of Kings, and that He will raise people from the dead'.

King Mutesa asked him, 'Are you not lying? Is there a resurrection from the dead?' They told him that indeed there was, and that those who learnt the words of God, when they died would rise again.

So King Mutesa said to Katukula, 'Well then, come and teach me to read,' and brought a Swahili called Makwega, who taught the king every day, and he learned Mohammedanism very quickly. Some others learned with him whose names are Musisi Sabakaki and Basude Sabawali of Kigalagala, who is now Mutola, and Myakonyi Omumyuka of Myu-

* An asterisk in the documents indicates a note at the end of the relevant document.

1

kanya, and later Kauta Mukasa, who was Katikiro, and Mujabi Omuta-buza, and Tebukoya, and Sembuzi and Wakibi.

These were first taught, but afterwards the converts were slow in coming forward.

When the king went from his capital, Banda, and went to Nakawa he persevered with his reading and fasted during the first fast, and he then ordered all his subjects to read Mohammedanism. He also learned to write in Arabic: the Arab Wamisi brought the Mohammedan Kibali who taught the king.

Then Mutesa came from Nakawa to Nabulagala, and thence to Rubaga, where he stayed some time. He again ordered his people to read, but he saw they were not giving their minds to it. So he said to his head district chiefs, 'I want to know if people are learning to believe in Islam well.' His chiefs told him they were. 'Well,' he said, 'if they are, how do they salute each other as Mohammedans?' They replied, 'Some salute thus – *Sala-maleku dekimu musalamu* – others, *Sibwakede bwatulise.*'

He saw they had not learned to salute, and found that those who had begun to really learn were very few indeed, and he gave orders that every man who had not learnt was to learn the salutation, *Salamu alekumu ale-kumu salaamu* or *Shabuluheri.* And in anger the king gave orders tha everyone refusing to learn was to be seized.

Many who would not learn were then seized, called infidels and killed. Then every married man fixed up a stone in his yard to pray at, and every chief built a mosque, and a great many people became readers, but were not circumcised, and all the chiefs learned that faith.

> – from the translation by C. W. Hattersley in
> *Uganda Notes*, May 1902, p. 35.

Suna: Kabaka Suna died in 1856 and was succeeded by Mutesa I, Kabaka 1856–84.
Medi Abraham: Ahmed bin Ibrahim, trader from Zanzibar.

2. THE INQUIRING MIND, 1875

Kabaka Mutesa I and his discussions with Ernest Linant de Bellefonds.

21, 22, 23 April – I have had many different discussions with M'Tesa during the last three days. Our conversation had dwelled on all the different powerful forces of the world in turn: America, England, France,

Germany, Russia, the Ottoman Empire, constitutions, government, military might, production, industry and religion.

The King's sister was present at these sessions. The daughters and sisters of the King never go on foot; they are always carried by their slaves.

25th April – M'Tesa summoned me at eleven o'clock at the same time as the Fakir of the Xoderia. Our talk therefore was exclusively about the Koran. The poor Fakir was at a loss as to how to answer all the King's questions. I had to give him some help.

I informed the King of the system of trade by means of money. The value of all goods is based on the tallari. This system makes trade and transactions easier.

27th April – In answer to all M'Tesa's questions concerning the earth, the sun, the moon, the stars and the sky and in order to make him understand the movements of the heavenly bodies. I had to make shapes on a board, the heavenly bodies being represented by little glass balls. The lecture took place today. The gathering was not very large. The two viziers Katikiro* and Chambarango,* four leading officers, the two scribes and a few favourites. The four cardinal points, the rotation of the earth, its movement round the sun, night and day, the seasons, the movement of the moon round the earth and its phases (which I did by means of a mirror) and the general movement of our system in space.

M'Tesa grasped everything perfectly. We were seated on the ground in a circle and there was a very friendly atmosphere. I have never seen M'Tesa so happy. It was the first time that we had spoken to each other directly without using interpreters, and this is against all the laws of etiquette. M'Tesa himself explained afterwards to the wonder-struck gathering. What was so surprising was that M'Tesa was able to inspire in his associates and in many of his people this quest for understanding, for self-instruction and for knowledge. There is great rivalry among them and they are very eager to improve. They are an inquiring, observant, intelligent people with minds longing for the learning of white people whose superiority they recognize; and with the help of a mission having farmers, carpenters and smiths amongst them, these Gandas will soon become an industrial people. This being so, Ganda would be the centre of civilization of all this part of Africa. . . .

I left the King at two o'clock after we had arranged to meet again at four. The same people were there as in the morning. The talk was or Genesis. M'Tesa had the story of Genesis from the Creation to the Flood taken down on a writing-tablet. We parted at nightfall. M'Tesa is spellbound and I shall be able to obtain all I want from him. . . .

17th May – Yesterday and today we had long discussions with M'Tesa concerning the duties of man towards himself and towards his neighbour. I gave him various precepts, a mixture of Socrates' philosophy and Christian morality. What troubled the King most is knowing what para-

3

dise, hell and the angels are composed of. Where are they set and what sort of joy and punishment await us after death? Is it true that the body lives again after death? If this is so and given that the body is matter, should not God then have a body? ...

26 May – ... In as much as M'Tesa believes himself to be of divine essence, so he is led by pride and vanity to continually brag and boast, and this makes him look ridiculous and sets people against him. In spite of his faults, he is certainly the most intelligent African living between Sobat* and Lake Ukerewe.* He learns about the customs, habits and governments of every country and all this not merely out of idle curiosity, but with the idea of becoming better informed and of bringing about some useful reforms in his own country.

Thanks to him, the people of Uganda are today as much above the other tribes I have visited, as civilized Europe is above the Bedouin Arabs, those primitive nomads of the desert.

The self-esteem of M'Tesa is extreme. He is very concerned about what the civilized world thinks of him and his greatest ambition, and very laudable it is, is that his name should go down in posterity. He wants history to think of him as the founder of the human race.

'I am called M'Tesa,' he said one day, 'which means in Ganda language, *reformer, benefactor*. I want history to say of me one day that if I had not been given that name at my birth, posterity would give it to me at my death.'

> – from E. Linant de Bellefords, 'Itinéraine et Notes. Voyage de service fait entre le poste militaire de Fatiko et la capitale de M'Tesa, roi d'Uganda. Fevrier–Juin 1875', *Bulletin Trimestriel de la Société Khédiviale de Geographie du Caire*, ser. 1, 1876–7, pp. 58–62, 73, 81–2.

Katikiro: chief minister.
Chambarango: Kyambalango, a county chief.
Sobat: the river Sobat now in the Sudan.
Ukerewe: an island at the south end of Lake Victoria.

3. KABAKA MUTESA I, COLONEL GORDON AND THE FIRST CHRISTIAN MISSIONARIES, 1876-7

Kabaka Mutesa I to Colonel Gordon,* 6 February 1876.

To Sir Canell Gorlden February 6th, 1876.

My Dear Freind Gorden hear this my word be not angry with Kaverega* Sultan of unyoro. I been head that you been brought two manwar ships but I pray you fight not with these Wanyoro for they know not what is good and what is bad. I am, Mtesa king of uganda for if you fight with governour if you fight with governour you fight with the king. I will ask you one thing but let it may please you all ye Europeion for I say if I want to go to Bommbey if the Governour and if the Governour of Bommbey refuse me to past will I not find the orther road therefor I pray you my friends hear this my letter stop for a moment if you want to fight put ships in the river nile take west and north and I will take east and south and let us put wanyoro in to the middle and fight against them but first send me answer from this letter. Because I want to be a freind of the English. I am Mtesa son of Suna king of uganda let God be with your Majesty even you all Amen.

Mtesa king of uganda.
February 6th, 1876.

Kabaka Mutesa I and Dallington to Gordon, 24 March 1876.

To Sir Colonel Gordon, My dear Friend, I wish you good day. It is I M'tesa, King of Uganda who sends you this letter. I wish to be the friend of the white men, Therefore, hear my words which I say.

1. I want a priest who will show me the way of God.
2. I want gold, silver, iron and bronze.
3. I want clothing for my people and myself to wear.
4. I want excellent guns and good cannons.
5. I want to cause to be built good houses for my country.
6. I want my people to know God.

Kabaka Mutesa I to Gordon, 3 April 1876.

From King M'tesa, the greatest King of the interior of Africa, 3 April 1876.

This letter is from M'tesa, the greatest King in Africa. It is I M'tesa, King of Uganda, Usoga* and Karagwe. Listen then to my word which I tell you. Oh! thou European, I have become your true brother, I am a Christian, only I have not yet been baptised.

I believe in God the Holy Father, Almighty, Creater of heaven and earth, and in the Lord Jesus Christ, the only true Son of God, begotten of the Father before the creation of the earth. He is God of God.

May your Queen be a mother to me and may I become her son. May her sons and daughters be my brothers and sisters. It is I, M'tesa, King of Uganda. Formerly the Mahommedans tempted me saying that Mahommed was the first and last of good people, but we find this is not the truth but a lie. May we both be united. Oh! Colonel Gordon, listen to this letter which says Oh! God, let there be peace between England and Uganda. Oh! may England be joyful always. Oh! Colonel Gordon, come quickly to me, and, if you do not come, at least send one of your white men, who you have with you, I want the reply to this letter to be printed.

May God be with the Queen, May God be with your Majesty and I beg you to send me paper, ink and pens, because all my paper is finished.

Kabaka Mutesa I to 'all the English' with Gordon [no date].

To all the English who are with Colonel Gordon.

Oh! all the men of England, hear what is said in this letter, for I am M'tesa, King of Uganda. I will tell you the truth, because I am a King and will not lie. Because I am on your side. If at times I say I do not want white men, it is in order to pretend, because if I always say it, others will say why does M'tesa want white men and does not ask for us.

Therefore I say in my heart I will receive in secret the English letter. Therefore I pray you, listen my friend to what I say. Send a letter to England and tell them that M'tesa wants one of the priests of England.

But you yourselves come here and quickly so that I can tell you all that I have in my heart and then you can go to England with joy.

May the Grace of Our Lord Jesus Christ, and the Love of God, and the Fellowship of the Holy Ghost be with us all always. Amen.

From M'tesa, King of Uganda, son of Suna.

Oh! Colonel Gordon, I will tell you the truth. I M'tesa tell the truth. I do not want your people, but I want you yourself to come, you yourself to me, or that you will send one of the white men you have with you. But I do not want Hammed Effendi* because he belongs to Islam. I have nothing more to say, but look after yourself.

Kabaka Mutesa I at Nabulagala to Gordon, 29 August 1876.

To Sir Colonel Gordon.

Oh Lord our heavenly Father King of all Kings Governor of all things power no creature able to resist to whom it belongeth justly to punish sinners and to be merciful to them that truly repent. Save and deliver us we humbly beseech thee from the hands of our enemies; abate their pride assuage their malice and confound their devices that we being armed with thy defence may be preserved ever more from all perils to glorify thee who art the only giver of all victory through the merits of the only Son Jesus Christ our Lord Amen.

Oh my Dear friend Gordon forget me not I have give all your soldiers and I never want your soldiers, but I want you yourself to come to me.

Oh God let there be peace between England and Uganda and you been tell me not to buy Zanzibar's powder what I shall I do for me hands is empty therefor I pray you to give me powders and guns and I been heard that you been toled Ikanagruba and send to him that all the guns which you got is for King M'tesa come let us be two powerful Country from King M'tesa son of Suna King of Uganda.

Kabaka Mutesa I to the missionaries of the Church Missionary Society at Ukerewe, 10 April 1877.

To my Dear Friend.

I have heard that you have reached Ukerewe. So now I want you to come to me quickly. I give you Magombwa to be your guide, and now you must come to me quickly. This letter from Mtesa, King of Uganda, written by Dallington Scopion Maftaa,* April 10, 1877.

– from Sir John Gray, 'The Correspondence of Dallington Maftaa' *Uganda Journal*, Vol. 30, No. 1, 1966, pp. 13–24.

Gordon: Colonel Charles George Gordon, of Khartoum fame.
Kaverega: Kabarega, Omukama (ruler) of Bunyoro.
Usoga: Busoga.
Mufta: Dallington Maftaa, Mafutah, an African boy from a Christian mission in Zanzibar who had travelled to Buganda with H. M. Stanley.
Hamed Effendi: in command of the Egyptian post in Buganda July–August 1876.

4. THE ADVENT OF THE OUTSIDE WORLD

Mathias Kalemba's story, c. *1880*.

My father had always believed that the Baganda had not the truth, and he sought it in his heart. He had often mentioned this to me, and before his death he told me that men would one day come to teach us the right way.

These words made a profound impression on me and, whenever the arrival of some stranger was reported, I watched him and tried to get in touch with him, saying to myself that here perhaps was the man foretold by my father. Thus I associated with the Arabs who came first in the reign of Suna. Their creed seemed to me superior to our superstitions. I received instructions and, together with a number of Baganda, I embraced their religion. Mutesa himself, anxious to please the Sultan of Zanzibar, of whose power and wealth he had been given an exaggerated account, declared that he also wanted to become a Muslim. Orders were given to build mosques in all the counties. For a short time, it looked as if the whole country was going to embrace the religion of the false prophet, but Mutesa had an extreme repugnance to circumcision. Consequently, changing his mind all of a sudden, he gave orders to exterminate all who had become Muslims.* A good many perished in the massacre, two or three hundred managed to escape and, with Arab caravans, made their way to the Island of Zanzibar. I succeeded with a few others in concealing the fact of my conversion, and continued to pass for a friend of our own gods, though in secret I remained faithful to the practices of Islam.

That was how things stood when the Protestants arrived. Mutesa received them very well; he had their book read in public audience, and seemed to incline to their religion, which he declared to be much superior to that of the Arabs. I asked myself whether I had not made a mistake, and whether, perhaps, the newcomers were not the true messengers of God. I often went to visit them and attended their instructions. It seemed to me that their teaching was an improvement on that of my first masters. I therefore abandoned Islam, without however asking for baptism.

Several months had elapsed when Mapèra [Father Lourdel] arrived. My instructor, Mackay, took care to tell me that the white men who had just arrived did not know the truth. He called their religion the 'worship of the woman'; they adored, he said, the Virgin Mary. He also advised me to avoid them with the greatest care. I therefore kept away from you and, probably, I would never have set foot in your place if my chief had not ordered me to supervise the building of one of your houses. But God showed his love for me.

The first time when I saw you nearby, I was very much impressed. Nevertheless, I continued to watch you closely at your prayers and in your dealings with the people. Then seeing your goodness, I said to myself, 'How can people who appear so good be the messengers of the devil?'

I talked with those who had placed themselves under instruction and questioned them on your doctrine. What they told me was just the contrary of what Mackay had assured me. Then I felt strongly urged to attend personally your catechetical instructions. God gave me the grace to understand that you taught the truth, and that you really were the man of God of whom my father had spoken. Since then, I have never had the slightest doubt about the truth of your religion, and I feel truly happy.

– from J. F. Faupel African Holocaust,
London 1962, pp. 30–31.

The killing of Muslims occurred in 1876.

5. THE DILEMMAS IN BUGANDA, *c.* 1883

Rev. Philip O'Flaherty, C.M.S. Missionary, Buganda, to Wigram, C.M.S. Secretary, London, 28 February 1883.

. . . the king sent for me to his royal presence. I went. We were almost alone except for his harem. He said, 'Philipo. I am sick and tired of the Arabs and their religion. But that religion having been taught me when I was young, it has taken a powerful hold of my imagination. My heart tells me it is wrong, and its Founder a liar. But Philipo you have seen me lying on this couch for two years. I have no strength of body or mind and I and my Chiefs, we cannot find it in our hearts to discard our women, and have but *one wife* for you see the women alone cultivate our country and get us food. The Baganda will not cultivate the soil and I cannot force them. It is a thing that one king alone cannot do. It must be done by degrees. And my mind tells me that while women cultivate the soil, the chiefs and Batongolis* will have a number of them as their choice. And this being the case, faithfulness to one wife is an impossibility. If there is one thing you have hammered into my head it is this, that I have no power, except in name, and by fits and starts, and that any amount of Royal power cannot change the hearts and thoughts of a people long accustomed to their own way, and especially a nation of conquerors as we have been and still are. Therefore it is best that things should correct themselves slowly and by degrees as your religion grew slowly and by degrees.

But one thing I am anxious – very anxious about – I don't like those Arabs and wangwana* taking away my people. These 2 years back I have not given away one single man or woman or child. I buy my stuff for ivory. But my people have no ivory, but slaves. And now, such a thirst for cloth has caught hold of them that they will sell men and women for guns, powder and shot and cloth and soap, etc. Now can I stop this? Can you inform me as to the way we can put an end to this purchasing and selling of slaves, while at the same time my people can get those things the Arabs bring? Can the English help me on this matter and will they?'

I saw at once what I have long seen before – the difficulty of the King's position. I said I would consult my brother Mackay and that I would lose no time in laying these thoughts before my society at home.

The *serious* manner in which His Majesty spoke – his grasp of the position of himself and people – his insight as to his own inability to *force* matters – and the futility of forcing religion down his people's throats as Mohammed did – the desire to see here a Merchant Company of Englishmen, which, having a steamer or boats of their own on the lake, would soon exclude the Arabs. All these things have raised Mutesa high in my estimation. He cannot do what he would. He says 'What can I do? Can you not find the way to assist me. Those cursed slave dealers really rule my people. This I myself formerly encouraged but it has assumed such dimensions that it cannot I fear be stopped. It would be folly in me to try it. God alone by a stronger power than a man on this couch has, can prevent this now. The Arabs all hate you and your country and often pestered me to wink at their murdering you. They also hate Mackay* because he hates slavery.'

– from the archives of the Church Missionary
Society, London.

Batongolis: Batongole chiefs, a category of chiefs appointed by the Kabaka.
Wangwana: here a generic term for Africans from what is now Tanzania who were associated with traders from the coast and Zanzibar.
Mackay: Mr A. M. Mackay, the noted missionary of the Church Missionary Society.

6. THE AFFIRMATION
OF THE CHRISTIAN MARTYRS, 1886

Denis Kamyuka's account

We set out with unconcealed joy, walking in single file; Gyavira, Mugagga, Kizito, Werabe and myself; each of us with a silent prayer on his lips. After ten minutes' march, we encountered Senkole and his following, their faces streaked with soot. He held in his hand the Sacred Fuse with which, as we filed past him, he tapped on the head each of those singled out for death. Me, he allowed to pass untouched, as if to say, 'Not fit for martyrdom! Too small, my boy!' 'My poor Kamyuka,' whispered Mugagga to me, 'you are going to miss the rendezvous in Heaven.'

Already, Senkole had singled out Charles Lwanga, our gallant leader, declaring, 'You, I am keeping for myself, to sacrifice to Kibuka, Mukasa and Nende. You will make a prime offering.'

In taking leave of the rest of us, Charles said, 'My friends, we shall before long meet again in Heaven. I stay here and go on ahead of you. Keep up your courage, and persevere to the end'. . . .

When all the victims had been laid on the pyre, the executioners brought more wood, which they piled on top of them. While this was being done, I heard the Christians, each reciting the prayers which came to his mind at that supreme moment. When the men began to spread wood over Mugagga, he cried out, 'Wait a bit! I must have something to drink first: I am suffocating in this jacket of reeds.' Mukajanga, informed of the request, agreed, saying, 'It is a last request which cannot be refused.'

Our joyous friend was carried down from the pyre, untied and given two small portions of plantain-wine, for which he gave thanks. Some of the pagans thought within themselves, 'Here is one, at least, who flinches.' After the executioners had allowed him time to get rid of his stiffness and recover his breath, they came to Mugagga saying, 'Now you must be tied up again.' 'Wait just a little longer!' he exclaimed. Then Mukajanga said to him, 'I think that the others will be leaving without you.' 'In that case,' he replied, 'a truce to fooling! Wrap me up quickly in my reeds. I am at your service.' Then noticing Sebuta, Werabe and myself, below and to one side, he called out 'Poor Kamyuka! I am going up to Heaven. We shall be separated for a time. Good-bye to you all, until we meet again.'

I was stupified and speechless, unable to utter a word in reply. My eyes filled with tears and my throat was dry and constricted with emotion. Gyavira, Kizito and Kiriwawanvu, who had heard Mugagga's farewell, hastened to add their voices to his. 'Good-bye, friends,' they called, 'we are on our way.'

When Mukajanga saw that all was ready, he signalled to his men to station themselves all round the pyre, and then gave the order, 'Light it at every point.' The flames blazed up like a burning house and, as they rose, I heard coming from the pyre the murmur of the Christians' voices as they died invoking God.

From the moment of our arrest, I never saw one of them show any lack of courage. The pyre was lit towards noon.

– from J. F. Faupel *African Holocaust*, London 1962, pp. 192, 196–7.

7. THE REVOLUTIONS IN BUGANDA, 1888

Rev. E. C. Gordon (from Usambiro at the south end of Lake Victoria) to Rev. H. W. Lang (Church Missionary Society, London), 7 November 1888.

The events that have taken place in Buganda during the months of September and October are of more than common interest. It is the unexpected which often happens. The story of the Baganda Mission has ever been interesting and remarkable. Many chapters of the story have been told, and the pages filled with strange facts. The contents of each succeeding chapter are more eventful and checkered than the preceding. Now the bare facts have been posted to Zanzibar and to England. The account of how the facts took place has yet to be told. It has been a very difficult matter to find out a good and correct story of the Revolution. It has been harder still to find out and get hold of a solid reason for the rebellion. At the same time it is a matter for sincere thankfulness and gratitude to All Mighty God that we are alive, in health and able to talk of this fact. Through the great Mercy of God Mr Walker* and myself passed safely through the uncertain waves and fortunes of a great Revolution in Buganda. The fact of the matter is that the whole business of the Revolution and Expulsion of Mwanga* passed off so quietly, quickly and skilfully as hardly to take the name of Revolution. The expulsion of Mwanga was the work of one brief day. It was effected very speedily and with great dexterity. There was but little resistance made on the part of Mwanga. It is true that he had but a very small portion of the Baganda soldiers at his command. Mwanga and his few followers and favourites offered no stout defence but made of their own position. They made but a short and feeble opposition to the forces who came against them. And the result was in consequence the hasty flight of Mwanga and some of his most faithful pages and favourites. The new king named Kiwewa was placed upon the empty throne the same day. In fact he was called to head the revolutionists and lead them to victory. But now some one will be inclined to ask not unnaturally several questions which are these. What caused the Revolution? How was a revolution possible? By whom was it brought about? To these suggested questions it is my hope and intention to make some attempted reply. To begin with the first question. What caused the revolution? The best answer to this question would probably be the bad management and misrule of Mwanga. For the late king had managed to excite much ill-feeling and considerable ill will against himself. He had made himself thoroughly unpopular amongst a large and very important portion of his subjects. Mwanga did not seek to win the affection of a large body of the Baganda, who have been daily growing in influence and power in Buganda. This body of people may be most conveniently and suitably called 'The Readers' or 'The Reformers'. This new company of Baganda was in great measure composed of the youth and strength of the country. This company may also be divided into two parties, namely the Christian and the Mohammedan Readers. If the numerical strength of either party were taken, we should probably find that the Christians and Mohammedans were equally strong on this point, neither surpassing the other in the matter of number of adherants. Under the name of 'The Christian Readers' must be included the Roman Catholics and Protestants, that is, all the pupils of the French Priests and our own. Now Mwanga had made himself both odious and offensive to the minds of these two powerful bodies of Readers or Reformers. He had by his conduct caused much offence. For some time past Mwanga had shown a growing dislike to all who were anxious to advance and depart from the old heathen method of worship. Why Mwanga should have shown displeasure and dissatisfaction with this portion of his subjects is probably known only to himself. It may be that he himself preferred to remain in ignorance and indifference with regard to religious matters. His line of conduct certainly indicated that he desired to remain as he was and live in a state of carelessness and thoughtlessness. He showed little inclination to favour any one of the three Religious parties of the country. Latterly however his manner of action seemed to indicate a settled purpose and intention to make an end of the new and foreign Religions by destroying the worshippers of both the Christian and Mohammedan persuasion. With this aim in view, he began to gather round himself a band of pages and favourites who were for the most part content to live in the same condition of careless ease as he himself. Then, the restless and suspicious mind of the king will be another thing which helped to make him mismanage his affairs, and caused him to lose the regard and esteem of his subjects. With a mind restless and suspicious, he was ever too ready to listen to the slanders and calumnies of the many who sought to procure his favour at all hazards. There were ever many who did not hesitate to maliciously accuse the Readers of both the Christian Religion and Mohammedan Religion of rebellion and revolt.

Mwanga seemed never to have felt himself secure, and was ever fearful of losing his throne. He was upset and disturbed by the slightest breath of discontent. There were not wanting audacious men who knew Mwanga's weakness, and such advisers were able so to work upon the fears of the king as to make him commit very rash acts.

In this manner Mwanga was led on by bolder and more adventurous spirits to the commission of numerous rash and thoughtless acts which finally cost him his throne. For it was not any one act in particular, but a number of hasty and headstrong threats and incautious actions which worked to bring about the expulsion of Mwanga. It will be well to give a short account of the imprudent steps which are said to have led up to the rebellion and to have caused the Baganda to revolt. It must be remembered that only a small portion of the Baganda people may be with all truth charged with taking an active part in this revolt against Mwanga. This portion of the Baganda we have named the Readers or Reformers. But at the same time, it is quite true that the whole of the people of Buganda had become disgusted and tired of the harsh and severe rule of Mwanga and his repeated acts of robbery. If we add to this yet another very forcible reason or cause, which probably affected much to produce the first action, it is this, *the strange and ardent love of change*, which is so strong and marked a characteristic of the Baganda. In this particular feature of the Baganda character, we have a reason at one time mighty and cogent enough to bring about the deposition, without even any other great substantial external exciting causes. There were doubtless several things which annoyed the Baganda people as a whole and made them ill-affected towards Mwanga. Probably one of the most offensive acts of Mwanga was the cruel manner in which he collected his taxes. This would be a grievance felt by all the Baganda, by those even, who followed the heathen customs of their ancestors. It used to be the custom of Mwanga to take almost regular monthly journeys in all directions through his dominions, for the purpose of robbing his subjects. These periodical raids of Mwanga became a matter of much offence and annoyance to the Baganda. For on such occasions [they had] to supply the king's bodyguard with food and provisions, the country through which the king would pass was robbed of its goats, oxen, and the fruit of the ground. Then more, if the king was charmed with the beauty of any of the females whom he might happen to see, he would not scruple to seize such of them as he deemed worthy, to be placed in his harem. The country people then had their complaints to raise against the king, all which called for redress. But let us pass on to learn about the heavier complaints made by the Reformers against the king. Ever since Mwanga came to the throne, it may be not far from correct to say that all reading had been carried on in secrecy. Neither the Christian nor the Mohammedan faiths were ever honestly recognized or fairly patronized by Mwanga. The Followers of these two respective faiths were necessarily obliged to worship God in much silence and secrecy. Though Mwanga was for the most part only indifferent, yet latterly he seems to have shown himself as increasingly more and more actively opposed to the profession and professors of either the Christian or Mohammedan Faiths. It is well known how Mwanga and his chiefs ordered the cruel massacre of the Christian readers in 1886. The only plea for such ruthless and cruel slaughter then was, that the Christians would join with their White teachers, and increasing in number, they would cause rebellion. Now however, the story runs, that the king lodged complaints and accusations against the followers of both Religions. The great complaint ever and always made by the king against the Mohammedans has ever been of the same nature. It has ever been the same charge of disrespect and dishonour toward their king. They will not eat of the meat which the king slaughters, in as much as it is slaughtered by one uncircumcised and the flesh is therefore unclean. There was a complaint laid against the Christian Readers, in that they too were disobedient and rebellious servants, who refused to do the king's work on Sunday. It is well to mention that there were rumours and scares floating about long before the actual storm of the wrath of Mwanga reached its height. It was rumoured that the Mwanga had decided to make a summary end of all the Readers. But the time was not ripe for the threats to be executed. About this time the king summoned the whole of Buganda to a great work. He called them together to enlarge the size and extent of his large pond or lakelet. He kept the big chiefs with their sub-chiefs and pages hard at this work for a very long time. He made the great chiefs build huts on the spot and refused them to go to their homes to sleep, or refresh themselves. He set over them a slave, a servant and favourite of his own. They were forbidden to shelter themselves properly from either the sun or the rain. They did the work by turns. The king would come down to see the work. He was surrounded by his favourites and pages well armed. It was now that the Christians were accused by the overseer of absenting themselves from work on the Sunday. It is also said that the king was angered by another act of disobedience on the part of the labourers, for instance. Mwanga ordered the companies who were working by turns to come unarmed, these refused to obey saying they brought their weapons to protect the king. Then Mwanga in much anger abruptly left this work unfinished and threatened to be avenged. Shortly after this, he was said to have changed his plans and we now began to hear of him holding secret private meetings with the Pokino* and one or two more large and powerful chiefs. You must understand that all the information I have been able to gather from first to last has been learnt from the Christian Readers, who many of them daily visited our station. The stories they related were diversely told, and the details of the events often very contrary, and hard to be reconciled or understood. In fact though I tried to make out some good solid sensible story, my efforts were not crowned with much success. This I have explained and now again say that I am writing from memory and stating facts. Now, in council the king and his advisers lit upon some other plan by which he hoped to rid himself of the Readers of the imported Religions. He worked in common with his counsellors to return to the happy days of Suna the father of Mutesa, when he would be surrounded by all those who preferred to follow or maintain the worship of their ancestors. In a few days time the king (following out his plan made in council) ordered a march to the lake. He was to be accompanied by the soldiers of his bodyguard and his own personal bodyguard of pages and favourites. The day arrived when the king started attended by the usual number of his followers. It is now time to ask the second question that is suggested to your minds. How was it possible that a rebellion should take place? The answer is, the king himself had made it possible to depose himself. Well how had the king made this possible? He had armed the leaders of his two large bodyguards with their followers and these leaders themselves were Readers. For the sake of convenience it is necessary to explain something regarding the nature and use of these bodyguards. It has been said that Mwanga had managed to surround himself with a personal bodyguard of young lads and favourites who were all non-Readers and were commanded by an especial favourite, a non-Reader. These pages and favourites were the king's constant attendants. Besides this bodyguard we have mentioned two other large bodyguards whose duty it likewise was to attend upon the king on all occasions of his departure from the capital. The leaders of these two last bodyguards were Readers of the Christian Religion. One Leader of them being a Roman Catholic, a pupil of the French Priests and a powerful and influential chief. The other leader being a pupil and leader with us. The followers or retainers of these two big chiefs were very numerous, and for as much as the Masters were recognized Readers, the servants and retainers were reckoned to be included under the same name as their Masters. Many of our Christians were therefore called to follow the king and they followed with some misgiving, recollecting the fierce threat of the king regarding themselves. The reported plan of the king seemed to have been somewhat as follows. The king with his personal favourite bodyguard of non-Readers were to cause the leaders of the other two bodyguards with their followers all Readers to enter canoes and depart for some island under orders from the king to rob and plunder the same island. The non-Reader chief who was to take these two leaders (Readers) to the island had orders to leave them together with their retainers on the island and also the Admiral (a Christian Reader), and if he succeeded in deceiving them, to bring away their canoes. The intention was to have them all; the two Leaders, Readers, the Admiral and readers with all their followers on the island to perish with hunger, for the tale about going to plunder was a hoax. At the same time the king had an accomplice in the Pokino who is a very great chief and was left behind at the capital to aid and succour the king. There is yet another large band of Readers of the Mohammedan

Religion, headed by a very powerful and well-known Chief, The Mujassi,* and of this band some mention must be made. The Mujassi it is said was ordered to go with the king on this occasion, but he refused shaming sickness. They came saying that the king was intending to drown them all in the lake. It has been said that the Readers before leaving the capital to go with the king fully believed that there was some treachery and foul plan. They were therefore prepared to make resistance. The whole army reached the lake, where the non-Reader chief was proceeding to execute the orders of his king. The king had gone off on to the water followed only by the non-Readers, the chief in command ordered the rest of the body-guards chiefs to follow. These replied that it was not their custom to go on to the lake except they saw the king and went together with him. Upon this the king seemed to see that his intention was discovered and had turned home. He returned home on Sunday afternoon saying to himself, they have rebelled. Nor was he wrong. The Readers had become so certain of this, that it had really been the cruel intention and fixed purpose of the king to try and drown them. Now therefore they determined to rebel. It seemed also clear that had the king been successful in this his design, directed chiefly against the Christian Readers he would immediately have turned upon the Mohammaden Readers for their destruction also. Therefore a combination of the two most opposite parties was required.

This then brings us to ask and answer another question. Who effected the Revolution and deposed Mwanga? And the answer is, the Readers and Reformers who had been armed by Mwanga with some of the best of his weapons and had thus been made so strong by the possession of firearms as to be rendered capable of resisting his authority.

On the Monday morning the Christian Readers, that is the leading chiefs of the bodyguards were holding consultation with the Mujassi and other leading Mohammedan Readers, who were chiefs. All the morning messages or messengers were passing backwards and forwards amongst them for all the Readers, both Mohammedan and Christian alike, were now heartily agreed on this one point, namely, the deposition or expulsion of King Mwanga. It is or was stated that the Mohammedan Readers were ready and prepared to undertake the work themselves without the aid of the Christian chiefs. Some of my informants said that the Christian leaders did not wish to go so far and to de-throne Mwanga, but were on the point of making their escape to Bunyoro, the only other alternative.

In the end however the leaders of both the Religious bodies joined together their united strength for the object of attempting to expel Mwanga. The one great complaint of both the discontented parties being that the king was intending and determined to put them all to death, some by drowning and others by some other violent means. A party of Mohammedan chiefs went to inform the Prince of their choice of the intention and mind of the Readers. As the day wore on, the attacking parties approached the capital by two different roads. The Mujassi and his soldiers had possession of the prince whom all intended to place upon the throne. The two Christian leaders with the Admiral and many other sub-chiefs reached the capital by another way. Poor Mwanga made little show of fight. He came outside the capital fired a few guns, then quickly retired and fled towards the Lake, followers by about 200 attendants. The Readers rushed forward and seated the new Prince upon the vacant throne.

That same day, the chief offices were distributed among the Leaders of the Readers, who had enthroned the new king, Kiwewa. Some of the principal posts were filled as follows. The Christian Roman Catholic leader was made the chief Judge, Katikiro. The post of Mukwenda* was filled by the Christian leader who read with us. Two other most important chieftainships were filled by the Mujassi and another Arabic Reader. The old Katikiro most wisely retired and took his departure and went to take up his abode near the place of the sepulchre of King Mutesa. The late Pokino was driven away or rather took refuge in flight. You will remember that he was suspected of taking an active share in the cruel intentions of Mwanga. His hasty flight gave good proof that he was implicated in the business. His houses were plundered and then burnt to the ground. The next day we were called up to see the new king. Many of the Arabs were also invited, a messenger came down to conduct us all up together. It was hardly possible to believe that anything extraordinary had taken place. There was no noise or disturbance. It is true that outside the capital, where some crowds were collected, there was considerable excitement. When admitted inside we preceded the Arabs into court or audience. Here again the excitement was considerable yet there was no quarrelling or noisy disturbance. The king was most lavish with his words and far too generous with his promises. He turned to the Arabs and proclaimed peace with Bunyoro and liberty to trade. No heavy customs duties or taxes upon goods imported or exported. He gave liberty for the Arabic Religion to be taught and announced that a Mosque would be built. He turned to us, and said, that there was liberty to teach on our part, and liberty for the Baganda to come to be taught without restriction or hindrance.

In this manner passed the first day of the reign of Kiwewa.* We went home most thankful that the great change had been brought about so peaceably and quietly. It is strange, yet I believe it to be a fact, that the deposition of the previous day was accomplished without the loss of the life of a single soul. It was a Revolution without bloodshed. Mwanga indeed was followed, but with promises that his life would be spared. The Pokino was caught, pardoned and degraded with disgrace. Many of the other big chiefs were deposed and degraded. Peace, quietness and justice began to reign in the land. That a great change had taken place came to be visibly felt and recognized. Many indeed began to believe that the change they had been anxiously looking and longing for had been granted a beginning. Many things indeed seemed to point in the direction of peace and prosperity and many things gave hope and expectation of a healthy and happy time to have been begun.

It must be borne in mind that during all this time the king was merely the tool of his advisers and counsellors, namely the chiefs of the Readers both Christian and Mohammedan who had seated him upon the throne. These chiefs began to regulate and set in order many matters of law and order needing important attention. As indication of the commencement of a milder rule, the executioners or court policemen were forbidden to attend court armed as formerly with ropes. They were now ordered to arm themselves with sticks. It was even said that the king was to be deprived of the power of passing the sentence of capital punishment for many offenders before criminal, and punishable only by death. Another manifest change must not be omitted. It was most interesting with respect to ourselves as Christian teachers. The Promises regarding Freedom of thought and liberty to be taught the white man's religion spread far and wide. These promises doubtless brought gladness to many who had secretly been reading the Arabs Religion. For those Baganda who were Christian Readers, and who had for a long time been in hiding, the news was most acceptable and welcome. Many who had been for a long time hidden and were thought to be lost or fled the country now boldly came forward without fear.

Many Christians now emerged from their places of concealment and flocked to the king's court and began to enter into his service as pages and messengers. Thus released Christians and seekers after the Truth began to come about our Mission station in crowds on Sundays and in great numbers on all the days of the week. Very many indeed were wanting alphabet sheets. Many more were asking for first syllables, then others were demanding more advanced papers and printed portions while a large number were imploring for prayer-books and New Testament gospels and single Epistles.

For a time the Baganda came about the station like swarms of bees, from the dawn of light to the dusk of evening they crowded both sides of the house and some of the rooms. Many Chiefs came to visit us, asking and beseeching us for Alphabet sheets, that they might teach their followers and slaves. Besides those who came for papers, books and alphabets, there were the many applicants for medicine now increased in number with the new change in affairs. On the Sundays the most noticeable change was to be seen. On the very first Sunday of the reign of Kiwewa, the congregation doubled in numbers, and the number of Baganda who remained for afternoon worship was more than treble the usual attendance.

As each several Sunday came round a larger number of people gathered together to hear and read the word of God. On the last Sunday before the unfortunate conclusion, the number of worshippers at the morning service was quite 300. On this occasion as also before, worship was held in the house as well as the room always used for such services. Many people had to be content to remain outside. On this very Sunday, there were present most of the important and influential Christian chiefs, including the Christian leaders and Reader of the bodyguard mentioned as one of our pupils. He was raised to the great chieftainship of Mukwenda. So matters were working and all appeared quiet and calm.

If the success of the movement proved the righteousness and justice of the cause, the deposition and expulsion of Mwanga was a righteous and just act. The whole business of the deposition and the necessary division of the land among new chiefs had been carried out successfully. All the work had been done so promptly and skilfully as to give great credit to the persons concerned in the execution. The work was beginning to look solid and we hoped for permanent peace and prosperity. We were not the only hopeful persons. That a great calamity was soon to completely darken the horizon and fall upon us was far removed from the thoughts of most, if not all, of our Christian Readers. After all the quietness and calmness which we enjoyed was not permitted to last. In fact the tranquillity which prevailed in Buganda was as the calmness which precedes the storm.

The greater the calm the more fierce the storm that follows. In this instance, the storm that has burst upon Buganda has probably been the most violent and disastrous that the checkered life of this country has yet seen. The peace and hope of prosperity and progress was rudely broken up in an unexpected manner. The daily life and routine of duties seemed to be progressing with more than usual smoothness, but alas the peace and quietness was wanting in solidity, because not founded nor established upon authority.

The poor king all this time was but a child in the hand of his officers and ministers. His time was chiefly occupied in giving his consent and approval to the distribution and division of the various chieftainships. This division of the land was performed at the instance of the few favoured chiefs already in power, as the Katikiro, the Mukwenda, the Mujassi and by a few other chosen representatives and Readers of both parties. Be it remembered that the offices of chief judge, and Mukwenda were filled by Christian Readers, the Katikiro being a Roman Catholic and the Mukwenda one of our Pupils. The few chosen representatives of both the Religions probably did more than the bigger men towards presenting and forwarding candidates for promotion or to fill the many vacancies. The bigger men after receiving their reward departed to take possession of their new houses and land. There was much of this work to be done, for besides filling vacancies, many of the old chiefs had to be dispossessed for various reasons, some for unfaithfulness to the new king in that they took no part in placing him upon the throne, others for other causes.

Now it was touching the distribution and division of the land that disturbances and disputes arose. Yet even here no real quarrelling nor passionate strife took place, and all such matters was passing on to a successful conclusion. So then, had there been no other foreign element and watchfully self-interested party in the country all would eventually have worked well and prosperously. But all through the changes which had been taking place the Arabs had awaited the results with eager anxiety. They were distressed and aggravated to find such posts as that of the Judge and the Mukwenda occupied by Christian Readers. The late Katikiro had always shown himself their friend, and had often and often stood between them and the angry king to ward off his wrath and covetousness. They felt his loss, it grieved them to the very heart, but chiefly because they feared the change might heavily affect their purses. Well, this new Katikiro was in their eyes a heathen and an Infidel. How could he befriend them. How could he help them. Thus were the Arabs prepared to interrupt the present order and peace if they could by this means devise some scheme for their own advantage. The Arabs had received fair promises from the king but they had not realized them. Many of them were much dissatisfied and complaining of the treatment they received at the hands of Kiwewa. Mwanga had owed them a quantity of ivory and the new king had promised to make every effort to pay off the debts of his predecessor. So indeed he had begun to pay the Arabs to the best of his ability and means. But here he found himself in difficulties at once. He had not got the ivory wherewith to pay, nor did he know where to look for or to find it. The king was therefore somewhat in trouble and the Arabs were discontented with their lot and condition. They now began to look about to seek out a way in which to better their state. While looking about with envious and malicious eyes, they met with another body of malcontents. The famous Mujassi, with several, in fact, all of his fellow chiefs, Mohammedan Readers, were likewise brooding over their injuries and grievances.

The nature of their troubles and grievances has already been hinted at. These Chiefs complained that the best and largest chieftainships had been given or had fallen into the hands of the more favoured Christians. It may be true that the most important offices had fallen into the hands of the Christians, yet all the same the greater part of the country was doubtless fairly evenly divided between the two parties. But with this division the Mohammedan Readers did not agree. Many of the leading complaining chiefs doubtless met the Arabs and talked over with them these matters of hostility, and at the same time consulted of and suggested the remedy.

The plot formed by the Arabs and the Mohammedan Readers in consultation was cleverly and deceitfully laid. The sequel shows how unjust and cruel it was. The very night before the unfortunate fight between the two parties, we were returning from the capital and saw what confirms our belief in the fact, that the Arabs and Mohammedan Readers were one and acted together in this matter. We met on this occasion the chief who now fills the office of the Katikiro and another large and influential chief returning to the capital after having paid long visits to the Arabs quarters. Then on the day of the actual fight many Arabs were present at the battle, some indeed whose names could be mentioned took an active part in the fighting. Besides this most of the Arabs sent a detachment of their slaves well armed to the assistance of the Mohammedans. Others of the Arabs went up early to the court that day and stationed themselves round about the king, poisoning and embittering his mind against the Katikiro and all Christian Readers. They made the king think or persuaded the king to believe that his life was really in danger; that an attempt would certainly be made to dethrone him in favour of a princess whom the Christian Readers had determined, as they said, to set upon the throne.

The king was thus led on and induced to regard the Arabs as his friends and protectors but the Christians as his adversaries and destroyers. Time was fast wearing on and yet nothing had been done to check the growing power of the Christians. There was yet wanting some tangible excuse to encourage and urge on the discontented to begin the affray and turn the Christians out of power. There must be some charge laid against the Christians. There must be an attempt to bring a plausible accusation against them. So an opportune occasion was siezed upon and a very lame story made up. The Christians were by this story made the movers of disturbance and rebellion, and made to appear as the dissatisfied party who struck the final blow.

A party of Baganda who had been sent down the west side of the Lake by Mwanga to collect his tribute and taxes from the various dependent tribes returned to Buganda the day before the fight took place. Now this party consisted for the most part of Christians. Their leader who had been a big man under Mwanga was represented as returning to the capital very wrath in mind because of the fact that no chieftainship had been left vacant for his benefit and reward. This man was reported to be fully prepared to dispute his right to some chieftainship by force of arms. He was also charged with rebellion against Kiwewa, in that he intended to overthrow and depose the king in favour of a Princess. The Christian Readers were all accused of being involved in this plot though this chief had had no possible opportunity for holding communication with very many or even any of them. His first duty after seeing the Katikiro was to present himself before the king with the tribute he had collected for his master. Now he never had time given him to see the king. On the very morning of his arrival near the capital on the way to visit the Katikiro and king he was further charged with firing too heavy a salute of guns the previous day announcing his arrival.

The exact details of the day of the fight have never been clearly explained to me. However this man was charged together with the other Christians of having in their company a Princess whom they intended to place on the throne. The meaning of the Princess was that the Christians wanted to be governed by a woman as was the custom in Ebulaya.* A story more false and groundless could never have been invented. When

Kiwewa was to be placed on the throne the drum announcing rebellion was beaten. There was no attempt or intention to rebel on the part of the Christians and the first guns were fired by the Mohammadans and their supporters. There was a court held that morning, and the Katikiro was questioned it appears in court about his fidelity to the king. Well, the Katikiro left abruptly and he had hardly got back to his houses, when he was summoned back to the open space outside leading to the kings courts. The fight had begun.

Thus taken by surprise, the Christian leaders and their followers had to fight for their lives. They had to fight at a great disadvantage and against desperate odds. The determination of the Mohammedans was to turn out the Katikiro. The battle waged fiercely for some time, but the Christians had not been able to collect in sufficient quantities nor yet in time. The Katikiro and Mukwenda had been heard to say that they never intended to fight, they were forced into the battle and defeated. Two if not more of the chief Christians Readers were killed, the young admiral and another chief. The body of the Christians fled with the Katikiro and the Mukwenda.

Now the fight being over the business of settling the new order of things was entered upon. A new Katikiro, new Mukwenda, new Pokino, new Koluji were soon chosen. The sub chiefs and subordinates were then appointed. . . .

– from the archives of the Church Missionary
Society, London.

Walker: the Reverend R. H. Walker, a C.M.S. missionary.
Mwanga: Kabaka of Buganda, 1884–97.
Pokino: a county chief of Buddu, Buganda.
Mujassi: Buganda's 'General'.
Kiwewa: short-time Kabaka of Buganda 1888.
Mukwenda: county chief of Singo.
Ebulaya: England, Britain.

8. KABAKA MWANGA APPEALS TO THE IMPERIAL BRITISH EAST AFRICA COMPANY, 1889

Kabaka Mwanga to F. J. Jackson, 15 June 1889

I am writing to the white men, Englishmen who are passing through Masailand towards Usoga. Many compliments to my friends who I love in the Lord. After salaams I will give my news. Hear it. First I was a very bad man to God and therefore my people turned me out of my kingdom. I ran away to the Europeans of Usukuma,* I joined the Christian religion. I repented of all my sins I had committed before God. The Christians who remained in the country with the Europeans fought the Mohammedans and drove them out. The Christians went and lived in Usugara.* They wrote letters to the Europeans to get me to return and fight again with the Mohammedans. I went back to my throne. Then Mr Stokes* arrived with letters and told me about you; he did not find me in Uganda. Mr Mackay was in Usukuma. They gave news that twelve Europeans with 1000 guns were coming up by Masailand towards Usoga wanting to go to Uganda. Well Mr Stokes gave me passage by his boat and brought me to the Christians (of Uganda): I found they had fought a second time and again a third time they defeated them (Mohammedans). I saw one Island in Nyanza.* I built on it. I took all the Islands and canoes from the Mohammedans, I did not leave them one. I am now living on the island. I send you the news that you may come here, and that we Christians may join together. By the help of God we will conquer. I pray you be good enough to come and put me on my throne. I will give you plenty of ivory and you may do any trade in Uganda and all you like in the country under me. Hear me a second time my father. If you come send word and I will send the canoes to bring you over. Send one European, Mr Last, to hold a shauri first. Stokes has left a letter here which I send you. He said if the Europeans come before I return give them this letter. Stokes has gone again to Usukuma to bring gun-powder. He said if the Europeans come to Usoga let them wait I will come back quickly I will not delay. The man I send is named Ukassa* when he reaches you he will give you all our news when you arrive at Akoli.* The first man I sent I don't know whether he reached you. The Lord bless and keep you – Believe me, Your brother and friend

Leon Mwanga
King of Uganda

– from Public Record Office, London, F.O. 84/2061.

Usukuma: at the south end of Lake Victoria.
Usugara: to the south-west.
Stokes: Charles Stokes, European trader, ex-C.M.S. missionary.
Nyanza: Lake Victoria.
Ukassa: Mukasa.
Akoli: Wakoli's in Eastern Busoga.

9. THE COMPANY'S OCCUPATION
OF BUGANDA, 1890

Apolo Kagwa, Katikiro, to Colonel Euan-Smith, British Consul-General, Zanzibar, 25 April 1890.

To the Consul-General of Victoria, Queen of the English, who lives at Zanzibar.

I, the Vizir of Uganda, under Mwanga, acquaint you with the whole state of affairs. All of us, the people of Mwanga in Uganda, are called Christians. But all of us people have no common counsel. We are divided into two parties. One party is the Katoliki (Roman Catholics). They had been taught by the French. And the other party are ourselves, the people of the religion of the Book (Protestants). We have been taught by the English. These Katoliki have become, as it were, half the land, and we, the people of the Book, have become as it were the other half. Well, when Mr Jackson* reached us at Uganda, when he was called by Mwanga, he found us in the dangers of war. We were fighting with our enemies, the Mahommedans.

When we asked him to help us, he said, 'If I help you, you must put yourselves under English protection, your King and all his people, and all his lands.' So we people of the Book at once agreed to Mr Jackson's words, but the Katoliki were persuaded into not putting themselves under English protection without making inquiry at the coast, and so we had a difference about this matter, and we separated, and at once agreed to follow Mr Jackson, and the Katoliki at once agreed to go elsewhere.

So, then, when we were leaving the land, Mr Jackson bade us wait quietly, as he agreed to what the Katoliki said, that we had better write to the important people in Zanzibar, and he agreed also to leave Mr Gedge* to stay and help us, while we went to the coast to get soldiers to give us

25

real assistance. He has left Mwanga his flag, that he may return to the coast with these our people, Samuel Mwamba and Victor Senkegi. They are great people at Mwanga's Court who bring these letters, so I tell you that I and all my connections in no way want any other plan, because we have already agreed to place ourselves under English protection, if they help us. Nor shall we change aught that we have agreed to.

This is the end. Many compliments to you.

I am, etc.

Apolo, Katikiro of Uganda.

Kabaka Mwanga to Colonel Euan-Smith, British Consul-General, Zanzibar, 26 April 1890.

I inform you of the news of Uganda. How that when the Mahommedans had driven me out I dwelt on an island. I sent to Mr Jackson to help me, and he refused, and said, 'I cannot help you now.'

So we fought by ourselves and drove them out. When I returned to Mengo Mr Peters,* the German, came and asked me for a Treaty of Commerce, and I gave it to him. Then Mr Jackson came and wanted a Treaty to farm the Customs of the land and to put his flag up, and that I should enter into his hands, and I refused, and my people refused.

Now, I am sending two of my people to the English Consul, and the French Consul, and the German Consul, named Samuel Mwemba and Victor Senkezi, great people at my Court, that they may know your counsel. If they want to help us, what repayment should we make to them? Because I do not want to give them (or you) my land. I want all Europeans of all nations to come to Uganda, to build and to trade as they like.

So I beg you to allow guns and powder to reach Uganda, that we may thoroughly drive out the Mahommedans.

I am, etc.

Mwanga, King of Uganda.

– from Public Record Office, London, F.O. 84/2064.

Jackson: F. J. Jackson, leader of an Imperial British East Africa Company expedition.
Gedge: Jackson's companion.
Peters: Carl Peters, German adventurer.

10. THE PROTESTANT VICTORY, 1892

Henry Wright Duta Kitakule* to a Missionary in Zanzibar, 5 April 1892.

I am writing to you a second time to tell you about Uganda. In my first letter I told you how we fought with the Catholics and drove out King Mwanga. Well, when we had driven out the Catholics Mwanga ran away and reached Kiziba, which is German territory, and remained there. We sent him many written requests that he would return to his throne, but he refused, and applied to the Germans to come and help him. They refused. So then Mwanga sent us a written proposal, saying, 'I wish to return to my throne', we invited him and he ran away from the Catholics and returned to us and we restored him to his throne. Further we assigned to all the Catholics a district of Uganda, viz. Budu, and there they lived apart. We told them, 'we do not wish to mix with the Catholics again'.

At the present time we Protestants have possessed to ourselves of a very large district, and all the islands; and now the Mohammedans are applying to us to assign them a district, where they may settle and cease fighting with us: but the terms are not yet finally agreed upon. We hope that the Protestants will now have chief power in Uganda, and I think the land will perhaps be at peace. King Mwanga proposed to make a formal statement to us of his wish to be a Protestant; but we told him 'Remain for a time in the Catholic Religion', as he was, because he was not yet a true or sincere believer. King Mwanga has hoisted the English flag and it is now flying before his house.

$$- \text{from Zanzibar Secretariat Archives, E. } \textbf{143.}$$

Kitakbule: an Anglican clergyman.

11. COMPANY'S TO IMPERIAL PROTECTORATE, 1894

Colvile's Treaty, 29 August 1894.

Treaty between Henry Edward Colvile, a Companion of the Most Honourable Order of the Bath, a Colonel in Her Majesty's Army, Her Britannic Majesty's Acting Commissioner for Uganda, for and on behalf of Her Majesty the Queen of Great Britain and Ireland, Empress of India, etc., her heirs and successors, and Mwanga, King of Uganda, for himself, his heirs and successors:

1. Whereas Her Majesty's Government has sanctioned the Agreement between Mwanga, King of Uganda, and Sir Gerald Herbert Portal, K.C.M.G., C.B., Her Britannic Majesty's Commissioner and Consul-General for East Africa, made at Kampala on the 29th day of May, 1893.

2. And whereas Her Britannic Majesty has been graciously pleased to bestow on the said Mwanga, King of Uganda, the protection which he requested in that Agreement;

3. I, the said Mwanga, do hereby pledge and bind myself, my heirs and successors to the following conditions:

4. I undertake to make no Treaties or Agreement of any kind whatsoever with any Europeans of whatever nationality without the consent and approval of Her Majesty's Representative.

5. I freely recognize that so far as I, the King, am concerned the sole jurisdiction over Europeans and over all persons not born in my dominions, and the settlement of all cases in which any such persons may be a party or parties, lie exclusively in the hands of Her Majesty's Representative.

6. In Civil cases between my subjects, the Court of Her Majesty's Representative shall be a Supreme Court of Appeal, but it shall lie entirely within the discretion of the said Representative to refuse to hear such appeals.

7. In criminal cases where only natives are concerned, it is left to the discretion of Her Majesty's Representative to interfere, in the public interest and for the sake of justice, to the extent and in the manner which he may consider desirable.

8. And I, Mwanga, the King, undertake to see that due effect is given to all and every decision of the Court of Her Majesty's Representative under Articles 6 and 7.

9. I, Mwanga, fully recognize that the protection of Great Britain entails the complete recognition by myself, my Government, and people, throughout my kingdom of Uganda and its dependencies, of all and every international act and obligation to which Great Britain may be a party, as binding upon myself, my successors, and my said Government and people, to such extent and in such manner as may be prescribed by Her Majesty's Government.

10. No war or warlike operations of any kind shall be undertaken without the consent of Her Majesty's Representative, whose concurrence shall also be obtained in all serious matters of State, such as the appointment of Chiefs or officials, the political or religious distribution of territory, etc.

11. The assessment and collection of taxes, as also the disposal of the

revenues of the country, are hereby made subject to the control and revision of Her Majesty's Government in such manner as they may from time to time direct.

12. The property of Her Majesty's Government and of their officers and of all servants of Her Majesty's Government, shall be free from the incidence of all taxes.

13. Export and import duties on all goods leaving or entering Uganda and its dependencies shall be leviable by Her Majesty's Government for their sole use and benefit. These duties shall be fixed in accordance with the provisions of the General Acts of Berlin and Brussels of 1885, and 1890 respectively, and of any International Agreements arising from the same and to which Great Britain is or may become a party.

14. The foreign relations of Uganda and its dependencies are hereby placed unreservedly in the hands of Her Majesty's Representative.

15. Slave-trading or slave-raiding, or the exportation or importation of people for sale or exchange as slaves, is prohibited. I, Mwanga also undertake, for myself and my successors, to give due effect to such Laws and Regulations, having for their object the complete ultimate abolition of the status of slavery in Uganda and its dependencies as may be dictated by Her Majesty's Government.

16. The present Treaty supersedes all other Agreements or Treaties whatsoever made by Mwanga or his predecessors.

17. This Treaty shall come into force from the date of its signature.

In faith whereof we have respectively signed this Treaty, and have thereunto affixed our seals.

Done in duplicate at Kampala this 27th day of August, 1894.

H. E. Colvile, Colonel.

Kabaka, King.

This is to certify that the above are the signatures of Colonel H. E. Colvile, C.B., and Mwanga, King of Uganda.

W. T. Ansorge.

Apollo, Katikiro.

Mugwanya, Katikiro.

– from Public Record Office, London, enclosure in Colvile to Hardinge, 28 August 1894, F.O. 2/72.

12. ASSOCIATION WITH EARLY BRITISH ADMINISTRATORS

Samwiri Mukasa to Captain Lugard,* 29 June 1894.

My dear Captn F. D. Lugard.

Many many greetings to you I cannot count the greetings from me and after the greetings thank you for my letter which you sent us, by the hand of Apollo K. it arrived this month June 28th 1894.

Now Uganda begins to have peace. Today there is no trouble which you were worried with in those days and war and strife and fighting, since these our Catholic brethren as they are now quiet, each person obtains his own property; there is now no robbery or quarreling. But I am amazed at your wisdom and your fellow feeling for us to remember us just like you remember your European friends. You have already got to Europe and yet you remember even us simple black folk, you have already met again your English friends and they gave you joy and you have talked with them and yet you remember constantly to write your letters to us, this is your third greeting. Oh! Bwana if we did not get anything from your hand for myself I have had more joy than from receiving gifts, well you look at us here from your place where you live. How is England? If the Queen writes you a letter of greeting then you rejoice don't you, and just as you rejoice so I, even I, must take joy in your letter?

Also I have never seen a Captn like you who left here to return to England and who wrote us his letters to me and Zakaria Kizito.* It is only the Europeans of the C.M.S. and you who write us their letters. I trust you like The Father for he cannot forget your very great work since it is you who were the beginning of our peace in Uganda and up till now the peace which you brought us we shall never forget you for bringing. In your letter I heard that if you want to return to Uganda you can return and we shall be glad to hear from you if you return here to Uganda.

There is not much news from here. The Governor of this place is in Ntebe.* He makes it a very fine town better than Kampala. As for King Mwanga, the Governor tried to convince him gently to leave here Kampala and Mengo, but Mwanga refused to leave Mengo but I think that in the future he will go to Ntebe.

The reason I shall not write to you about Kabalega* is that Capitn Macdonald and Major Owen have already explained to you all the news of Unyoro* and its wars and at present Kabalega has taken refuge deep in his country of Bululi. He has built there his city of hiding perhaps so that he may make a stand here and fight for his old city, just a fortress. He cannot even return to Kibiro.* And those Nubis who remained behind at the mutazinge* (Muttanzige) house have now left there and are in service as soldiers. I think that the Kingdom of Kabalega will be lost perhaps just a half will be left. But we are very sorry that the brother of the Governor Portal has died here in Uganda and also another Governor arrived when he left to return to England. But he had only a few days in England and had not yet given all the news of here in Uganda and he died suddenly like this amazingly quickly.

Here in our country he died for our sake only for he came to administer the country for the affection you great ones of England have for us. But our grief is not excessive for we have a word of joy here in the Gospel of Saint John. The Lord Jesus said, John chapter 11 verse 25, John chapter 6 verses 39, 40, if we remember these words which are really true we accept them with joy and they will prevent our grief for those who depart from this world.

And I have left the ranks of chiefs of the country of my own choice, now I am just an ordinary person. I am not Mulondo who held the chieftainship of Mulondo and Sira who was before Mukubya is now Mulondo. I now work in teaching the children of the C.M.S. Namilembe.* That is my only work. My friend Zakaria is in his position of Kangawo even now.

Greetings to all your family also. I write this letter now of mine Samuel Mukasa at Mulago.

Believe me ever your friend Samuel Mukasa.

Apolo Kagwa to Captain Lugard, 4 July 1896.

To my very dear Cap Lugard, very many greetings. After the greetings I remember you always, I have not yet forgotten you. I remember all the good that you did for us. Nowadays in our country all is peace and quiet. We are at rest, there are no disturbances and bad events and all the important Europeans who work here in Buganda are very good, we have made friends with them and get along with them.

Also my new house which I built of brick is finished, I have gone into it. All the chiefs whom you know who are your friends have sent their greetings, and also my wife as well.

May God bless you and keep you always
I your true friend
  Apollo Katikiro Kagwa

      – translations; from Lugard Papers, Rhodes
        House, Oxford.

Lugard: Captain Frederick (later Lord) Lugard, representative of the Imperial British East Africa Company in Buganda 1890–92.
Samwiri Mukasa, Zakaria Kizito: prominent Baganda Protestant chiefs.
Ntebe: Entebbe.

Kabalega: Kabarega, Omukama (ruler) of Bunyoro.
Unyoro: Bunyoro.
Kibiro: in Bunyoro.
Mutazinge: Lake Albert.
Namilembe: Namirembe, the Anglican headquarters in Buganda.

13. THE 1900 NEGOTIATIONS

The Regents of Buganda to Sir Harry Johnson, 3 January 1900.

To the Commissioner,

Greetings, and after greetings we want to thank you for what you told us. Yes, that is very good sir. And we to help ourselves as far as our land can manage. As concerning every 'hut' to pay 3 rupees, yes, but it is better for every 'hut' to pay 2 rupees this year, and 3 rupees in the following year. It is not that we are refusing to pay, it is because our land has been very much devastated by the enemy and we have not yet recovered. Your ivory has not yet been prepared even, and people have not settled down to cultivation in order to get wealth.

Again, Sir, we chiefs of the land request you to give us 1 rupee out of every 3 rupees collected from each hut, and the Government to get the remaining 2 rupees, for we are friends of Her Majesty the Queen as you said. It is not good for us to be poor and people to laugh at us saying 'look at those who call themselves friends of the Queen being short of money'.

Again Sir, in connection with the gun licence of 4 rupees – that is all right, but we beg you to give us a period of three years in which to settle our country down. This is because our guns, together with those possessed by the askari in the service of the Queen are needed in defending our country. Again we are serving the Queen with those guns and we are not entirely serving ourselves. In case of emergency, we, and the askari of the Queen are the people who shall be first to go to the front. We therefore request you to give us a period of three years, and after that, those who shall be unable to pay 4 rupees shall take back the guns to our Government. Again, some of the big chiefs have got guns; one may have 100, another 50, another 20, another 10 and another 5. All these guns help the askaris of the Queen. It is just the same, as you said, that the guns of the Police do not require a licence because they are defending the country.

Even now, Kakungulu* is serving the Queen at Bukedi.* He is trying to make the Bakedi obey the Queen. What about the guns he has? They have not yet stopped serving the Queen. Even in Buganda we have got many posts for defence. There are 7 in Budu, 2 in Koki, 3 in Kabula at Lumama's, 1 at Kitunzi, 2 at Luwekula, 1 at Kyambalango, 3 at Kimbugwe, 1 in Bugerere, 18 in Kyagwe. And what will happen to these? As for taking possession of the land, this is all in the prerogative of the Queen, and we ourselves are placed in the very positions which we hold by the Government, witness our acceptance of the Government's orders, and also the assistance we give to the Government in ruling Buganda. For it is the rules of the Queen which we seek to put into force in Buganda. Failure on our part to carry out any request is due to the immaturity of our country which is not yet used to carrying out the orders of the Queen. Because of that inexperience we shall proceed slowly in all spheres until we are able to proceed on our own. This indeed is the reason for our begging you to leave us to rule so that we may under your tutelage rule wisely. For our country, you should remember, Sir, is unique in Central Africa. For years we have been friends of the Queen, and even you yourself said so. It is on account of this friendship that we have agreed to speak our minds before you. For you have told us, Sir, to consult you about anything we do not understand so that you can explain to us. It is because of your kindness, and the mercy of Her Majesty the Queen, that we request you to read our letter and understand. We are complaining about various things which is why we have informed you. These days we are just complaining like a hen crying to go back into the egg. We are thinking of the same thing if we lose all our respect. We who are called friends of the Queen are afraid of losing respect for this will make some people laugh at us. We beg you not to be angry with us if there is anything in our letter which will make you angry, for we are but your children and you are our father and so forgive us. May God keep you.

The Regents of Buganda to F. J. Jackson, 16 January 1900.

. . . We will therefore ask what was far above our understanding and which puzzled us as much as if we had been mere children.

  1. Our first enquiry is in respect of guns – we agree to pay Rs 3/–; but will a person finding himself unable to meet the tax have the option of handing the gun in to you for keeping? And should a person, after paying the tax for a year or two find himself unable to meet the tax anymore, and wishes to hand in the gun, will you be willing to take it?

  2. We agree to the annual Hut Tax of Rs 3/– a hut, which is a reasonable tax. We would, however, ask you how invalids and old men and women are to obtain means for their sustenance while they have to meet the Rs 3/– tax?

3. With regard to the houses in the enclosure of the Kabaka and chiefs, owing to incompetency to put up proper houses, the walls that would have constituted one building have been spread to so many houses which stand in one enclosure.

Had we known the art of building, one house could have done instead of so many houses, which could have provided accommodation for servants, cooks, and stables for goats and fowls. Now the question is how these are going to be accommodated.

4. We would further enquire if our king is no longer so and what is the reason for his removal? We invited Europeans in this country of our own free will so that we may receive help at their hands; we did not do so because we had been conquered by force. We gather, however, that our Kabaka is being set aside as the government will rule the country without a king.

5. We also would ask if our Council is abolished. The Regents had acted as ˌleaders in the Kabaka's Council. Now when the Kabaka in whose behalf they were instituted Regents no longer exists, what other designation will they be known as, and how are they ʃgoing to be maintained? Will they be maintained from the Queen's revenue?

Perhaps you will ask why the Lukiko* should not be abolished. Many of our neighbours have repeatedly warned us that Europeans will possess our country, but we protested against what they said. We pointed out to them that they could see for themselves that the Europeans, although powerful, respect our customs for the sake of friendly relations. Now our neighbours will defeat us in this contention of ours.

6. We would also ask you what is going to be done about the Bakungu* and other chiefs. How will they be maintained? These chiefs are not included in the £200 category of Saza* chiefs; what then will become of these chiefs? Will they rank as Bakopi*? If our fellow chiefs are to be so degraded, how will our contentment exist? You may ask how it is that they will become Bakopi. These chiefs had surveillance over the Bakopi because the former were entitled to count fees and to a reasonable percentage on the yearly tax collection. These chiefs, excluding the Batongole,* number 783 and perform the following duties:

They go out with askaris on expeditions, supply men to do government work. Some of them decide cases in the country and thus prevent disturbances which would be dangerous to life in the villages. Some of them construct and take canoes wherever government send them, such as Sukuma and other places. Some act as the Kabaka's bodyguard while others are the Kibuga's police. The most elderly assist in deciding cases with us in the council. These chiefs are prepared to perform any other duties there may be and to learn to do any work which they at present do not know and which the government may wish to see performed in this country.

7. We are specially worried about the abolishment of our council, the Kabaka, and members of the Lukiko.

8. We also would ask why all the other Agreements drawn up previously by the Queen's representative have been abolished. Have we been guilty of any misdemeanours? We had put much trust in these Agreements and hoped they would benefit us as they were made in the Queen's name. For this reason, although Mwanga was our Kabaka, we refused to part with him as by doing so we would have rendered these Agreements invalid. We were therefore much annoyed with him and siding with the government fought and captured Mwanga.

9. We would also wish to know if the capital is no longer to be known as such. Each Saza Chief, we gather, is to remain and will no longer leave his Saza and the European officer there, in order to come up to the capital as was the former arrangement with you namely that every Saza Chief will remain for 4 months at the capital leaving a Musigire* in charge at his headquarters. What will make a Saza Chief attend at the capital in future? There will no longer be a Kabaka or Council which made him come up in the past.

10. We would also enquire the reason which has prompted the Queen to degrade her faithful and loyal subjects by placing us on the same level as the Kavirondo, Masai and others. The Queen's representatives, who came to this country before, had assured us that as long as we remain loyal, we shall retain our Kabaka and our honour. We therefore did our utmost to discharge our duties faithfully and well. We had presumed that we would retain jurisdiction over the natives and that the government will only deal with matters between non-natives and capital offences, as is the custom at present. We were quite satisfied and pleased with this arrangement.

11. With regard to forests, we would enquire where we shall collect firewood in the future, as well as fell trees for building purposes, for the construction of canoes, and for burning charcoal for the use of smithies. It has been stated by you that persons in the neighbourhood of a forest will get those commodities (or land where wood is obtainable). What about those not living near a forest?

12. As regards the taking from us of all waste land, we would state that we grow crops on such lands which also serve as pasturelands for our cattle, goats and sheep. Again where shall we obtain one or clay for making our pottery?

13. There is also the question of accommodating our youths who marry and thus require land to settle on. Where will they settle? 2,000 of them marry every year.

Are we going to live as strangers in our country? Formerly there used to be very little waste land in Buganda, but the wars which have went on for 11 years have depopulated the country. We would ask therefore that we be allowed to utilize waste lands for agricultural and pastoral purposes, and that you will only sell to non-natives such places as will be unoccupied for these purposes, the revenue accruing from such transactions going to the government.

14. We would also enquire what will maintain the Queen-Mother who has had so many estates.

15. How will the princesses and princes, relatives of the Kabaka, obtain means for their subsistence?

16. What will be the position as regards the estates purchased or of those for which promise to sell has been made.

17. There are certain coffee forests which were planted by our forefathers. What is to become of these.

18. What will be the regulation regarding big game – such as buffalo, elephant and hippopotamus and small game such as bush-buck, reedbuck, etc., which supply meat.

19. What of animals that destroy life such as lions, and leopards, and what will be the position regarding our landing places where we used to beach our canoes; where will these canoes be landed in the future?

This is the conclusion of our views.

We remain,

Your sincere friends

> Apollo Katikiro Regent
> Sitanislas Katikiro Mugwanya Regent
> Zakaria Kangawo Regent

> – translations; from Entebbe Secretariat Archives A6/8 and S.M.P.C. 450.

Kakungulu: Kakunguru, a very notable Muganda of the period.
Bukedi: in north-eastern Uganda.
Lukiko: Buganda's parliament.
Bakungu: the most important category of appointed chiefs.
Bakopi: the ordinary people of Buganda.
Batongole: a further category of appointed chiefs.
Saza: a county.
Musigire: messenger, representative.

14. THE UGANDA AGREEMENT, 1900

Extracts from the Uganda Agreement, 1900.

We, the undersigned, to wit, Sir Henry Hamilton Johnston, K.C.B., Her Majesty's Special Commissioner, Commander-in-Chief and Consul-General for the Uganda Protectorate and the adjoining Territories . . . on the one part; and the under-mentioned Regents and Chiefs of the Kingdom of Uganda on behalf of the Kabaka (King) of Uganda, and the chiefs and people of Uganda on the other part: do hereby agree to the following Articles relative to the government and administration of the Kingdom of Uganda . . .

3. The Kingdom of Uganda in the administration of the Uganda Protectorate shall rank as a province of equal rank with any other provinces into which the Protectorate may be divided . . .

5. The laws made for the general governance of the Uganda Protectorate by Her Majesty's Government will be equally applicable to the Kingdom of Uganda, except in so far as they may in any particular conflict with the terms of this agreement, in which case the terms of this Agreement will constitute a special exception in regard to the Kingdom of Uganda.

6. So long as the Kabaka, chiefs, and people of Uganda shall conform to the laws and regulations instituted for their governance by Her Majesty's Government, and shall co-operate loyally with Her Majesty's Government in the organization and administration of the said Kingdom of Uganda, Her Majesty's Government agrees to recognize the Kabaka of Uganda as the native ruler of the province of Uganda under Her Majesty's protection and over-rule. The King of Uganda shall henceforth be styled His Highness the Kabaka of Uganda. . . . The Kabaka of Uganda shall exercise direct rule over the natives of Uganda, to whom he shall administer justice through the Lukiko, or native council, and through others of his officers in the manner approved by Her Majesty's Government. The jurisdiction of the native Court of the Kabaka of Uganda, however, shall not extend to any person not a native of the Uganda province. . . .

9. For purposes of native administration the Kingdom of Uganda shall be divided into the following districts or administrative counties:

(1) Kiagwe; (2) Bugerere; (3) Bulemezi; (4) Buruli; (5) Bugangadzi; (6) Buyaga; (7) Bwekula; (8) Singo; (9) Busuju; (10) Gomba (Butunzi); (11) Butambala (Bweya); (12) Kiadondo; (13) Busiro; (14) Mawokota; (15) Buvuma; (16) Sese; (17) Buddu; (18) Koki; (19) Mawogola; (20) Kabula.

At the head of each county shall be placed a chief who shall be selected by the Kabaka's Government, but whose name shall be submitted for approval to Her Majesty's representative. This chief, when approved by Her Majesty's representative, shall be guaranteed from out of the revenue of Uganda a salary at the rate of £200 a year. To the chief of a county will be entrusted by Her Majesty's Government, and by the Kabaka, the task of administering justice amongst the natives dwelling in his county, the assessment and collection of taxes, the up-keep of the main roads, and the general supervision of native affairs. On all questions but the assessment and collection of taxes the chief of the county will report direct to the King's native ministers, from whom he will receive his instructions. When arrangements have been made by Her Majesty's Government for the organization of a police force in the province of Uganda, a certain number of police will be placed at the disposal of each chief of a county to assist him in maintaining order. For the assessment and payment of taxes, the chief of a county shall be immediately responsible to Her Majesty's representative, and should he fail in his duties in this respect, Her Majesty's representative shall have the right to call upon the Kabaka to dismiss him from his duties and to appoint another chief in his stead. In each county an estate, not exceeding an area of 8 square miles, shall be attributed to the chieftainship of a county, and its usufruct shall be enjoyed by the person occupying, for the time being, the position of chief of the county.

10. To assist the Kabaka of Uganda in the government of his people he shall be allowed to appoint three native officers of state, with the sanction and approval of Her Majesty's representative in Uganda (without whose sanction such appointments shall not be valid) – A Prime Minister, otherwise known as Katikiro; a Chief Justice; and a Treasurer or Controller of the Kabaka's revenues. These officials shall be paid at the rate of £300 a year. Their salaries shall be guaranteed them by Her Majesty's Government from out of the funds of the Uganda Protectorate ... Her Majesty's chief representative in Uganda shall at any time have direct access to the Kabaka, and shall have the power of discussing matters affecting Uganda with the Kabaka alone or, during his minority, with the Regents; but ordinarily the three officials above designated will transact most of the Kabaka's business with the Uganda Administration. The Katikiro shall be *ex officio* the President of the Lukiko, or native council; The Vice-President of the Lukiko shall be the native Minister of Justice for the time being; in the absence of both Prime Minister and Minister of Justice, the Treasurer of the Kabaka's revenues, or third minister, shall preside over the meetings of the Lukiko.

11. The Lukiko, or native council, shall be constituted as follows:

In addition to the three native ministers, who shall be *ex officio* senior members of the council each chief of a county (twenty in all) shall be *ex officio* a member of the Council. Also each chief of a county shall be permitted to appoint a person to act as his lieutenant in this respect to attend the meetings of the council during his absence and to speak and vote in his name. The chief of a county, however, and his lieutenant may not both appear simultaneously at the council. In addition, the Kabaka shall select from each county three notables, whom he shall appoint during his pleasure, to be members of the Lukiko or native council. The Kabaka may also, in addition to the foregoing, appoint six other persons of importance in the country to be members of the native council. The Kabaka may at any time deprive any individual of the right to sit on the native council, but in such a case shall intimate his intention to Her Majesty's representative in Uganda, and receive his assent thereto before dismissing the member. The functions of the council will be to discuss all matters concerning the native administration of Uganda, and to forward to the Kabaka resolutions which may be voted by a majority regarding measures to be adopted by the said administration. The Kabaka shall further consult with Her Majesty's representative in Uganda before giving effect to any such resolution voted by the native council, and shall, in this matter, explicitly follow the advice of Her Majesty's representative. . . .

12. In order to contribute to a reasonable extent towards the general cost of the maintenance of the Uganda Protectorate, there shall be established the following taxation for Imperial purposes, that is to say, the proceeds of the collection of these taxes shall be handed over intact to Her Majesty's representative in Uganda as the contribution of the Uganda province towards the general revenue of the Protectorate. . . .

15. The land of the Kingdom of Uganda shall be dealt with in the following manner:

Assuming the area of the Kingdom of Uganda, as comprised within the limits cited in this agreement, to amount to 19,600 square miles, it shall be divided in the following proportions:

	Square miles
Forests to be brought under control of the Uganda Administration	1,500
Waste and uncultivated land to be vested in Her Majesty's Government, and to be controlled by the Uganda Administration	9,000
Plantations and other private property of His Highness the Kabaka of Uganda	350
Plantations and other private property of the Namasole	16
Plantations and other private property of the Namasole, mother of Mwanga	10
To the Princes: Joseph, Augustine, Ramazan, and Yusufu-Suna, 8 square miles each	32

	Square Miles	
For the Princesses, sisters, and relations of the Kabaka		90
To the Abamasaza (chiefs of counties) twenty in all, 8 square miles each (private property)	160	
Official estates attached to the posts of the Abamasaza, 8 square miles each	160	
		320
The three Regents will receive private property to the extent of 16 square miles each	48	
And official property attached to their office, 16 square miles each, the said official property to be afterwards attached to the posts of the three native ministers	48	
		96
Mbogo (the Muhammedan chief) will receive for himself and his adherents		24
Kamswaga, chief of Koki, will receive		20
One thousand chiefs and private landowners will receive the estates of which they are already in possession, and which are computed at an average of 8 square miles per individual, making a total of		8,000
There will be allotted to the three missionary societies in existence in Uganda as private property, and in trust for the native churches as much as		92
Land taken up by the Government for Government stations prior to the present settlement (at Kampala, Entebbe, Masaka, etc, etc.)		50
Total		19,600

. . . As regards the allotment of the 8,000 square miles among the 1,000 private landowners, this will be a matter to be left to the decision of the Lukiko, with an appeal to the Kabaka. The Lukiko will be empowered to decide as to the validity of claims, the number of claimants and the extent of land granted, premising that the total amount of land thus allotted amongst the chiefs and accorded to native landowners of the country is not to exceed 8,000 square miles. . . .

Her Majesty's Government, however, reserves to itself the right to carry through or construct roads, railways, canals, telegraphs, or other useful public works, or to build military forts or works of defence on any property, public or private. . . .

20. . . . should the Kabaka, chiefs, or people of Uganda, pursue, at any

time, a policy which is distinctly disloyal to the British Protectorate, Her Majesty's Government will no longer consider themselves bound by the terms of this Agreement. . . .

Done in English and Luganda at Mengo, in the Kingdom of Uganda, on the 10th March, 1900.

> H. H. Johnston
> Apollo, Katikiro, Regent
> Mugwanya, Matikiro, Regent
> Mbogo Noho, his X mark
> Zakaria Kizito, Kangawo, Regent, etc. etc.

> – from N. Turton, J. B. Griffin, and A. W. Lewey, *Laws of the Uganda Protectorate*, London 1936, Vol. VI, pp. 1373–84.

15. BRITISH POLICY, 1909

Opinion of a senior British administrator in Uganda [1909].

. . . The existence of the Agreement is the central fact of the Protectorate, and I am unable to think that it could be relegated to 'its proper position', presumably the background, even if it were desirable so to do. Even if the Protectorate was amalgamated with the whole of the British possessions in Africa, the Uganda Agreement would nevertheless remain the central fact of administration in Uganda, unless the British Government was prepared to go back upon its solemn assurances and treat it as null and void. This proposal [for the amalgamation of the Uganda and the East Africa Protectorates] cannot for one moment be seriously considered. . . . The conditions in the two Protectorates [Uganda and British East Africa] are almost entirely different as regards administration, native government and produce. Many travellers, distinguished and otherwise, have remarked that upon crossing the Lake they appear to have come to an entirely different country. The relations existing between Officials, Civilians and Natives bear no resemblance to those of the East Africa Protectorate. In this Protectorate there is an organized scheme of native government of considerable importance; and it is not too much to say that the whole scheme of administration is entirely different to that of the East African Protectorate and requires special knowledge which can only be acquired in the Protectorate. . . . As regards the native governments, I know that they would greatly demur to any amalgamation which would tend to reduce their rightful importance. Administrative Officers of experience in this Protectorate are agreed that the best method of developing the country is through the native governments, and that these governments should be upheld and established in every possible way . . .

> – from 'Memorandum containing rough notes for a despatch to the Secretary of State upon the question of Amalgamation between the Uganda Protectorate and the East African Protectorate'. Confidential [Unsigned, but by Stanley Tomkins, 1909], Public Record Office, London C.O. 533/63.

16. ENTRENCHING THE OLIGARCHY, 1912

Proposal by the Regents of Buganda for 'The Council of Bataka (Chiefs and Princes), being a Constitution of a new Chieftainship and a Council for those Chiefs who hold most land in Buganda', 5 June 1912

Whereas it has been seen that the country is progressing very fast in wealth and education, and that owing to thè rapid progress of the country those Chiefs who now possess most land in the country by allotment under the Uganda Agreement, will on retiring from their present official positions, become mere peasants in spite of the fact that they possess most of the land; whilst before we had our hereditary Butaka Chieftainships which governed the country with the Kabaka, but which have been mixed up by the introduction of Mailos or allotment of land.

Now therefore we the undersigned wish to constitute a Chieftainship in our new Butaka lands which we have acquired, and to give the right to those holding this Chieftainship of expressing their opinion on matters relative to land and wealth of the country, as follows:

I. The Chieftainship to be established shall be called 'Bakungu na Balangira' (Chiefs and Princes).

II. The right to be given to those holding the above-mentioned Chieftainship shall be in the form of a Council of their own which shall be called the 'Council of Bataka' (Landowners), subject to the following provisions.

I. (1) It must be clearly understood at the outset that this new Chieftainship shall have nothing to do whatever with, or effect in any way the present positions held by Chiefs under the Government, nor interfere in the government of the country, but that it is an Honour conferred on great Landowners of the country.

(2) For this reason therefore this Chieftainship shall be conferred only on the following classes of Chiefs under condition that each of these Chiefs has more than ten square miles of land; ten square miles of land is the minimum amount of land required in this Constitution, and no one with less than this amount shall be allowed to be conferred upon him this Chieftainship, except in the cases of Princes who may be allowed to sit in the Council of Bataka and be styled Balangira (Princes), even if they do not possess more than five square miles of land. Chiefs of the following classes who are qualified to have this Chieftainship conferred upon them shall be called 'Bakungu' or Balangira according to their ranks and shall enjoy the privileges and rights of the 'Bakungu na Balangira'; the following are the classes of Chiefs to whom this Honour can be conferred under the above conditions:

(i) The five Princes who are:

Bwana Nuhu Mbogo
Yusufu Suna Kiwewa
Joseph Musanje Walugembe
Augustine Tebandeke
Alamanzani Ndaula

And their respective heirs.
These shall be styled princes.

(ii) The three Regents while in their present positions or retired.

(iii) County Chiefs while in their present positions or retired.

(iv) Gombolola* Chiefs while in their present positions or retired, subject to the above-mentioned conditions as to land.

(v) Heirs of Chiefs mentioned in classes (ii), and (iii) and (iv), subject to the above mentioned conditions as to land.

(vi) Any other Chiefs upon whom the Kabaka with the advice of the majority of the Council of Bataka shall, from time to time, confer the privileges of a 'Mukungu' and the right to sit in the Council of Bataka, provided always that such chiefs satisfy required in this Constitution to the amount of land they possess. However the Kabaka shall not create any one a 'Mukungu' without the approval or consent of the majority of the Council of Bataka.

II. (1) The above mentioned Chiefs and Princes who are qualified for this Chieftainship of 'Bakungu na Balangira' shall compose the Council of Bataka.

(2) The Kabaka is the nominal head of the Council of Bataka, but in practical business there shall be a President of the council elected by the majority of the Council in consideration of the amount of land he possesses and what he is doing on his land to promote the wealth of the country, but this does not take away the right of the council to elect any

43

other man more suitable to fill his place if they find that the man with most land is of no use as a leader in the Council.

(3) In addition to the President above-referred to the majority of the Council shall elect a Vice-President, a Treasurer and a Secretary in precisely the same way as they elect the President, and these four together with three other members of the Council who shall be elected by the majority of the Council, shall form a 'Committee' which shall decide from time to time, the time and place of the meeting of the Council, and shall in this case authorize the Secretary to inform each member of the Council in writing the time decided for the meeting of the Council. The Committee moreover shall deal first with every other subject submitted to the Council, before it is brought before the Council for discussion. In the meetings of the Council of the Committee, in absence of the President the Vice-President shall take the Chair, or failing him the Treasurer shall take the Chair, who in addition to this shall look after all financial matters of the Council. The Secretary shall keep minutes of the proceedings of the Council, and issue notices, etc., to Members of the Council if authorized by the Committee or the President of the Council.

(4) Any member of the Committee has the right to submit to the Committee any name of a Chief who in his opinion should have the privileges of a 'Mukungu' and the right to sit in the Council of Bataka, conferred upon him, and if the Committee approve of him his real name shall then be submitted to the Council, and if the majority of the Council approve of him, the President of the Council shall recommend him to the Kabaka, who alone has the power to create any Chiefs a 'Mukungu', and to give him the right to sit in the Council of Bataka. In creating such a 'Mukungu' the Kabaka shall give him a letter signed by himself, the President, Vice-President, and the Treasurer which confer upon him the title and privileges of a 'Mukungu' and the right to sit in the Council of Bataka. A 'Mukungu' created in this manner shall pay to the Treasurer of the Council the sum of Rs 500/– which money when collected shall be at the disposal of the Council of Bataka.

(5) Any chief belonging to this Chieftainship, when being written to shall be designated by the title of 'Mukungu' put after his surname, and no other person may put this title after his surname who does not belong to this Chieftainship, and if such a person is found he shall be sent to the Lukiko to be tried for this offence.

(6) Any 'Mukungu' and a Member of the Council who shall sell his land in such a way so that he is left with less than the minimum amount of land required in this Constitution, shall be deprived of the privileges and title of a 'Mukungu' and the right to sit in the Council of Bataka.

(7) The President of the Council can always warn any 'Mukungu' whom he thinks is not behaving himself as he should in the Council, and if such a 'Mukungu' does not seem to take any notice of the President's warning on several occasions, the President may, if he thinks fit, submit

his name to the Council and if the majority of the Council decide that he should be deprived of his right to sit in the Council, the President shall then send up his name to the Kabaka and advise him to depose such a 'Mukungu' from their Council; such a 'Mukungu' who is deposed from the Council in this manner shall not forfeit his title of 'Mukungu'.

(8) The chief object of this Council of Bataka is the consideration of Laws, Ordinances, or Agreements relative to land and wealth of the country – such as Land Laws, Ordinances, or Tax Agreements, etc. – which the Lukiko wish to enact or make or contract. In these cases the Lukiko shall inform the 'Bakungu na Balangira' first of all of what they propose to do, and then afterwards send to their Council draft of Laws or Agreements which they wish to enact or contract and ask for their opinion, which when given should be carefully considered by the Lukiko. Nothing in this clause shall be construed as giving the Council of Bataka any power to interfere in the management of affairs by the Lukiko, the native Administration, but simply to express their opinion on matters referred to above.

(9) The Council of Bataka however can always submit to the Lukiko or the Kabaka resolutions or protests passed by the majority of the Council on any subject which in their opinion is the cause of universal grievance. This Council has also the right to appeal to the Government through the Lukiko, in special cases against the decision of the Lukiko.

> – from Entebbe Secretariat Archives, C/113/1910.
> enclosure in Knowles, Provincial Commissioner,
> Buganda, to Chief Secretary, Uganda, 18 June
> 1912.

See Michael Twaddle, 'The *Bakungu* chiefs of Buganda under British Colonial Rule, 1900–1930', *Journal of African History*, x, no. 2., 1969, pp. 309–22. *Gombolola:* sub-county.

17. THE AUTONOMY OF BUGANDA, 1914

Katikiro and Omuwanika of Buganda to Provincial Commissioner, Buganda, 26 February 1914.

We beg most humbly to draw your attention to the following points which, in our opinion, are ruining the power of the Lukiko, and violating the provisions and intention of the Uganda Agreement, 1900, in connection with the Administration of our Country.

2. As you know, Sir, for judicial and Administrative purposes, it was laid down in the Uganda Agreement, just mentioned above, that the Province of Buganda should be divided into twenty different counties, with a Chief at the head of each County, who should be directly responsible to the Kabaka through the Lukiko, except in the matter of collecting the Government Tax. At present, however, some Saza Chiefs disregard the Lukiko altogether and consider themselves directly responsible to the District Officers. Some of them have even begun to send in reports of their Counties etc, to the District Commissioners without the Lukiko's knowledge, which they are really not supposed to do except through the Lukiko. The District Officers have not discouraged this, with the result that sometimes, some important Administrative point is discussed and settled by the Saza Chiefs and the District Commissioners without our knowledge, or sometimes when the matter has been referred to the Lukiko by the District Commissioner for discussion in the Lukiko, we do not know what correspondence has already passed between the District Commissioner and the Saza Chief. For example, we have only to quote the recent case of the Saza Chief Kangao in connection with the allotment of surplus estates and lapsed areas. If the Kangawo had a complaint against Sir Apolo Kagwa, in his capacity as the Katikiro, with reference to a particular allotment of a surplus estate or lapsed area, why could he not bring his case before the Lukiko, instead of writing direct to the District Commissioner? This was a purely native matter triable by the Lukiko, against whose decision, if he wished, he could have appealed to the Provincial Commissioner. We beg to draw special attention to this Chief Kangawo, and we would ask you to demand an explanation from him, for he has on several occasions disregarded the Lukiko.

3. Again, Sir, at present a great many cases allowed to come up before you, which really could be finally settled by the Lukiko. Of course, no one whose case has been decided against himself, will ever see the justice of such Judgment and will always wish to appeal against the decision. We do not, Sir, mean that no cases should be allowed to come before you, but we only wish to point out to you that by allowing every petty case to come before you, a great many Baganda, especially the Chiefs, are apt to disregard the Lukiko and to appeal in every single case before the Provincial Commissioner.

4. In conclusion, we would add, Sir, that it is most important to go into this question of the power of the Lukiko thoroughly and to settle it before His Highness the Kabaka comes of age, as it is otherwise quite evident that it will be very difficult for him to rule his country. Everyone will only be too ready to disregard the decision of his court, and to appeal at once to the Provincial Commissioner, however small the case may be. We would therefore ask you, and to remind the Saza Chiefs of their duty towards the Lukiko.

5. Briefly the following are the points that we would beg to submit for your consideration:

(1) That for Administrative purposes the Saza Chief should be directly responsible to the Kabaka through the Lukiko, except in the matter of collecting tax.

(2) That District Commissioners should, as far as possible, discourage this disregard of the Lukiko by the Saza Chiefs, and should when writing to the Saza Chiefs send a copy of such letter to the Lukiko for their information.

(3) That appeals of petty and useless cases should be discouraged as far as it is consistent with justice.

6. It is most important that the power of the Lukiko should be properly recognized by all the Baganda if the Lukiko is to maintain its proper place, as the Final Native Court and the Headquarters of the Native Government of Buganda.

We beg most humbly to apologize for troubling you so much with such a long letter.

We have the honour to be, Sir, Your most obedient servant,

Apolo Kagwa Katikiro
Zakaria Kizito Kisingiri

Andereya Kaima to Provincial Commissioner, Buganda, 6 March 1914.

I have the honour to inform you the reason why I refused to sign the letter which the two Regents wrote you on the 26-2-14.

1. I know that I am Regent as the others are, while they were arranging the matters they did not let me know about that, so they discussed it secretly.

2. In their letter they said that District Commissioners must not write letters to county Chiefs without letting them know and also the Saza Chiefs must not write letters to D.C. before letting the Lukiko know. If the Mengo Lukiko surpasses Kampala's (Lukiko) it is true, but we all know that we are under the Kabaka and his Lukiko. But we are prevented from introducing any word to Kampala. Sir, I have seen this matter is very important and it deserves to be put right in ruling the Kabaka as he is grown up. Because I think he will judge his subjects as well as possible. But to prevent Saza Chiefs from introducing any word to D.C. who rules them, it will not be good, because the Saza Chiefs are under the P.C. and D.C. Sir, remember the matter which Katikiro said to Kyambalango, Luwekula and Kiimba that I will persecute you so much for your (Master) Mugwanya appointed the Muhammedans to take our Saza for that reason, all the Saza Chiefs rely on D.C. and P.C.

3. If that matter was good and profitable to our country, they could not

hide it from me, so they should have called me to complete it. And I wish to plead that matter before you, on account of putting right such a matter concerning the Kingdom of Buganda by themselves. And they put me aside as I am not Regents as they [are].

4. They state that any man who has a small case he is not worthy to go to Kampala to plead it.

They refused a man who has stopped 4 or 5 months before plead his case to state it before them. But who will help that man if he does not go to P.C. and the D.C.?

For the reason (which) I mentioned above, I therefore refuse to sign the letter.

I have the honour to be, Sir, your obedient servant,

Andereya Kaima.

Provincial Commissioner Buganda (F. A. Knowles) to the Regents and the Lukiko, 9 March 1914.

With reference to the letter dated the 25 February 1914, signed by Sir Apolo and Kisingiri, and the Acting Regent's Kaima's letter of the 6th instant on the subject of upholding the 'Kitabwa'* of the Lukiko, I regret to see that you cannot agree with one another, and have to write separate letters on such a subject, concerning which you certainly should be of one mind.

2. The Acting Regent should have been consulted before the letter above referred to was written, the fact that he was not so consulted shows, I regret to see, that there is still ill feeling between you.

3. The Acting Regent's letter of the 6th instant points to the same fact, and I am very sorry to see it, in spite of His Excellency's recent advice to you on the subject and my repeated warnings that your duties must seriously suffer while you keep up your petty quarrels. One of your most important duties as Regents is to work *together* with one accord for the good of the country. I hope I shall not have to speak to you again on the subject.

4. It has always been Government policy to uphold the 'Kitabwa' of the Lukiko, in so far as is compatible with the welfare of the country, and I quite agree that the Saza Chiefs should realize that they are subject to the Lukiko, though at the same time it is very necessary that they should report to the District Commissioners in the course of their duties. They can send copies to you of all such reports that are important.

5. With regard to the petty cases where no appeal lies these are invariably returned to the native Court for trial, and only those received in the British Native Courts which the authorized Officers find it necessary to hear in the exercise of their revisional powers.

6. The Saza Chiefs will be assembled at the end of this month and you

should inform them what I have said in the matter. The District Commissioners will also be informed.

– from Masaka District Archives.

The Kabaka referred to was Daudi Chwa, 1897–1939.
Kitabwa: Kitibwa, respect, honour, prestige.

18. BRITISH ADMINISTRATIVE POLICY, 1917

Provincial Commissioner, Buganda, to District Commissioner, Masaka, 6 July 1917.

The general policy and native administration of Buganda must of necessity owing to the Uganda Agreement, 1900, vary to a considerable degree to what is in vogue in other Provinces and this memorandum is written as a general guide mainly to officers newly posted to the Province and to those who have previously never served in Buganda. Broad lines only are given as it is recognized that in such matters and especially in individual circumstances much must be left to the discretion of the officer in local charge judging from local aspects but it is of utmost importance that the spirit of the policy should be followed in order to insure a sympathetic and united policy throughout the Province not only between the British and Native Governments but between the administrative officers of the Province.

2. Buganda is different from other Provinces in that although divided into 4 Districts for the convenience of administrative routine, it is necessary to treat it as one large area for the purposes of administrative policy and the administration of all 4 Districts by one method and policy is of the first importance.

3. The Provincial Commissioner is placed in charge of the Province to guide and advise the Native Government with the assistance of his staff of District Officers and in addition to these functions to supervise all work carried out by the Native Government, and as far as it is possible the main idea is that all executive work should be in the hands of the Native Government subject to the powers of guidance, advice and supervision already stated.

4. By these powers in accordance with the Agreement British Officers have with regard to Poll and Gun Tax sole executive control and this

k is carried out by them through their chiefs exercising full control supervision and by the Uganda Agreement (Payment by the Government, 1913) they have the power to recommend to the Governor any reduction of authorized salaries in case of neglect of duty in these respects, further British Officers are accorded the right of recommending candidates for Saza and Gombolola* Chieftainships for the approval of the Native Government and final approval of the Governor, and equally they have the right of recommending men for dismissal from these posts in all such cases recommendations should only be made after consultation in the case of Gombolola Chiefs with the Saza Chief and in the case of Saza Chiefs with the Lukiko through the Provincial Commissioner.

5. In judicial matters, vide para 6 of the Agreement and further explained by the Courts Ordinance, 1911, the powers allowed to British Officers are both ample and sufficient and without taking from the Native Government the executive power which it is necessary for it to have the British Officer, by these powers is given full and ample scope for complete supervision.

6. In neglect of administrative duties it is advisable as far as possible to work through the Native Administration, advising it as to the most suitable punishment to meet the particular case and in more serious matters utilizing the powers outlined in para 4.

7. In exercise of the powers of guidance and supervision the Kabaka, Ministers and Lukiko are directly dealt with by the Provincial Commissioner while Saza and Gombolola Chiefs are dealt with by the District Officers and by the Provincial Commissioner only through the District Officer.

8. Similarly it must be remembered that the different parts of the Native Government are centralized in the Lukiko under charge of the Kabaka's Ministers and just as with the British Administration so with the Native Administration is it necessary for there to be a united policy throughout the Province and the position of the Lukiko in executive matters as far as Chiefs are concerned is much the same as the position of the Provincial Commissioner to the District Officers, and in order to strengthen and bring together all parts of the administration both British and Native all copies of instructions issued to the Lukiko by the Provincial Commissioner and copies of instructions issued by the Lukiko as approved by the Provincial Commissioner are sent to District Commissioners for information and co-operation.

9. In all indirect matters of administration such as agricultural progress, dealings with non-natives and Government laws not in conflict with the Uganda Agreement which consequently affect the Province and in Township work, etc., the executive lies with the British Government though in many of these cases it is often advisable to consult the Native Government especially when their help is required so as to insure sympathetic co-operation.

10. These are the broad lines which should be followed by the British Administration in order to conform to the obligations laid down in the Agreement and to carry out the policy which is considered to be the best for the Province and which is in accordance with the general lines of British Native Policy, namely to give self-Government under adequate and sympathetic guidance and supervision.

11. In dealing with all matters affecting natives the aspect from the native point of view though possibly at first sight not considered of great importance by the European mind must never be lost sight of and requires careful consideration and in addition in a country such as Buganda where there is a considerable amount of educational veneer legislation and reform should be made from the point of view of the general public not from the point of view of the more advanced sections only. It must be remembered that even with the best Chiefs it is difficult for them to free their minds of religious and personal bias when questions arise affecting national matters and before decisions are come to District Officers should try to view the matter from all sides and cultivate the sense of gauging fairly accurately what is going on 'on the other side of the hill'.

– from Masaka District Archives.

Gombolola: sub-county.

19. STATEMENT TO A VISITOR, 1919

Sir Apolo Kagwa, Katikiro of Buganda to the Reverend C. F. Andrews,* 22 December 1919.

With reference to our Meeting with you in our Native Parliament this morning, we beg to confirm in writing our opinion we expressed on the following two points which came out, namely:

(*a*) We do want the Indians to remain in our country, as we consider that their being here would improve our country, and would do us a lot of good, and would do no harm to the country. Besides, we find them moral people. We would, of course, like better Indians.

(*b*) We do not want our country to be united to any other Protectorate for, we consider that if this was done, it would greatly interfere with our Uganda Treaty, 1900, and our customs. We have other reasons besides. Therefore, we would very much like this Protectorate to remain as it is.

We thank you for coming to see us and our Native Parliament, and we wish you a pleasant voyage.

> – from Public Records Office, London, Colonial Office 536/107.

Andrews: the British clergyman who was a close associate of India's Mahatma Gandhi.

20. THE YOUNG BAGANDA ASSOCIATION, 1919–21

The Secretary, The Young Baganda Association to the Reverend C. F. Andrews, 22 December 1919.

We are very glad to have this privilege of welcoming you amongst us today. When inviting you, Sir, we are not unmindful of the important duty you have to perform during your short stay in Uganda; the kindness with which you accepted it, shows clearly how much you are interested in the welfare of the natives of this country.

First of all, we beg to introduce ourselves to you, that we are the Young Baganda Association, a society newly formed and in its infancy. We are very sorry we have not got our Assembly Hall at present to receive you in, but Sir Apolo Kagwa, the Katikiro, has kindly consented to let us have this room to receive you; for which we thank him very much.

This is a good opportunity for us to be able to disclose our grievance to you, so that you may see your way to help us.

1. Now, Sir, Uganda is a country which is growing amongst the civilized people and races and is in very bad need of high education to enable her people to meet the modern affairs. The present schools we have in Uganda are under the management of the Missionaries, whom we thank very much but the standard of these schools is very low. It is so low that one who leaves these schools after having obtained 1st class certificate hardly gets any good job in offices. The girls' education is much lower than that of the boys and you know perfectly well that if girls do not receive good education the nation cannot progress. Therefore Sir, we entreat you to see your way to recommend us for high education and this can only be done when the Government schools are introduced in Uganda.

2. It appears now that cases are tried by the Government of long imprisonment without asking for the assessors.

3. Now, Sir, we are proud to say that we are true friends to the British Government, far better than any other colony, because the famous King Mutesa invited them and preferred the protection of British Government to any other Government but on the other hand Government do not trust us as they should. The 1900 Agreement gives every Muganda who can pay tax to possess at least five guns, but now if one applies for even a shot gun, it appears, sometimes that no permission is given to applicant. When the War broke out all Baganda for the love of the Mother Country volunteered and great number lost their lives during the fight, and it was never reported that any of them failed his duty.

4. Trade. We need not say that in a country like this free trade is necessary for welfare of the natives, because Baganda would appreciate it if restrictions on cotton, etc. trade are removed, to encourage people to go in trading, because if no taxes are imposed on our produce and the Government undertakes to find markets for all produces Uganda would become a big Commercial Protectorate. Also we are very glad to know that you are very much connected with the Indians, therefore we sincerely hope that you will be able to convey our message to big firms in India to come down as we need them to carry on trade with us by leasing our land, etc., because we can get on quite well with the big Indian Merchants.

The Secretary, The Young Baganda Association, to the Negro Farmers' Conference, Tuskegee Industrial and Normal Institution, Alabama, U.S.A., 13 September 1921.

I beg most sincerely to introduce to you my infant African Society – the Young Baganda Association – and to inform you that we be allowed the friendship with you.

2. This Association was established in 1919 and is in Central East Africa in the Uganda Protectorate (on Lake Victoria), a country under the British Flag with her Treaty constituted in 1900 entitling us to so many privileges. We have in our country our own Native Government with the King to reign and Ministers to govern. And land tenure is not here a matter of difficulty as in other African Colonies because under the above Treaty almost half of the whole country is in our hands. The best land are in the hands of natives.

3. The following are the objects of this Association and same are recognized by both British and Native Governments:

(1.) To improve Uganda in every possible way,
(2.) To give a helping hand to deserved Muganda who may be in distress,
(3.) To see the best way to enable us to get and maintain our education.

4. With regard to the first object, this Association was advised more

than twice by Political men and lovers of Africans that we ought to affiliate with our brothers who are over-seas such as yourself here in United States of America and others in Africa and elsewhere. Not only to the friendship but also to seek co-operation and support from time to time. You know, dear brothers, that unless we Negroes get proper education and understand modern civilized ways, we will never be advanced and enjoy all the privileges of the citizens of today; we should therefore love one another.

5. We particularly appeal to you to come and help us in developing our land. People from India and elsewhere come and trade in this country but with no intent to make us good traders and farmers. We have land but we have no leaders in this line.

A party of your deligates is welcomed to come and study the local problems with a view to determining this task of uplifting us in this way.

6. I am glad to inform you that the National Association for Advancement of Coloured Peoples in New York accepted to help us in any possible way if we ask for it.

7. We shall be very thankful and trust you will be good enough to send us an answer at your earliest convenience.

> – the first item is from Public Record Office,
> London, C.O. 536/107, the second from the
> Tuskegee Institute Archives,
> Alabama.

21. ANIMOSITY TOWARDS ASIANS, 1921

Letter from Z. K. Sentongo (in Nairobi) to the Uganda Herald, *29 July 1921*

With regard to Mr K. M. Khandwala's open letter to the President of the Young Baganda Association, published in your issue of July 15th, I would like to take up some of the points put forward.

In the commencement of his long and illogical letter so beloved by the Indian mind, he mentions the 'very cordial relations . . . between native and Indians'. To apply the term 'cordial' to the conditions existing between the exploiter and exploited shows the height of his impertinence. Who but the Indians are exploiting us? – and in turn smuggling our hard earned money into India for their own benefit – robbing us doubly. He also mentions that the 'Indian soldiers defended the shores of East Africa during the war'. Where did this happen pray? General Charrington's figures published in the Press give the number of Indians killed in action Nil. Indians died of wounds Nil. But he charitably refrains from saying how many Indians were shot as spies. It is also stated on good authority, that the Indians (British subjects) in German East Africa were not interfered with during the war when real British subjects were put in detention camps.

The performance of the native carrier corps without mentioning the native soldiers, stands out, in glaring contrast to the Indians. The members of the carrier corps gave their lives not by the thousand but by the ten thousand to uphold the supremacy of British arms in this country and sacrificed themselves as surely as those who died in action; without them the operations in this country could not have been carried out.

His mention of presenting Mr Jeevanjee with an address means nothing, and is on a par with another Indian effort in Kenya to blind the natives with the late 'Tea Party' – these incidents merely show that we are no match for the Indians in their cunning. The resolutions wormed out of the natives in Kenya have now no authority as they have been repudiated by all responsible bodies.

The absurd assertion of Mr Khandwala that where there are two opposing civilizations 'the native, who will be a product of the assimilation of the two cultures will be a better, more enlightened and more cultured man', simply points out Mr Khandwala to be one of those individuals who can state as a fact what he would like others to believe. Fortunately for us in this country, who have an English education, the literature of two continents are open for us to learn from, and from it we learn unmistakenly that where two civilizations are opposed the native of the country learns the vices of both with none of their good qualities. The other misstatements in his letter are too childish to deal with.

Let me finish with an appeal. It is now becoming increasingly evident day by day that Indian influence is operating against our economic advancement. Indian artizans and fundis with their unsanitary and low style of living, oppose an almost insurmountable barrier to the native who wishes to engage in skilled labour. If the European community would establish technical training schools, accept some of our young natives in the workshops as apprentices and promise to employ trained native workers wherever possible, the standing menace of the Indian to native advancement would be killed in a few years.

– from *Uganda Herald*, 5 August 1921.

22. KABAKA OR PROVINCIAL COMMISSIONER?

Memorandum to R. L. Buell [mid 1920s]

... At present, however, as has been pointed out before in this Memorandum, the Kabaka occupies a position which is tantamount to that of an ordinary Paramount Chief of one of the second-rate native tribes of Africa. He no longer has any power or control over his own Chiefs and all and sundry officers of the Protectorate Government appear to possess the right to 'have direct access' to the Kabaka, which right was exclusively reserved to the Governor alone. This practice is clearly contrary to the old native principles and system of Government of Buganda Kingdom, and is certainly in direct conflict with the terms of the Uganda Agreement of 1900. At present, in matters of the native administration of Buganda Kingdom, the Provincial Commissioner in charge of Buganda Province appears to occupy the position which was intended for the Kabaka in the Agreement. The Provincial Commissioner is now the direct ruler of the native chiefs of Buganda through his District Officers. Any order issued to the chiefs by the Kabaka or his Government has to be countersigned and approved by the Provincial Commissioner before it can be transmitted to the Chiefs concerned with the natural result that the Chiefs now are beginning to lose their sense of loyalty towards their Kabaka, since he has now come to be looked upon by these Chiefs as merely the headman or superior Chief of the Natives of Buganda on more or less the same level and receiving an annual salary from the Protectorate Government in the same way as they themselves. This is the effect brought about solely by the practice pursued by the Administrative Officers of the British Government, a practice which is entirely unjustifiable and clearly in conflict not only with the time-honored customs, traditions, and principle of native administration of Buganda, but also with the terms and intention of the Uganda Agreement of 1900 which is the basis of the Constitution of the Native Government of Buganda Kingdom.

– from R. L. Buell *The Native Problem in Africa* Vol. I, pp. 576–7.

23. AUTOBIOGRAPHY OF A MUGANDA CHIEF

Extracts from 'The Record of my service to the kingdom of Buganda and the important Government of Britain, the protector of this nation Buganda', by Samwiri Mukasa, [c. 1925].

1. Under<u>During Mutesa I's reign:</u> My father, Ibulaimu Nkata, was one of the important cooks to the Kabaka and he let me serve the Kabaka in this palace at Nabulagala (Kasubi). Soon after I was given an important position, considering my age which was not above 13 or 14 and this was cleaning the Kabaka's garments and making his bed, and thus started my services to the nation.

2. <u>During Mwanga's time:</u> I was soon promoted to the position of Kabaka's personal treasurer; this too was a high post for a boy of my age. The time for the persecution of the Christians was drawing near. There occurred a fire which burnt a big part of the Kabaka's palace and treasury. In those days the Kabaka sent me to collect his taxes in Kiziba. On my way back, I was told that the Kabaka had killed off all the Christians both inside and outside the palace, and that he was waiting for me to get on to those in the treasury. I was advised by many, including the Reverend Mackay and Ashe, not to get to the palace, but run away. But I could not leave the Kabaka's things unattended. So I handed them over to Omuwanika,* Kulugi, and escaped to the islands of Busi, until there was a battle at Mengo and the Kabaka escaped to the Lake. When I came back, Kiwewa was Kabaka.

3. <u>Under Kiwewa:</u> He did not stay on the throne for long, but owing to my previous good record of service I was made the Omuwanika of Buganda 1889, and I trustfully served as such until the wars with the Moslems, and our retreat to Kabula, under Nyonyintono, the then Katikiro. Kalema (Moslem) became Kabaka. . . . In 1890 though, we fought the Moslems, defeated them and Mwanga was back on the throne.

5. <u>As Makamba, the Sabaddu of Busiro, under Mwanga:</u> Mwanga gave me this chieftainship and the islands of Ssese were under me with the following chiefs on the mainland: Munawa, Mukebezi, Sebugwawo, Nawamba and Kabega Nawuwa Ekatale.

The important event was the battle of Nanziga, the last against Kalema, when I proposed dividing up our troops into two, one to attack and the other to act as reserve. This plan was worked and we defeated Kalema. Yona Waswa Mukwenda applied to the Kabaka that I be made his deputy because all his chiefs had deserted him during the battle and he had remained with me. This was accepted.

6. <u>As Muwemba, deputy Mukwenda, under Mwanga:</u> I did a lot in this position but I will just mention two things: (i) the restoration of order in

57

Buddu where the protestants were fighting the catholics in the first of the religious wars. I was appointed leader of the mission to stop the trouble spreading to all Buganda and I succeeded in doing this. (ii) Peters. The Kabaka was about to appoint an army leader to attack Kalema who was cutting off his kingdom in Kijungute when the German, Peters arrived. Two days afterwards, and before Peters told the Kabaka why he had come, Frederick Jackson, the British Government representative arrived. This fulfilled the promise Stanley made to us two who represented the Buganda Government and who were responsible for the co-operation and understanding which resulted in the British Government's undertaking to protect us. . . .

8. Bishop Tucker's invitation, immediately after the battle of Buvuma, for Christian Baganda to serve in the Church.

Bishop Tucker asked for volunteers from the Baganda Christian chiefs to serve in the church. I volunteered to forsake the importance of a chief and serve my country in this sphere. I was accordingly ordained a Reverend by the bishop and I took to preaching the gospel. I established a church where I was posted, at Nakiwate in Kyaggwe. With Reverend Blackledge we established other churches under this one. When one of us was inspecting the churches, the other remained behind, ministering in the church.

When I had served as a church minister for two years something happened which is important in the history of this country. The Kabaka left the throne and for a time the country was looking around for a Kabaka. Nuhu Mbogo would have been made the Kabaka if it were not for the Reverend Senfuma and myself pointing out to Sir Apolo Kagwa that this would plunge the country into an even worse civil war, and that the new Kabaka follow the old line of descent, must be a descendant of Mutesa. That there was no war then or afterwards I account for by the fact that we took this move. . . .

I got the idea that I should go back to being a chief. I therefore wrote to Bishop Tucker, telling him that owing to the disorder that my country was in I regretted I had to leave church ministry, which I had joined voluntarily, to help and bring about peace as an administrator. He agreed. I then wrote to the Regents and the Lukiko who were pleased by the idea. . . .

Soon afterwards Mr Andereya Luwandagga, who was the Mukubira was promoted to become Kimbugwe, and I took his place as Mukubira.

9. As Mukubira: Every other chief in Bulemezi, accept the Kangawo, was under me. My village Luwero, had a population of 1200, and the total number under me was about 3,700. Being the Mukubira I was responssible for peace and order, for I was quickly referred to when there was a major battle or minor rising, of both of which there were about six. I worked for the peaceful administration of the two governments and me

and my guns were like the 4th K.A.R.* in relation to the protectorate government.

10. As Kangawo, under Kabaka Daudi Chwa II: Kisingiri was Kangawo but he was promoted to the Treasury and on March 25th 1900, I succeeded him as Kangawo. I did a lot but I will just mention the most important services.

I started the collection of the 3 Rs tax. I realized how poor we were because it was difficult for people to get 3 Rs. It was decided that people should pay 2 Rs in cash and the third as a bag of flour of dried Matoke, but it was still difficult to get 2 Rs. The government therefore decided that those who could not get 2 Rs could pay by presenting a python, or bunches of processed sisal, pepper, a male sheep, maize, sim-sim, etc. One man named S. Munaku of Singo brought a python once. This all illustrates how poor Buganda was. It was very difficult to collect the taxes from everybody, and this was done by me personally for the present gombololas were non-existent then. After a period of 3 years people started committing suicide because they could not pay their taxes, or they ran away from their native country into the surrounding countries. . . .

. . . I was appointed to act as a regent, 1902 when the Katikiro was going to Britain.

11. As Acting Katikiro and Regent: This is an important post for the Katikiro deals with all the important affairs of the country. Much more was this so during this time when the Kabaka was still an infant. Sir Jackson had been succeeded by Col. Sadler and George Wilson (Tayari) was P. C. Buganda.

Some of the important services were:

(a) To bring up and look after the young Kabaka.

(b) To confer well with the protecting government.

(c) To put up a house for the Kabaka replacing the old round one; the idea was initiated by me and my fellow regents.

(d) The putting up of the Glorious Bulange* and the 'Coronation Ground'.

(e) Concluding the Boundaries between the protectorate town of Kampala and Mengo. P. C. Wilson wanted to extend Kampala towards Mengo but I wrote a letter to the governor suggesting that the protecting government town should expand towards Nakasero. The governor agreed with this and this prevented the swallowing up of Mengo.

12. Back as Kangawo after Sir Apolo Kaggwa's return, 1904
The services were:

(a) Tax – Considering the difficulties already pointed out and looking through government reports one realizes that I did tremendous work in this field. For a long time I collected more taxes than any of the other 19 Saza chiefs and this I did honestly. I started the issuing of receipts on payment of taxes. For instance in 1904, there was some suspicion about my collection of taxes and D. C. 'Munala' was sent to investigate and report. He got to each and every village and found no evidence of corruption. Again there were about 3,000 exempted from paying taxes either because of age or disease or some other physical deformity. It was said that I did so for no sound reason and I was instructed to send all of them to Kampala for re-inspection. I first sent a batch of 900 who were returned exempted; then another one of 700 who were also returned exempted; then one of 600, who were returned the same. I was collecting a fourth batch when I got a letter telling me to stop and that the allegations made against me were false. For these two reasons, D.C. Munala's report and the confirmation of the exemptions, I count myself to have been a very diligent worker in the collection of taxes.

(b) Roads – When I became Kangawo there were 2 roads to speak of. But even these had no bridges over streams. From then to 1925 I directed the construction of about 16 roads and now one can travel from one side of Bulemezi to another on a bicycle, motor cycle or in a car. No longer do people carry trade goods on their heads but on lorries. This is all due to my work in road construction which has accounted for Bulemezi's leading place among the Saza's. It should be pointed out that this kind of thing was never directed from above but was a result of the Saza Chief's initiative to see how best he could improve his county.

(c) Cotton – Because of the importance of cotton to Buganda and Uganda both here and abroad, I count myself to have done great work for I was the person who introduced the first cotton seed to this country. As I said above, I was trying to eradicate poverty from this country and I had heard how useful cotton was where it was grown. In 1903 I went to Mr Borup and asked for some cotton seeds. He however wanted me to take them after signing an agreement and that I was to pay 250 Rs if I did not fulfil the conditions therein. He then handed me 375 lbs of cotton seed. I was to plant it first and then extend the growing to other people.

It was not enough introducing cotton; I urged people to grow it. Although some said at first that it brought leprosy, my urging has in the long run brought wealth to Bulemezi, which county has always led in the growing of cotton, and to Buganda, and all Uganda. There are no more suicides although people are paying higher taxes. . . .

13. During World War I: This is one of the most important services that I have done for the peace of the protecting government and for the peace of the whole world. A war against Britain was a war against Buganda and so when I was appointed to lead some soldiers I at once left for Kampala with 5,000 men. There I was told not to go to the battlefield at once, but to wait in my country and do as I was directed. While waiting these are some of the things I did:

(a) I did all I could to recruit men for the armies.

(b) I sent in a lot of carriers.

(c) I very much encouraged the growing of food in my county for feeding the troops.

(d) I encouraged further the growing of cotton which, I was told, was useful for the production of gunpowder.

(e) Because I very much wanted peace I tried my best to get into contact with the British armies for I did not want the enemy to get to our city London. Therefore I wrote to the man in charge of war in England what I thought about the war. Although no action was taken according to what I suggested I was informed by Mr Cooper P.C. Buganda on behalf of the Chief Secretary that the British Commander had been impressed by my enthusiasm.

The important government mission: In 1917 H.E. the Governor and the Kabaka sent Prince Suna, 6 Saza Chiefs and 4 Gombolola Chiefs on a mission to Bukedi to instruct the people in the running of the government and to teach them to obey the protecting government like the Baganda were doing. We toured all Bukedi with the Protectorate Government representative D.C. Rubic and addressed many councils. This was an important mission intended for the better running of affairs in Busoga and Bukedi.

14. Acting Katikiro for the 2nd time: I worked for 1½ months as Katikiro on the invitation of the Kabaka, when the Katikiro was on leave. I need not mention what I did for everybody knows what a Katikiro does. Suffice it to say that when the Katikiro came back from leave, everything was alright.

The Buganda Government Luwalo: In 1920 it was decided to take a tax from the natives of Buganda. Just as I worked over the poll tax, so over this I worked hard for its collection to give some revenue to our government. I also suggested to the Kabaka and his Lukiko how this money might be used and some of my suggestions were worked upon and are still in application even today.

15. As acting Omulamuzi:* The Omulamuzi went to inspect Budu and Mubende in 1924, and the Kabaka invited me to act as Omulamuzi for 1 month. In that month I dealt with 9 important cases and a host of minor ones.

These are the important services which I thought fit to mention that I have rendered to the protecting government and my native country. . . .

– from a translation in Residency Archives,
Buganda, Old Series 1823A.

Omuwanika: Treasurer of Buganda.
K.A.R.: King's African Rifles.
Bulange: the Lukiko building.
Omulamuzi: Chief Justice of Buganda.

Abataka to Chief Secretary, Government of Uganda, 6 May 1921.

We have humbly addressed to you this letter while emploring you to kindly consider that is embodied therein and which have made us approach His Excellency the Governor, and which runs thus:

We have eventually realized that a considerable length of time has been taken in our country of Buganda Kingdom, since the Abataka brought up their complaints for the re-acquisition of their Butaka lands: notwithstanding the fact that they have put up their rightful claims to the authority of our Buganda Government which should do justice, nothing is yet done for them because of the reason that those who are expected to arbitrate are the ones who unlawfully acquired their fellowmen's butaka lands by reason of the 1900 agreement: which provided that each one should survey his own estates which he held in possession. Having realized our rights as the lineage sons of the Bataka in Buganda: who preserved our country from long ago on the system of butaka land tenure, have to be recognized as well as our ancestors.

We, some of the Abataka, having discovered that a serious mistake was made in this matter, and are of the opinion that unless we try to put it to an end, it will ruin our kingdom, therefore humbly pray you to grant what we are asking you in this petition – which is that, 'We have formed an association with the aim of preserving our Butaka estates in Buganda and is known as Ekibina ky'Abaganda Abataka' (The Association of Baganda Ancestors or Bataka); and the following are the chief aims of its formation:

1. To start the reorganization of Butaka estates that existed before the advent to this country of His Majesty's Government of England;

2. To give back all butaka estates to the original proprietors in accordance with our native customs;

3. To preserve and to see that each one gets his original butaka estate and the British Government ratifies and preserve same;

4. To recognize all clan institutions that existed in the country and their relative duties to our Kabaka and for each clan to have a representative who airs her interests in the central legislature as we used to do in the olden times.

This association declares to be loyal to all good laws and to serve George V and all his successors as all other countries are directed to do in the Empire of His Majesty George V.

We humbly pray to the British Government to sympathetically consider the petition of the Abataka of Buganda, because of the grave error committed in our nation of Buganda and referred to above. We further humbly state that we realize that it will be difficult for our country to progress as is planned and promised by Government (unless the above error is remedied).

We have come to realize that the foundation of our country based on 1900 (agreement) tends to develop a smaller section of the country whereas the larger section is on the contrary discontented and petitioning about the preservation of the good customs of Buganda: we visualize the difficulty in the way of progress by Government without the support of the Abataka who form the nation of Buganda. Without the Bataka, there is not Buganda. We assume and hope, Sir, that you will agree to grant what we ask you in this letter and to receive and entertain whatever we shall submit to you for consideration and to sympathize with our case, as without such assistance, we feel we shall not endure and win what we are aiming at; we have formed this association not because of planning a rapid progress, but solely to have a proper foundation laid upon which progress, may be based. The agreement to send up this petition has been reached at the time when the chief signatories to the 1900 agreement are still alive because after their departure, it will be most difficult for the younger generation to come to settlement of such historical affairs now in dispute.

We earnestly pray soliciting your sympathy for any of our petitions and for your excuse in having appended our signatories on matters of such an important nature as these.

We are, Sir, Your humble servants:

> Daudi Basudde
> Yuda Musoke Kasa
> The Secretaries of the Association of Bataka of
> Buganda.

Kabaka Daudi Chwa to Abataka. 13 May 1922.

Having carefully read and considered your letter addressed to me on 6th February and in which you embodied your grievances against the mailo estates* allocations by the Regents based on the 1900 agreement, in comparison to both letters from the Regents dated 18th March 1822, when they answered detailing the system adopted in allocating mailo estates, I have come to the following findings:

2. From the reading of the three letters, and to answers to my cross-examinations of both sides as well as examinations by either side, which lasted for a whole week, I have found that the main issue in dispute, which aggrieved the Abataka and against which they are petitioning is due to the fact that the Regents as alleged by the Abataka failed to properly follow section 15 of the principal agreement which provides: 'that all other people will have the allocation of their estates as they possess them now.' And also the provision of the Forests Agreement of 1907 which provided

in the first paragraph thereof that: 'whereas it was agreed that some of the chiefs and the Abataka were to be allocated to their original estates of which they are in possession of at the time and the Lukiko was required to check the genuineness of claim by individuals'.

3. Having carefully considered the matter before me, I have found that your submissions are justified. The Regents themselves in both their written defence and in my cross-examination, admitted that some of Butaka estates were allocated and acquired by people who were not entitled to same at the time; while they themselves deserted their own estates held according to their title of office and acquired new estates which did not belong to them before. When one considers the provisions of section 15 of the agreement and compare same with what the Regents said in paragraph 8 of their letter to the effect: 'that the Lukiko members shall decide all matters concerning the allocation of estates', one finds that although the Lukiko was authorized by the principal agreement to allocate the estates, and by particular provision to allocate some to people who deserved same, but it did not alter the first section which provided the allocation to chiefs and other people of their original estates in which they were found in possession then; and still further it never ordered or authorized the Lukiko to expel people from their estates in which they were in possession of.

4. With regard to para. 6 of the Abataka's memorandum referring to the exhumation of bodies of ancestors, I have found as a fact that some of the dead bodies were disinterred although two of the Regents who are still surviving disagree but as this is an accepted Buganda custom, anyone whose dead body was exhumed in this way, has a right to bring up an action.

5. As you all the Abataka know, we have quite a number of Butaka estates: there is the clan Butaka estates known as 'Kasolya' which are the chief Butaka Estates. As you will remember my examinations of the 25th of April 1922, I questioned the Abataka whom you presented to me of the 35 clans who attended my examination, at the end of which I eventually found out that the 'Kasolya Butaka Estates' were held by the rightful owners – the Abataka; and that additional allocations had been acquired by them to have the whole estate covered. The second Butaka estates are the Amasiga estates (branch estates), many of which appear to have been acquired by other people although some estates remained within the clans. The Butaka estates of a third order of sub-branches were eliminated. These kinds of estates were individually held and others belonged to deities (Balubale), the latter of which were abolished by religion.

As I have explained above it appears that the Butaka Estates of a major importance known as the 'Busolya' were preserved and held by the rightful owners who surveyed same as mailo estates.

6. With regard to the point raised by the Abataka in para. 16 of their

memorandum and which was answered in para. 19 of the Regents' first letter, regarding the Kibuga (township) after carefully considering same and consulting the chiefs, I have found that personal holdings or plots never existed before but such Bibanja (plots) were only held in the official capacity of chiefs and that the system of personal ownership of plots in the Kibuga (township) was introduced only recently with the mailo allocations.

Having been so informed, I have found that the Kibuga should be planned and entrusted in the hands of the Kabaka and the Lukiko to decide the good form in which it should be administered.

7. With regard to the question of having the Land Office searched raised in para. 14 of your memorandum, I have found that it will take a considerable long time to find out how mailo estates were allocated to individuals and to compare such findings to records of both the Government Land Office and the Lukiko Land Office.

I have therefore decided to give my decision on the main issue of your complaint submitted to me and then later appoint my inspectors to the office of mailo, to investigate all details, during which investigation the question raised by you in para. 5 of your memorandum to the effect that mailo estates were reserved for minors at the time of the allocation which was denied by the Regents as untrue allegations of paragraphs 5 and 7 of your memorandum.

8. I have found it impossible to accede to the Abataka's request in para. 16 of your memorandum – for the return of mailo estates in the hands of the Kabaka who should re-allocate same anew: I do not want to do this as I am convinced, if done it is likely to confuse the whole system of mailo estates allocations in the whole of Buganda Kingdom, but have directed that the chief Butaka Estates should be put in order: because every Muganda, who is known as a proper Muganda, has the feeling of one's butaka at heart and should therefore be sympathetic with his fellow Baganda in this question since this is not the first time for Butaka Estates claims to be pleaded before the Bakabaka of Buganda Kingdom. It is a fact that from olden times all the Bassekabaka were bound to accede to their requests. Now the matter having been proved that some of the Butaka Estates were indeed disallocated or acquired by other people, I therefore order that a law be enacted by the Kabaka Sabataka together with the Lukiko of Buganda and approved by His Excellency the Governor to be known as 'The Exchange of Butaka Estates Law in the Kingdom of Buganda'. Whenever such lands will be proved to be Butaka Estate whose rightful Mutaka was disposed for no just cause, during the time of mailo allocations, the Lukiko shall allocate to him a mailo to enable him redeem or exchange his Butaka Estate. Provision shall be made in this law, regarding the conditions or procedure to be followed for the exchange of any Butaka lands.

9. I have not considered every detail contained in the various long letters as the subject matter was summarized in my cross-examinations and have

not considered the period of the Bassekabaka but I have started from the time the mailo estates were introduced.

10. I have also left out the question raised by the Abataka regarding the Katikkiro himself as it is not relevant to the Bataka issue. But as it was requested by the Regents in para. 14 of their letter to have same separately treated, I have accordingly left it out.

Daudi Chwa,
Kabaka of Buganda.

Bataka petitioners to Britain's Secretary of State for the Colonies [1923].

We, the assembled heads, elders and representatives of the majority of the natives of Buganda most respectfully and humbly beg leave to introduce our elected delegates to explain fully and properly the real state of affairs affecting we the Bataka, i.e. our Native Government and our Butaka Land questions which are of extremely vital importance to the existence and welfare of Baganda community at present and in the future.

2. Under the agreement of 1900, according to which His Most Gracious and Imperial Majesty undertook to protect us and our country; 8000 square miles of land were reserved to be allocated to us and live in them in our own way, as the Right Honourable Mr Winston Churchill, then the Under-Secretary of State for the Colonies and K.C. thus ceremoniously commanded to the respect of the people, in 1907. When he had the honour of officially visiting this country. He said: 'Under that agreement all their rights and liberties are guaranteed and all their lands, possessions, and ancient privileges. Under that agreement they may preserve all the old grace and simplicity of their lives which have always so honourably distinguished the Baganda people. And that the Justice of the British Crown will be evenly administered between all classes, and all those who come under the authority of the King.'

3. But on account of the causes briefly stated in our petition and other memorandums that have been already despatched to your office by His Excellency the Governor of Uganda as it appears from His Excellency's letter No. 1704 dated the 26th January, 1923 to us, which reads as follows:

No. 1704

Provincial Commissioner's Office, Kampala,
26th January, 1923

To,

The Vice-Chairman,
Bataka Community, Mengo

I have the honour to inform you that His Excellency the Acting Governor has decided to refer the claim of the Bataka for a reconsideration of certain areas of land already allotted under Article 15 of the Uganda Agreement 1900, to the Secretary of State for the Colonies for decision. A delay of three or four months must thus be anticipated before a reply can be sent to the petitioners.

2. A despatch setting forth in full the case both for the Native Government and for the Bataka is being prepared, and copies of the more important Memoranda written to this Government by both parties will be forwarded.

I am directed by His Excellency to convey this information to His Highness the Kabaka and the Lukiko and to the Associations of Bataka.

J. de G. Delmege
Ag. Provincial Commissioner,
Buganda.

4. And for the purpose of explaining our petition fully and clearly to His Majesty's Government we have sent this deputation of our following most trusted delegates.

Saulo Lugwisa
Seruwano Kulubya
David S. Bassude

5. We beg to submit that the present state of affairs is most unjust and inimical to the best interests of the great bulk of Baganda population and has been causing endless ruinous litigations and disquietitude all over the country. We therefore most humbly beseach you to consider and decide this burning question with due regard to our immemorial and most highly cherished native law, customs and traditions affecting our land tenure so that the Baganda natives of this country whose perfect loyalty and faithfulness to His Imperial Majesty is a fact of undoubted veracity may be reserved, the value of the land and freedom of access to it for the present and future generations of your protected Subjects, and also be able to live in peace and harmony for the future.

6. We have empowered this party to act in our name and to engage anyone else to help them if necessary in putting the case before you, and in case of any difficulty which may arise they shall consult us by cable.

7. It will be very kind of you Sir, if you would be so kind enough to consider if any useful purpose would be served by your granting some interviews to our delegates in London, with the object of discussing with them the salient points in the petition.

We are
Your Honourable,
Your most humble and obedient subjects.
On behalf of the Baganda Bataka Community.

[.................. various signatures]

Speech by E. B. Jarvis, Acting Governor of Uganda, to the Lukiko, 7 October 1926.

I have come to read out the decision in the case of the Abataka from the Secretary of State for the Colonies.

Ssabasajja Kabaka,

Chiefs and all people of Buganda:

I asked Ssabasajja to summon an unusual Lukiko so that I could deliver to you the decision of the Secretary of State for the Colonies in the Butaka land question which is the subject of much grievance in Buganda; and which question, you all know, has been the subject of disagreement and correspondence for some years past.

2. You will recollect that a Commission of Inquiry was appointed in the year 1924, which was directed to carefully inquire and submit findings on the allocation of land by the Lukiko and to certify as to whether it was done in accordance with what had been stipulated in the 1900 agreement, and as to whether the allocation was based on the national custom of the olden days, and to recommend a measure of solution to be adopted, satisfying both parties and remedying any miscarriage of justice, upon finding that what was laid down in the agreement was not followed and the national customs or traditions were respected.

3. The members of the Commission of Inquiry, having carefully inquired into the matter, eventually found from the èvidence put before them, that some of the Abataka were unlawfully expelled from their butaka and their butaka estates were allocated to other people who were not entitled to same according to the Buganda Agreement and the Secretary of State for the Colonies has accordingly directed that the Buganda Government be informed that he also agrees with what the members of the Commission of Inquiry have found as a fact. In spite of the fact that the above was the situation, the authority of Buganda Government had failed to find a way out to solve the problem and the matters then left with the British Government were two items only: (a) a complete refusal to consider this matter at all and (b) to appoint a committee with powers to consider everything recommended by the Commission of Inquiry.

4. With regard to the last question of appointing a committee, the Secretary of State for the Colonies, although satisfied with the findings of the Commission of Inquiry into this difficult problem, and while appreciating their sympathetic considerations aimed at finding a solution satisfactory to both parties, believes that the majority of the people concerned will also appreciate the difficulty of formulating a set of safeguard rules to be followed by such a committee which might be appointed and that to try to do so now after such an elapse of a long time although with good intentions, presents more difficulties as it has been established for many years, which fact limits the possibility of a successful change over. For a considerable time in the past, it was an accepted policy without any

dispute even from those who are now petitioning for an inquiry to a reversion; the Secretary of State for the Colonies has further considered that there will not be enough unacquired fertile land which could be exchanged with the proprietors of the lands sought to be acquired.

5. The Secretary of State for the Colonies agrees with the findings of the Commission that the question of large estates to an individual ownership when compared to the welfare of the country as a whole is not so important as safeguarding the interests or well-being of the native tenants who might settle on the land.

6. Because of the foregoing explanation, the Secretary of State for the Colonies intimates that the Government of Buganda and people should be informed that he has decided not to interfere in the matter under dispute and to have nothing to do with the Crown Provisional Land Certificates issued to landowners and confirmed by the British Government.

7. The Secretary of State for the Colonies desires it to be publicly understood that the Abataka Association's petition to him regarding land allocations in Buganda Government has received due consideration and therefore this decision should be treated as final.

8. The Secretary of State for the Colonies, however, hopes that the Buganda Government will not fail to follow what the Governor may find fit to be done to take to reserve and preserve as may be practicable, the places known as burial grounds and which existed at the time of the Uganda Agreement.

9. It is further required to inform you that the Secretary of State for the Colonies is of the opinion that land allocation by the Lukiko and the procedure adopted by the Regents in land matters, which were referred to them, during the minority of the Kabaka, were neither carried out with justice nor with the trust attached to their office; and has therefore felt much sorrow and forced to point out that the Buganda Government should be more strictly supervised than has been hitherto the case in land dealing matters; the rights of landowners in their estates and the safeguards to tenants who settle on such estates should be watched.

10. In conclusion I should like to remind you that it was first agreed when the Commission started its inquiry into the Butaka issue, that each party would be bound to accept whatever decision the Secretary of State for the Colonies may arrive at.

And I therefore sincerely hope without any doubt in my mind that both parties because of what was agreed before, will accept and humbly submit to this decision and forget (or bury) all what has been creating differences and start working together in good spirit for the welfare of Buganda development.

> — the first two and the last item are from a translation of J. K. Miti Kabazzi, *Obulamu Bw'Omutaka*, pp. 105–8, 113–17, 121–4. The third item is from a printed copy in the editor's possession.

Abataka, Bataka: clan heads.

Mailo estates: estates having their origin in allocations under the terms of the Uganda Agreement 1900, in square miles, or portions thereof.

25. KAGWA'S PERSONAL PETITION, 1926

Sir Apolo Kagwa, Katikiro of Buganda, to Leopold Amery, British Colonial Secretary, 30 March 1926.

I most respectfully beg to submit herewith my humble Petition regarding certain complaints which I brought before His Excellency the Governor of the Uganda Protectorate against one of the Officers of the Protectorate Government of Uganda – Mr Postlethwaite, at present holding the post of Acting Provincial Commissioner in charge of the Buganda Province . . .

2. In my capacity as the Katikiro of Buganda or His Highness the Kabaka's principal Minister, I have to deal a great deal with the Officer of the British Government holding the position of the Provincial Commissioner in Buganda Province, and as I had to come in constant contact with Mr Postlethwaite during the time that he was stationed here at Kampala as Acting Provincial Commissioner of Buganda Kingdom. In the middle of 1925, however, our official relationship became somewhat strained, and I had reason to believe that it was due to his personal animosity which he entertained towards me, and I was consequently compelled to bring the matter officially before His Excellency the Governor, and made a full representation of the matter in my letter dated the 30th November, 1925. . . . The Governor considered the matter and decided that my complaints against Mr. Postlethwaite were groundless; and he thought fit to communicate this decision of the matter to me in a letter addressed to the Officer against whom I had complained, dated the 18th January 1926 . . .

3. Being, however, dissatisfied with His Excellency's decision of the matter on the ground that the matter had not been given sufficient consideration by His Excellency, and as I thought that the Governor's decision was not justified by the evidence laid before him, I decided to approach the Governor again on the subject, and I addressed him my letter of the 14th February, 1926 . . . in which I explained fully to His Excellency the reason of my dissatisfaction with his decision and treatment in the procedure adopted in communicating to me his decision through the Officer against whom I had brought my original complaints; and I requested His Excellency at the same time that the matter may be referred to

the Secretary of State for the Colonies. Unfortunately, however, His Excellency the Governor took strong exception to the wording of the last part of paragraph 4 of my letter just mentioned above . . . the passage to which His Excellency took such strong exception reads as follows:

'with all due respects, Your Excellency, I beg to submit that I cannot but feel that the procedure adopted in this connection was derogatory to myself as well as to my position. This action on the part of the Protectorate Government clearly shows that no consideration whatever is given to the natives or to their welfare by the British Government in spite of the fact that Your Excellency's principal duties and obligations as the Governor of Uganda Protectorate is to protect and guide the natives of this Protectorate who have been entrusted to your care by His Majesty the King of England'.

His Excellency the Governor felt so strongly about this part of my letter he wrote to His Highness the Kabaka on the 25th February, 1926 . . . requesting him to inform me that His Excellency considered the wording of that part of my letter grossly impertinent and improper. Again on the 1st March, 1926, at an interview held at Government House, Entebbe, between His Excellency the Governor and His Highness the Kabaka together with his three Ministers, I being present as the Katikiro of Buganda, after His Excellency had discussed with us some other important matter he considered it right to allude to this subject of the wording of this part of my letter in which he had taken exception in the presence of the Kabaka and Ministers; and I was severely censured before Mr Postlethwaite – the Officer against whom I had brought my original complaints . . .

4. With all due respects, Sir, I most humbly beg to submit that my intention in writing the last part of paragraph 4 of my letter referred to above was only to emphasize the fact that I had not been shown proper consideration from the Government which was due to me as the Katikiro of Buganda and principal Agent in inviting the British Government to this country, and that if no consideration had been shown to me, how much less consideration, if at all, could be expected by the other natives in general who are inferior to me in rank and the mere peasants. I submit further, Sir, that no disloyalty or insubordination was intended to be conveyed in the wording of this passage of my letter. Unfortunately, however, as it is clear from the excerpt of the Minute of the interview . . . I was not afforded an opportunity to offer my explanation regarding the intended meaning of the wording of the passage of my letter complained of by His Excellency the Governor or to defend myself in the matter of my original complaints which I had brought against Mr Postlethwaite, in spite of my repeated application and entreaty to His Excellency to allow me to do so at the close of the interview referred to above, but he refused to give me permission to do so and ordered me to leave the room.

I realize, however, that it was not right for me to write paragraph 4 of my letter of the 14th February, 1926, and I have already tended my apology to His Excellency the Governor through His Highness the Kabaka and have requested him to allow me to withdraw that passage of my letter referred to.

5. I have considered, however, that it is right that I should submit the whole matter to His Majesty's Principal Secretary of State for the Colonies for his consideration and final decision, as I am not satisfied with His Excellency the Governor's decision on the following grounds:

(a) I still maintain, Sir, that my accusations of private and personal animosity and hatred entertained against me by Mr Postlethwaite were quite justified, as I produced sufficient proof to support them such as the letter I produced addressed to me by my old friend and adviser Dr Cook who had been induced to write it by Mr Postlethwaite ... As it will be seen from the letter Dr Cook advised me to retire with dignity and honour on Medical grounds; but as this advice was not asked for by me prior to his giving it, and as Dr Cook has not examined me medically just immediately before writing the letter, I felt suspicious of the genuineness of this advice, so I decided to approach him, when he informed me verbally that it was Mr Postlethwaite who had induced him to write it, as he gave him to understand that the Protectorate Government was contemplating to force me to retire (which amounted to summary dismissal), and that it would be much more dignified, therefore, and honourable if I retire on 'Medical grounds'. I explained all this in my two letters addressed to the Governor already referred to ... but I regret His Excellency could not see his way to accept my statement. I also submitted, for His Excellency's information and proof of Mr Postlethwaite's anxiety to get me to retire as soon as possible, a Memorandum addressed to His Highness the Kabaka written by Mr Postlethwaite ... in which he suggested certain names of chiefs who, in his opinion, were the likely candidates to fill my post, which I did not know I had been asked by my Kabaka to vocate. But His Excellency did not consider that this was sufficient proof on the matter, and still held that my accusations were groundless.

(b) Moreover on the 28th October, 1925, the Provincial Commissioner, Buganda, arranged an interview between him and us the Kabaka's Ministers, but on the instructions of Mr Postlethwaite, I was refused admittance to that interview, and I had to stand waiting outside while my fellow-Ministers went inside and saw the Acting Provincial Commissioner, these instructions were communicated to me by Mr A. H. Cox, District Commissioner, Mengo, who was then in his place. I naturally resented this treatment as it was clearly derogatory to my position as the Principal Minister of His Highness the Kabaka. I endeavoured to explain all this to His Excellency the Governor at the interview referred to above in paragraph 4 of this Petition, but His Excellency would not allow me to do so.

6. In conclusion, Sir, I would most humbly beg to point out, with all due respects, that as I contemplate retiring very soon, I considered it only right to submit the whole matter to His Majesty's Principal Secretary of State for the Colonies for his information and consideration, so that the circumstances leading up to my retirement may be placed on record. As pointed out before in this Petition, I was the Principal Agent in inviting the English people and introducing the British Government into this country; and I sacrificed the best part of my life for the good of my countrymen, as well as for the welfare and safety of the lives of the Europeans – especially the English people – who were in this country during the turbulent times of the civil wars and religious strifes with the attendant unsettled condition of the country at that time; and moreover being the leading chief of His Highness the Kabaka in his Native Government of Buganda Kingdom, and his principal adviser, and having held the position of principal regent for eighteen years, I naturally expected to be treated by His Majesty's Government with special and personal consideration having regard to my length of service in the Protectorate Government in my capacity as the Katikiro of Buganda – Buganda Kingdom – a position which I have held since 1889, a period of thirty-seven years.

For the above reasons, therefore, I have decided to submit this Petition before His Majesty's Secretary of State for the Colonies for his favourable consideration, since I have not been satisfied with His Excellency the Governor's decision on the matter.

– from a copy in the Johnston Papers, Central African Archives.

26. EAST AFRICAN FEDERATION PROPOSALS, 1927

Memorandum on the proposed federation of the British East African dependencies. Its effects on the Constitution of Buganda Kingdom. By His Highness the Kabaka of Buganda [29 October 1927].

The purpose of this Memorandum is to deal fully with the questions of the proposed Federation as it affects the constitution of the Buganda Kingdom which forms one of the most important Provinces of the Uganda Protectorate.

In order to understand the importance of the position accorded to the Kingdom of Buganda in the composition of the Uganda Protectorate, one must necessarily look back and study the history of Buganda just prior to the advent of the first European to this Country about 1862, when Captain Speke arrived in Buganda at the Court of my august grandfather Kabaka Mutesa. It is stated that prior to this date my great-grandfather, Kabaka Suna, first heard of the existence of the white men somewhere in 1850 from a runaway Baluch soldier of Zanzibar. During the reign of Kabaka Mutesa, prior to the arrival of Captain Speke the Kingdom of Buganda prospered and was recognized as one of the most powerful of the native tribes in East Africa, west of the great Lake Victoria. That Buganda kept up its supremacy up to the time of the annexation to the British Crown is a well-known and indisputable fact. Buganda differed from its neighbouring native tribes in every way, especially socially and politically. Although possessing no civilization on the modern lines, yet Buganda had a peculiar civilization of its own, and, strangely enough, its system of government differed very little from a constitutional government of modern days. It is quite clear from the study of the history of Buganda that it was the unique position it occupied among its fellow-native tribes that compelled the British Government, when its annexation to the British Crown was effected to recognize all its ancient customs and to respect its system of government. In fact it was on these customs and system of government that the present constitution of Buganda Kingdom was built up by the late Sir Harry Johnston in his memorable and most generous Agreements made between himself and the Regents and Chiefs of Buganda in 1900 on my behalf during my minority.

Before turning to the effect of the proposed Federation on the constitution of Buganda Kingdom, it would not be out of place to deal briefly here with the present constitution of Buganda as laid down in the Agreement of 1900 already alluded to above. In that Agreement, after describing fully the boundary of Buganda Kingdom, the Kabaka of Buganda formally renounced, in favour of His Majesty's Government, all claims to tribute which the Kabaka of Buganda had on the adjoining provinces of the Uganda Protectorate. It is clear that such formal renunciation presupposed the recognition by the British Government of the Kabaka's prior rights over those claims. Following upon this renunciation, the status of the Kingdom of Buganda in the administration of the Uganda Protectorate is guaranteed, by the British Government. Further on in this Agreement the British Government formally recognized the Kabaka of Buganda as the supreme Native Ruler of Buganda under the British protection. In this Clause (6) of the Agreement it is definitely provided that 'The Kabaka of Buganda shall exercise direct rule over the natives of Buganda to whom he shall administer justice through the Lukiko or Native Council and through others of his officers in the manner approved by Her Majesty's Government'. It is needless to point out that by this provision the British Government intended to guarantee the preservation of the Kabaka's suzerainty among his own subjects, and to ensure the internal administration of his Kingdom by his Chiefs, subject to formal supervision of the British Government. Still further down in the Agreement (Clauses 9, 10, 11) the system of Government of the Baganda which Sir Harry Johnston found in existence on his arrival in 1899 was recognized and amplified in detail in this Agreement. These clauses now form the foundation of the present constitution of the Buganda Kingdom, which is further safeguarded by a special provision inserted in the earlier part of this Agreement (Clause 5) to the effect that all laws made by the British Government for the general governance of the Uganda Protectorate shall be equally applicable to the Kingdom of Buganda 'except in so far as they may in any particular conflict with the terms of this Agreement in which case the terms of this Agreement will constitute a special exception in regard to the Kingdom of Uganda'. The meaning and intention of this provision is too clear to require any further explanation. While the laws made by the Protectorate Government are applicable to Buganda, yet its constitution is safeguarded from the operation of any of those laws which are in direct conflict with the principles of this constitution as laid down in the Agreement under review. It is clear, therefore, that although Buganda is part of the Uganda Protectorate and administered by His Majesty's Government, yet in its internal administration the Protectorate Government has to respect its constitution solemnly guaranteed in the Agreement. It is, therefore, necessary that when any measure for the better government of the Protectorate is considered desirable to be applied to Buganda, but which on the face of it appears to be repugnant or in conflict with any provision of this Agreement, the Protectorate Government has to obtain prior consent of the Kabaka and Chiefs and people of Buganda to this measure before it can be made applicable to Buganda Kingdom, and this consent is always recorded in a formal Agreement which becomes a supplementary Agreement to the original Agreement of 1900. There are several such Agreements entered into by the British Government with the Kabaka and Chiefs of Buganda since the original Agreement in 1900. In theory, at any rate, Buganda Kingdom still retains its internal self-Government under the protection and advice of His Majesty's Government of the Uganda Protectorate; and in the administration of the native tribes of the Protectorate, the British Government has to give special consideration to the interests of the Baganda in the light of the terms of the Uganda Agreement of 1900 – in fact the British Government in administering Buganda Kingdom has always to be guided by the principles and provisions laid down in that Agreement. I trust I have made it clear from the foregoing that it has never been, and I hope will never be, the intention of the British Government to annex Buganda Kingdom as an ordinary Crown Colony or to deprive its Kabaka of his suzerainty among his subjects. Subject to the protection and advice guaranteed by His Majesty's

Government of the Uganda Protectorate, the internal self-Government has been left intact and has been reserved to the Kabaka and his Chiefs under the Agreement of 1900. This Agreement is binding upon the British Government except in the event of the Buganda Kingdom at any time failing to raise 'without just cause or excuse an amount of native taxation equal to half that which is due in proportion to the number of inhabitants'; or in the event of the Kabaka, Chiefs or people of Buganda pursuing at any time a policy which is distinctly disloyal to the British Government. (Clause 20.) None of these events have taken place, so that no breach of this Agreement has been made so as to release the British Government from the trust which it solemnly undertook to preserve under the terms of this Agreement which is binding on both parties that made it.

I now pass on to the burning question of the Federation. It is true no definite proposals have as yet been formulated upon which such Federation would be based. It is feared, however, and quite naturally, that whatever form the proposed Federation will ultimately take, there is no possible hope of any benefit accruing therefrom to the Baganda and the constitution of this Kingdom. In the first place, Buganda Kingdom is a very small country relatively speaking, and its importance is only felt in the light of its composition in the Uganda Protectorate and its status among its fellow-native tribes forming that Protectorate. It must be remembered in this connexion that the Uganda Protectorate was originally declared over Buganda and derived its name from the Swahili interchanging the word 'Buganda' into 'Uganda', and it only extended to the other native tribes now composed in the Uganda Protectorate gradually. Buganda must, therefore, of necessity, occupy the most important place among the native tribes in the Protectorate. It is clear, on the other hand, that if this proposed Federation of the British East African Dependencies is effected, the importance of Buganda will necessarily and proportionately be diminished, without, of course, any intention on the part of the British Government to subordinate it to any other native tribe. Again the present status of Buganda, although not intentionally destroyed, will necessarily be lost sight of in view of the vast numbers of the various native tribes with their relative importance that will be included in the proposed Federation. With all the best intentions on the part of the Central Government of the Federation, it is feared that it will no longer be possible to accord special consideration to the interests of the Baganda and the constitution of their Kingdom as has hitherto been done by His Majesty's Government of the Uganda Protectorate, and which was also the express intention of the Uganda Agreement of 1900. Both the interests of the Baganda and the administration of their Kingdom will necessarily form part of the uniform policy calculated to be the best for the general welfare of the native tribes comprised in the Federation. It is presumed that it will be necessary to create a special Department under the control of the Central Government of the Federation to deal with Native Affairs of the various Colonies and Protectorates composed in the Federation, and naturally such a Department will be confronted with numerous difficulties of native administration of the Federation, that it will be impossible for it to give special consideration to questions of minor importance affecting the individual Protectorates or Colonies; so that in its administration, it will be necessary for this Department to be guided by a uniform policy of Native Administration. Again even assuming that such a Department will not be necessary and that domestic affairs of native administration of each Protectorate or Colony will be left in the control of the Government of each Colony or Protectorate, yet there will arise, in the future progress of the Federation, questions of general interest which affect the welfare of the majority of the native tribes of the Federation upon which the Central Government will be called upon to legislate or offer its advice, and such legislation or advice may be in direct conflict with the terms of our Agreement of 1900 or repugnant to the principles of the internal native administration of Buganda Kingdom, in which case the general welfare of the majority of the native tribes of the Federation is bound to prevail over the interests of the single tribe of the Baganda; and the Agreement of 1900 will necessarily have to be interpreted and employed in accordance with the condition of the general native affairs of the whole Federation, and it will become almost impossible to accord the special consideration to Buganda Kingdom guaranteed under the Uganda Agreement of 1900. As pointed out above, the present position occupied by Buganda Kingdom in the Uganda Protectorate is quite unique, since any legislation introduced by the Protectorate Government which is inconsistent with the terms of the Uganda Agreement of 1900 is not applicable to Buganda Kingdom except with the prior consent of the Kabaka and his Lukiko. It is only natural that some apprehensions should be felt by all the Baganda that by the inclusion of Buganda in the proposed Federation it will not always be possible for the Central Government of the Federation to observe or give effect to this most important provision of the Agreement, which specially safeguards the interest of the Baganda and preserves the internal native administration of the Buganda Kingdom. For instance, it is naturally feared that Ordinances enacted by the Central Government of the Federation for the better government of the Federation as a whole or for the proper administration of native affairs in particular, will necessarily be applicable to the Kingdom of Buganda irrespective of the above mentioned provision in the Uganda Agreement; and, as already stated in the earlier part of this Memorandum, Buganda being a small and unimportant country compared to the other native tribes in the Federation, it will not always be possible for the Kabaka and chiefs of Buganda to remonstrate against any such legislation and assert their rights conferred upon them by the terms of the Agreement of 1900.

It may be argued, on the other hand, that the proposed Federation only contemplates amalgamation of certain public services such as Postal,

Transport, Medical, and Customs and such like, which do not in any way affect the native administration of the various Protectorates and Colonies and that the Government policy of each Protectorate and Colony in connexion with their respective native affairs will not be interfered with. I am well aware that the amalgamation of such public services is essential, and has already been effected in certain special cases between the Uganda Protectorate and Kenya Colony. If only the Federation of such services is contemplated, then I, as the Kabaka of Buganda, have no voice in the matter and have no suggestions or objections to offer thereon. It would be presumptuous on my part if I were to do so, since such matters are outside my province.

My desire in preparing this Memorandum is to give the Commission a clear idea of the present position of Buganda Kingdom in the formation of the Uganda Protectorate. I trust I have endeavoured to do this, and to impress upon them the importance of the present constitution of Buganda Kingdom as provided in the Uganda Agreement of 1900 and the internal native administration, which has been solemnly reserved to the Kabaka and his chiefs by the terms of the same Agreement. I have also tried to show how the position of Buganda will fundamentally be changed in the composition of the proposed Federation and how it will be no longer possible for the present constitution of the Native Administration of Buganda Kingdom to be safeguarded and reserved to the Kabaka and his Chiefs. This Memorandum is, moreover, written in the hope that the members of the Commission will gain therefrom some useful information and will learn the views expressed by the head of the Native Government of Buganda Kingdom on behalf of his Chiefs and people, which may prove of some assistance to the Commission in their work of investigation into this important question of Federation.

In addition to the foregoing, I consider it only right to place on record my appreciation of the attitude taken by the local Government in this matter. When the question of the amalgamation of the Uganda Protectorate, Kenya, Tanganyika and Zanzibar was first brought up in 1921, I and my Chiefs put up a petition to His Excellency the Governor in which we set out our anxiety and fears as well as our strong protest against such amalgamation, and in March of 1922, we received a reply from the Honourable the Chief Secretary to the Government (18th March, 1922), which contained the following assurance:

'. . . . the Secretary of State for the Colonies has requested that you may be informed that, if it should be decided to make any arrangements for effecting closer co-ordination between the Administrations in East Africa, whether by federation or other means, you may rest assured that no action will be taken involving infringement of the Uganda Agreement of 1900, and that in any event it is not contemplated that the Kingdom of Buganda or the Uganda Protectorate generally should be placed under the jurisdiction of any external legislative body in Eastern Africa, or that the Secretary of State's responsibility for the administration of the Protectorate should be reduced in any way.'

It is clear, therefore, that from the very beginning the local Government recognized the Secretary of State's responsibility for the due observance of the provisions of our Agreement of 1900.

Again when this burning question was revived in 1924, I and my Ministers on behalf of the Native Government of Buganda addressed a letter (5th May, 1924) to the Honourable the Chief Secretary in which we informed him that we had heard through the local Press that the amalgamation of the British Protectorates and Colonies in Eastern Africa was again under contemplation, and we expressed our fear for such amalgamation in the 2nd paragraph of our letter referred to above in the following terms:

'2. We have therefore ventured to approach you, Sir, to ascertain whether there is any truth in this rumour that we have heard, and if so, to find out whether this amalgamation, after it has been approved by His Majesty the King of England, will introduce any change in the British Administration of our country; and whether it will in any way affect the Uganda Agreement of 1900 and all the other subsequent Agreements that we have hitherto entered into with the British Government; and whether it will interfere with the native customs of the Baganda since this amalgamation will necessarily embrace many African tribes.'

To this expression of our anxiety, the Honourable the Chief Secretary was kind enough to give us a detailed reply containing some definite assurance and explanation calculated to allay our fears on this subject in his letter of 24th July, 1924, addressed to the Kabaka of Buganda, the most important extracts therefrom are these:

'2. Your anxiety in this matter was then (i.e. in 1921 and 1922) reported to the Secretary of State for the Colonies, whose reply was communicated to you in this Office Memorandum, dated 18th March, 1922 (already quoted above). This reply was to the effect that, should it be decided to make any arrangements for effecting closer co-ordination between the Administrations in East Africa, whether by federation or by other means, you may rest assured that no action will be taken involving infringement of the Agreement of 1900, and that in any event it is not contemplated that the Kingdom of Buganda or the Uganda Protectorate generally should be placed under the jurisdiction of any external legislative body in Eastern Africa, or that the Secretary of State's responsibility for the Administration of the Protectorate should be reduced in any way.'

'4. His Excellency the Governor is sending copies of this correspondence to the Secretary of State for his information, but he is confident that neither you nor your Ministers need have any anxiety in this matter.'

As a result of the Honourable the Chief Secretary's promise contained in the last paragraph of his letter just quoted above, he communicated to His Highness the Kabaka later in 1924 in his letter of the 18th October, 1924, the Secretary of State's approval of the assurance already given to us by the local Government on the question of the amalgamation of the British East African Dependencies. This letter reads as under:

'With reference to your letter, dated 5th May, 1924, on the subject of the federation of the British Colonies and Protectorates in Eastern Africa, I have the honour to inform you that a despatch has now been received from the Secretary of State for the Colonies to the effect that he approves the terms of the reply sent to you from this Office, Memorandum dated 24th July, 1924.'

In view of the correspondence just quoted above which passed between the Protectorate Government and the Native Government of Buganda Kingdom since 1921 on the subject of the amalgamation of this Protectorate – Buganda Kingdom in particular – with any other Protectorate or Colony of British Eastern Africa, there is not the slightest doubt that this matter has always caused us a great deal of anxiety and fear since 1921, and we have always steadily and strenuously opposed such amalgamation; while it is equally apparent that the Protectorate Government has always realized and appreciated our anxiety and has taken every opportunity to allay our fears on this subject by obtaining from the Secretary of State his formal approval to the assurance already given to us by the local Government. I have, therefore, considered it right to express my gratitude to the Protectorate Government for the attitude and view that it has always taken in reference to this important question. I feel quite sure that nothing will be done by the Imperial Government to shake the confidence of my chiefs and myself in the guarantee that has already been so freely and repeatedly given to us by the Protectorate Government, and which, moreover, has been formally approved by the Secretary of State for the Colonies.

In conclusion, I cannot refrain from making a few humble suggestions in the event it is ultimately decided that the proposed federation is imperative and should be put into operation at some future date. These suggestions are quite simple and are made without prejudice to the rights acquired by the Kabaka, Chiefs, and people of Buganda under the Agreement of 1900:

(a) That if the Federation is effected, Buganda should be excluded therefrom as regards the constitution of the Kingdom of Buganda, provided under the Uganda Agreement of 1900, and that no legislation made by the Central Government of the Federation shall interfere with the internal native administration of Buganda Kingdom; and that any measures introduced by the Central Government of the Federation in connexion with the general government of the native tribes composed in the Federation shall not be applicable to the Baganda.

(b) If, on the other hand, it is considered undesirable to exclude Buganda alone from the Federation as indicated in (a) above. I would humbly beg to suggest, with all due respect, that my country, being the most important native state in the Uganda Protectorate, may receive the same consideration and treatment as was accorded to the Protectorate of Basutoland. It is understood that when the subjection of Basutoland to the control of the Cape Government proved unsatisfactory, the Basuto appealed to the Imperial Government to take them over, and in 1884 Basutoland ceased to be a portion of the Cape Colony. In our case we are quite convinced as pointed out above in detail, that the inclusion of Buganda Kingdom into the proposed Federation will not prove beneficial to the interests of the Baganda, since it will necessarily involve the breach either directly or indirectly of the fundamental principles of the constitution of the Kingdom of Buganda laid down in our principal Agreement of 1900. I would, therefore, humbly submit that when the Federation comes into force, Buganda Kingdom should be taken over by the Imperial Government, and a special Resident Commissioner, with the necessary staff, appointed by that Government to look after the interests of Buganda Kingdom and the welfare of its people, stationed in Buganda, as is done in the case of Basutoland. This would prove most beneficial to the Baganda as they will have special British Administrative Officers allotted to Buganda to look after their interests and to advise them in matters of native administration of their kingdom; and no other native interests or outside influence will interfere with the policy of the internal native administration of Buganda Kingdom. This is all the more necessary and desirable since it is a well-known fact and admitted by the Administrative Officers of the British Government that the Baganda are quite different from the surrounding native tribes of Eastern Africa, east or west of Lake Victoria.

> – from *Papers relating to the Question of the Closer Union of Kenya, Uganda, and the Tanganyika Territory*, Colonial, No. 57, London, His Majesty's Stationery Office, 1931, pp. 80–5.

27. PROPOSAL FOR REFORM OF THE LUKIKO, 1929

Letter and enclosure from Yusufu Bamuta to the British Colonial Secretary, 3 October 1929.

We most respectfully beg to write and inform you that after very careful consideration we have come to the conclusion that if this country hope to progress and enable Baganda to run their own Government on modern lines and that if our suggestions meet with your kind and sympathetic consideration we are sure that our country will prosper and that as time goes on we will be able to become a self-governing people in the true meaning of the term.

We the undersigned, leaders of the different political parties in this Kingdom, after full consultation with hereditary Chiefs and others have come to an agreement to present to you with this petition.

We attach our suggestions for your kind consideration.

We have the honour to be

Sir,

Your most and humble servants

Yusufu Bamuta

Chairman Bulungi Bwa Buganda Party

[here follow 211 signatures]

Notes on a Scheme of Representative Government for Buganda Kingdom

1. The Historical Position

It is clear from a perusal of the Uganda Agreement, that the framers of it found a form of limited monarchy in being.

The Kings had it is true very arbitrary powers, but they were not removed from the influence of the chiefs, and on the death of a King the big chiefs and ministers both governed the country, and chose the successor.

Thus the limitations of Royal Power were apparent.

In fact, leaving out the various acts of extreme cruelty, due usually to the excess of the reigning monarch, and to the lack of religion, many things in the Native State of Buganda followed much the same course as they would have taken, and as similar things did take, in other times, in Europe.

In such circumstances, the early British Administrators saw their duty very clearly, and acted upon it. They retained the form of Native Government and developed its constitutional side.

Thus we find in the Agreement, a constitutionally governed state consisting of:

1. The King.
2. The Ministers.
3. The Committee of Notables.
4. The Council of Chiefs.

The functions of the King, the Ministers, and the Notables are advisory, but the King with His Council or Lukiko, becomes the Executive.

At the time when these persons were appointed, that is to say the time that the Uganda Agreement was made, it would not have been possible to select anybody, for the reason that any election must pre-suppose literacy, and practically the whole country was illiterate. This then is the reason why no such machinery, e.g. that of election, was provided for in the earlier political arrangement.

In passing we may note also, the difference in the status of certain members of the Council, etc. The Ministers, for example, to be appointed in co-operation with the British Representative, the County Chiefs, to be authorized by both parties, because they were responsible for the Imperial Tribute, the Poll Tax, as well as for the purely native taxes.

2. The position of the King and his relations with The Imperial Government.

In many parts of the Uganda Agreement we read: 'And in such matters the Kabaka shall be exclusively guided by the advice of His Majesty's Representative.'

These expressions are vital to the status of the Buganda Kingdom, what do they mean? If they are an imposition on the acts of the native Kings in all matters, then there is no sovereignty in the Native Government. From a study of the context however, it is clear that this is not the correct meaning, and that the only occasions when the Native Government must follow the advice of the King's Representative, without question, is on matters of purely imperial import, that is to say:

The appointment of chiefs who collect the Imperial Tribute.
Peace and War.
Reserved Taxation.
Reserved Legislation, fiscal, etc.

On all other matters the use of the passages quoted from the Agreement to limit the powers of the Native Government would be *prima facie* contrary to the Agreement, itself, and definitely *ultra vires*.

With these limitations, therefore, the Kabaka of Uganda, acting with his Lukiko, or Council is to all practical intents and purposes the head of a sovereign state.

3. The Position of the Present Government Machinery, in Uganda.

From the time that the Agreement was entered into up to the present, a great change has taken place in Buganda. An educated population has grown up, estimated as being as high as 65% of the men and 25% of the women. That is not to say that all these people can read an English newspaper. No, although some thousands of them could, it means to say that this number of the population could read a notice in their own language, and could record a vote in written characters.

An elective assembly is therefore decidedly possible.

In lieu thereof there is a system whereby mostly uneducated men occupy the teaching positions in the country, for which they are not fitted. This system is favoured by what is known as the Provincial Administration, which seems to seek to curtail the status of the Buganda Government, and to treat only with the uneducated and backward Baganda to the practical disfranchisation of the mass of the advanced population.

4. <u>What is wanted as a Remedy?</u>

The present system in Buganda is rather on a par with putting a horse to draw a motor car. It is antiquated and impossible of repair, and wants scrapping.

Within the limits of the Agreement, there should be an elective body in place of the Lukiko. The Provincial Administration as regards the Kingdom, should be entirely altered, and the Office of Provincial Commissioner, abolished. In place thereof there should be a single British Official, to act as Resident or liaison between the Native and the British Government. The Officer should be instructed to confine himself to the terms of the Agreement and not to render his presence irksome, by scheming, or interference.

5. The following Franchise qualification is suggested:

(a) <u>Men.</u> Ability to Read and Write to a simple standard in the vernacular language.
Ownership of not less than 5 acres of land containing an occupied homestead, or being cultivated up to four-fifths of acreage.
Possession of an earned income of not less than £25 per year.
Proof of continuous education extending to not less than five years with a good leaving certificate.

(b) <u>Women.</u> Legitimately married only, who could pass a single reading and writing test in the vernacular.
(There are many intelligent women in Buganda, but owing to moral slackness it is necessary to support the steadier type of women as much as possible, and as an inducement to others to reform).

6. Numbers

As the present Buganda Government consists of nearly 90 persons, it is presumed that if each Gombolola* voted for a candidate, and the county chiefs held seats by virtue of office, about the same number, certainly not more, would result.

Ministers would in the circumstances have to be elected, for a fixed period, from the Lukiko, and the present County Chiefs, should while remaining in the Lukiko for the term of their office, be replaced by elected office holders appointed by the Lukiko, according as vacancies took place.

Thereafter they should become officials only with no further say in Administration, than their European compeers.

Where a matter required Imperial Sanction, the decisions of the Lukiko would require ratification by the British Authority but the right to originate the recommendation would still rest with Lukiko, and the Secretary of State would still be the Umpire in case of dispute.

In the course of time it would be natural to expect the enlargement of the possibilities of African Advancement in Buganda to include many positions now held by Europeans or Asians.

7. Functions of the Lukiko

The present Council meets once a year and its chief business is the passing of money supplies.

A representative Lukiko should meet more often, say 3 times a year, and there is no limitation on their legislation powers other than as regards the reserved matters in the Uganda Agreement.

There is no reason why they should not pass resolutions and frame their own legislation within the limits laid down.

8. The Present System

The present system is iniquitous because it deprives the African of his ligitimate advance, and creates continual ill feeling between the King's Protected Baganda Subjects, and His Other Subjects. It is British Policy to meet the need for expansion and provide for it, not to repress things until there is an explosion of ill feeling. This is the case for the early re-arrangement of things in Buganda.

As things go at present our people will be swept into the whirlpool of 'Federation' without the means of articulate protest.

– from Public Records Office, London, C.O.
536/157.

Gombolola: sub-county.

28. PRO AND CON, 1930

Speech by Kabaka Daudi Chwa, 14 August 1930.

The Provincial Commissioner, Ladies and Gentlemen, Ministers and Chiefs.

I wish to express my gratitude for the kind congratulations tendered by the Provincial Commissioner on behalf of the Protectorate Government on the occasion of the celebration of my 34th birthday.

It has given me the greatest pleasure to hear the Provincial Commissioner's congratulations on the progress of my country. It is only fair for me to state here that what little progress has been effected in the native administration of my country has been mainly, if not solely, due to the fact that we have been fortunate in securing sympathetic Administrative and other Officers who take a keen interest in the welfare of my people and country and who are ever ready to offer sound and useful advice, which, I am glad to say, I and my Chiefs have always received most gratefully. The spirit of confidence and co-operation which exists between my Native Government and the Protectorate Government has been the backbone of the present progress and prosperity of my people. I would, therefore, take this opportunity to thank the Provincial Commissioner most heartily on behalf of the Protectorate Government for the interest shown by its members in the welfare of my people.

A very unfortunate incident which occurred during the early part of the current year and which has caused endless anxiety in the minds of my people, has been the buying of this year's cotton. Owing to the formation of a Syndicate of Cotton Buyers at the beginning of this year and other circumstances the price of cotton has been extremely low with the result that the native growers have been very reluctant to sell their cotton. This naturally has had the result of rendering the collection of taxes and other dues very difficult, and consequently the present collection of Poll Tax in Buganda is very backward. This unfortunate incident has also had another far-reaching effect on the cotton industry. From the reports I have received both from the Officers of the Protectorate Government and my Chiefs it is clear that the planting of cotton this year is not at all as extensive as it should have been, simply due to the fact that the growers not having been satisfied with the price of cotton of last year's crop, are naturally not very anxious to put in as much labour in planting cotton this year as they did last year, anticipating the same trouble in disposing of their cotton next year. In this respect however, I rely upon the influence of my chiefs and their co-operation with the Officers of the Protectorate Government to overcome this difficulty, and I have every confidence that my chiefs will, as they have always done, convince my people of the necessity of planting cotton, since this is the only source of wealth open to my people especially the Bakopi.

In conclusion I would again thank the Provincial Commissioner for the kind congratulations he has offered on behalf of the Protectorate Government; and I would at the same time take this opportunity to assure him, as Representative of His Excellency the Governor in this Province, of the staunch loyalty which I and my chiefs and people have always entertained towards His Majesty, the King and His Government, and which I have every confidence shall never be impaired. . . .

– from *Uganda Herald*, 15 August 1930.

29. CLOSER UNION
AND OTHER QUESTIONS, 1931

Serwano Kulubya, Omuwanika [Treasurer] of Buganda in reply to the Chairman of the Joint Committee of both Houses of the British Parliament on Closer Union in East Africa, London, 12 May 1931.

. . . I am sent by His Highness the Kabaka, Chiefs and the people of the Kingdom of Buganda to confirm the Memoranda written by His Highness the Kabaka on the question of Federation. There are also copies of the correspondence, which has passed between the native Government and His Majesty's Government in Buganda, of which, I believe, copies have been supplied to the members of this Honourable Committee. We in Buganda are in the peculiar position of having an Agreement with the Imperial Government whereby our interests are safeguarded and our internal independence guaranteed. Whilst it is scarcely doubted that the terms of the Agreement will be observed strictly by the Imperial Government, we cannot help showing some alarm that in all the Official Memoranda on the question of Closer Union no guarantee is given nor is any indication given that any guarantee will be given in the future that in any scheme of Closer Union the terms of the Buganda Agreement will be left entirely unimpaired. In the absence of any specified guarantee and in view of the almost studied avoidance of such guarantee we cannot help but feel that there are official doubts as to the possibility of bringing Buganda into Closer Union during the existence of the Buganda Agreement as it stands today. For ourselves we cannot understand how Closer Union can be effected without seriously impairing our rights and privileges as provided for in the Agreement. Whilst recognizing that no change might be

87

made in the letter of the Agreement it is almost certain that in course of time changes will be forced upon us, and eventually (it might be in our children's time), we would find that our Kingdom had been absorbed into a great organization. Quite apart from the question of the impairing of our rights under the Buganda Agreement should Closer Union be effected, we fail to see how a uniform native policy could ever be adopted for the whole of Eastern Africa. It is well known how vastly the various African tribes differ intellectually and how some have reached a more advanced state of civilization than others. How can any policy be devised which would be suitable to all these varying elements in the population? We, in Uganda, my Lord, are quite satisfied with our present position and enjoy a large measure of consideration from the British Government. The question of 'Paramountcy' does not cause us much anxiety at present. But what would be the position under Closer Union? Can it be denied that our interests would suffer greatly? Where we now enjoy the benefit of the advice of our local administrative officers – men who understand local conditions and whose sympathy we possess, and who can give us undivided attention without fear or favour, seeing that they have had a long training for this work and, therefore, great experience of what is best in all circumstances for our State. Under the suggested Closer Union we would be compelled to deal with a central body which would be largely influenced by a section of the population who are sincerely convinced of the imaginary evils which are implied in the doctrine called 'paramountcy'. Can it be wondered that we object to laying ourselves open to such a retrograde step? Are we not entitled in all fairness to oppose a scheme which will literally rob us of our birthright and substitute therefor a mess of pottage which in all possibility will have acquired a bad taste, but which we know will be the means of introducing discontent where heretofore has been almost perfect harmony? Without prejudice to our objection to the whole scheme of Closer Union, we would say that in view of the great differences between the various tribes of Eastern Africa, both socially and politically, it is difficult to see how a universal system of Government could possibly be devised which will meet the needs of all sections of the population. To deal alone with the question of the representation of native interests upon the said central governing body, would such representation be undertaken by European officials and missionaries or would representative Africans be elected by their fellow countrymen? In the latter event, is it certain or even probable that all the varying elements concerned would be capable of producing individuals sufficiently advanced and enlightened to take their place in the counsels of the governing central body with any degree of efficiency? So far as Buganda is concerned, nothing short of a large measure of actual native representation would meet the case and we consider here we meet one of the greatest stumbling blocks to the whole scheme. We are left in doubt as to anything approaching details of this scheme, which means such a lot to us, and, in the circumstances, we hold firmly to the belief that to let well enough alone is the safest policy affecting the Kingdom of Buganda. In all the examination of witnesses, expert and otherwise, which have preceded our examinations we find only here and there a passing reference to the Buganda Agreement. This Buganda Agreement is the very lifeblood of us as a nation – by it we have risen to our present status through the wise administration, the studied sympathy, and the deep-seated personal interest taken in us by the officers of the Imperial Government. We have no desire to forget these great helping hands which have been the means of placing us where we are today; and we dare not agree to the dangerous principle either in practice or precept of swopping horses whilst crossing the stream. Our one desire is to be left alone to carry on in the same way as we have been going since the Solemn Promise which marked the signing of the Buganda Agreement when it was first signed by the two parties. To attempt a new untried policy in the face of a tried one which has meant so great an expanse to us, is asking for more than we are prepared to give, and is asking for more than we should be expected to give. On the one hand we have been told by many people on many occasions that the integrity of the Buganda Agreement is fully ensured – that the British Government and the European element in the population are the trustees for the African population – that paramountcy of native interests is the order of the day. On the other hand, what do we find? The statement of His Majesty's Government on Closer Union contains not one word as regards the Buganda Agreement – no guarantee of the integrity of the Agreement is mentioned therein. A very large portion of the European population is shocked at the very word 'paramountcy' when applied to native interests. Is it to be wondered that we in Buganda wish to remain apart? Is it to be wondered that we fear for our national future under any scheme of Closer Union? Is it to be wondered that we are forced to adopt such an uncompromising attitude to a proposal which can only end in the subjection of Buganda interests to the benefit of other and more powerful sections of the community?

Honourable Members, we are a small Community, comparatively, but we ask for fair play, we ask for a continuance of the redemption of the Promise given us, we ask that the Justice and the Justness which has made the British Empire the mighty power it is today, be still further guaranteed to us and that we be permitted to carry on on the lines which have brought us to the measure of prosperity which we enjoy today....

5634. There is a question which has been referred to, which I should like to hear your views on. We have had various evidence regarding the official language to be used in the three Dependencies. I understand that at present the language of Swahili or Kiswahili is being adopted as the official language? – Yes.

5635. It is being adopted, I think, very largely in Kenya, very largely in Tanganyika, and, I believe – you will put me right if I am wrong in this –

that it is being gradually introduced into Uganda to replace existing native languages, the Mother tongues. Now, perhaps, you would give your view on the advantage or the disadvantage of the introduction of Kiswahili as the language of the Courts and of official communication between people? – My lord has just pointed out that it is being introduced. I should say that in most cases it is being forced, instead of being introduced. I think these two terms are distinct. The question was brought up and we in the Buganda Province opposed it, because we do not see what we will gain by putting aside our own Mother tongue and adopting some other language which has no foundation. Swahili is just as it is spoken on the Coast, but when you come to the point of asking who are the Swahilis, you will not be able to be informed that the Swahilis live in such-and-such a country, and we do not think it is a good policy to force people to give up their own pride of race, their own language, and ask them to take on a new language altogether. I do not think, as a race, we would tolerate that. In some provinces, it was forced in that way, but I am glad that in Buganda, as you have just pointed out, the officers were very sympathetic, and it has not been forced so much in Buganda; but, of course, we never know what will happen. Things keep on changing, and we would say that most of the people in the Uganda Protectorate do not like it, and they do not think that it will benefit them in any way. My Kabaka, as I may point out, has put in a Memorandum to that effect, which is in the hands of the Colonial Office. It is a Memorandum on the use of the Kiswahili language as the official native language in Buganda, by His Highness the Kabaka of Buganda, Kampala, 1929. . . .

5640. And in the matter of education, you wish the education to be given in Luganda, to start with? – The question of education is already taken in each race, in each nation, as they think it will justly fit their requirements, and the present arrangements is that those vernacular schools should be trained in Luganda or in their different tribes, and the Bunyoro will carry on in the same way.

5641. As a second language to be learned, what second language do you think is preferable? – English, of course, my Lord, which is the key to everything, as it is. . . .

Lord Passfield: 5661. I have just one question to ask. You expressed the fear of the Kabaka that any form of Closer Union would really be inconsistent with and opposed to your Treaty, the rights of the Kingdom of Buganda. That was so, was it not? – That is so, yes.

5662. You remember that in 1927, four years ago, when the Hilton Young Commission was going out, my predecessor, the former Secretary of State, wrote to the Kabaka giving him an assurance that nothing would be done contrary to that Agreement, and that, if it had to be altered, it would be altered only with the full consent of the Kabaka. That was in 1927? – And we were very thankful for that, my Lord, but it was quite clear that the feelings of the Zanzibar Government were mentioned in the

Hilton Young Report; and also in the White Paper it was clearly set aside as to those kingdoms or territories which will be put together, but there is no mention made of the Buganda Kingdom. Quite naturally when that White Paper is being read, it is quite possible that it may be read by a man who does not know what is happening between the Colonial Office and the Kabaka, and naturally he will not understand exactly what sort of guarantees have been given, unless it is shown on a common and public paper which is in circulation.

5663. You will remember that in February last year I, myself, wrote to inform the Kabaka that if a central authority were constituted the agreement of 1900 with the Kabaka will not be varied without the full consent of himself and his councillors. I repeated in 1930 the declarations which had already been given in 1927? – You repeated that, my Lord; I quite remember it. It has also been stated quite clearly in the Kabaka's last memorandum that he is very thankful for all those promises, but anything which is put aside is quite likely to be forgotten sometime, if I may say so, and therefore we ask that where you may write anything in that way in your reference, or the letters which you may write to us, it should be stated that the position of Buganda is to remain intact, as is stated in my letter to so-and-so of such-and-such a date.

5664. I quite understand, but I was anxious to make it clear that that Government, just as the present Government, has undertaken the same as the late Government, so any future Government will keep the promise which has been made to the Buganda? – I know, and I have already stated in my paper which I have just presented before this honourable Committee, that we have got no doubt; but at the same time we would ask that everything should be put on a full record which can be seen by the public. I should say, my Lord, that I am right in saying that that letter has only passed between the Colonial Office and the local Government in Entebbe, and the Kabaka himself; it would be worth while to put it down on paper in black and white.

5665. It has been published here? – It has been published here, but that is quite recently. The point you have put to me, I believe, was not circulated in Buganda.

5666. I do not want to carry on the conversation. I was only anxious to repeat once more that the Government has no intention of attempting to alter the agreement of 1900, without the full consent of the Kabaka and his councillors. I say that again? – I am very thankful to hear it, my Lord.

Mr Amery: 5667. Then I gather that, from your point of view, it would make a great deal of difference in the case of any scheme of Union if it were accompanied at the same time by a public declaration of the British Government about the status of the Buganda Kingdom, that you would attach great importance to a public statement on record that the position of Buganda would remain unaffected? – That is so; we would like whatever is going out to be pointed out exactly in that paper. We get the promises; we do not doubt those promises, but when an official paper comes out there is nothing mentioned with regard to the position of the Buganda Kingdom.

5668. You would like any official paper that dealt with the future constitution of East Africa to include a reference to the position of the Buganda Kingdom? – That Buganda would remain intact in accordance with the 1900 Agreement.

5669. You would not say, would you, that the present railway and customs agreement, the railway agreement between Kenya and Uganda and the customs agreement between all the three countries has prejudiced the position of the Kingdom of Buganda, would you? – That is very difficult, because we know nothing about those later agreements or customs agreements, so it is very difficult for me to answer questions on railways and customs and things like that. All the Governors know quite clearly that we are not brought in contact with the working of railways, customs and post offices and things like that.

5670. But you have had no reason to believe that you have been injured by it? – I cannot express an opinion upon anything which I am not quite clear on.

5671. But what I meant is that, at any rate, you have not any positive reason for feeling that an extension of the railway agreement to Tanganyika would injure Uganda? – Our fears are always there in these new proposals, unless everything is laid on the table and we know clearly where we stand.

5672. It is the unknown that you are most afraid of? – It is strange to us, and I cannot express an opinion unless the whole thing is put upon the paper, so that we can understand after considering it, and digesting it properly.

5673. But a scheme which is put forward by the White Paper, with very general powers to a High Commissioner, you are afraid of. That has been published? – We are afraid of the whole White Paper as it stands at the present time, and, as I said in my statement, we would rather be left alone where we are now. . . .

Mr Wellock: 5718. There is one question on the matter of intercourse and communication. You said just now you could speak each other's languages. That rather suggests that there is considerable intercourse between the tribes; is that so? – That is so. There is considerable intercourse between the tribes.

5719. Has there ever been any attempt to have meetings or conferences or discussions between the tribes in regard to general questions affecting Uganda as a territory? – Not as far as I can remember.

5720. Has any proposal of that kind been discussed at all? – It was brought up by the Kabakas themselves, and it was a private discussion between the Kabakas of the four provinces.

5721. Are there any matters in particular which you discuss between members of one tribe and another? – I do not remember any occasion of that being done.

5722. Have you discussed this question of Closer Union amongst the different tribes, or has it all been done within your own tribe? – Each tribe discussed this question separately, and there was no combination or working together in any way.

5723. Could you tell the Committee a little about the constitution of the Lukiko; how it is composed, and whether there is anything approaching an electoral method adopted in making your Lukiko? – The constitution of Lukiko is as defined in the 1900 Agreement; that is, the Kabaka, his three Ministers, 20 County Chiefs, three Chiefs from each County, and six Chiefs nominated by the Kabaka which makes it 89 in all. The people appointed in this way by the Kabaka make the Lukiko Council.

5724. That is to say, the Kabaka nominates all the members. And has it ever been discussed or suggested that there should be a method of election of the various Chiefs? – The Kabaka, of course, does all that in accordance with the agreement which he entered into with His Majesty's Government in 1900 and the Lukiko, and there was a question brought up by some young people to that effect, but he thought it would disorganize the tribal constitution and so he opposed it, and at the same time wrote to His Excellency the Governor telling him of the impossibility of this, and in paragraph 4 of his letter he says: 'With regard to the desire on the part of the signatories of the petition to introduce democracy government in all its technicalities in this country at one sweep, this can only be viewed as absurd at this state of civilization and progress of the country since it would not only be undesirable, but absolutely unworkable, and would only result in dislocating the present system of the good administration of this country.' That is the Kabaka's letter to His Excellency the Governor dated the 25th November, 1929.

5725. Do I understand from that then, that, although you have the agreement of 1900, it would be possible for the Kabaka, if he so desired, to introduce a measure of democratic government? – I think that is a question which has to be left entirely in the hands of the Kabaka, and about which I cannot express an opinion.

5726. Could you tell me if there is much agitation in Buganda for a change of government in that respect, a change of procedure in regard to the election of your Lukiko? – If I may say so, Sir, being one of the native Government officials in a high position, I do not see any agitation that there may be, and I should say the proper course of finding out that is through the Colonial Office, if I may suggest it, who consulted the Governor to see the actual position in Uganda.

5727. In regard to your smaller Councils, how are they composed, and how are they elected or appointed? – They are elected on the same basis of the 1900 Agreement.

5728. Do I understand then that the Kabaka appoints every individual on every local Council, or is it done through advice? – The constitution has always been there, and we have got our various ways of nominating or appointing these people. The Kabaka has got certain powers to appoint up to a certain grade, and then the other lower Chiefs carry on for the lower grades, and the Kabaka does not interfere very much in those.

5729. Just one further question with regard to the land. I understood from Mr Bruton, I think it was, that there were 19,000 square miles in Buganda? – Mr Bruton: 19,600 I think it was.

5730. Yes; I am not getting the odd figures. I understood that 8,000 of those 19,000 were in the control of a comparatively small number of people at the head, and that left 11,000 for the rest of the community. I should just like to ask about those 8,000 square miles. How many people really control that land and draw the rent from it, or whatever term you use? – Serwano Kulubya: The question of land as I have just said, is clearly laid down in the Uganda Agreement, paragraph 15, and the people who own that land are clearly shown there; but I would like to point out that nobody is stopped or prevented from occupying any piece of land he requires in Uganda; although he is not a landowner, he is at liberty to use that land, and the Government is there to see that no excessive rent or anything of that kind is charged.

5731. Is that matter strictly supervised? – It is supervised by a law which was passed entitled the Nvujo law.

5732. And you are allowed generally to buy and sell land by your tribe in Uganda? – From native to native.

5733. Not outside the tribe? – No, not non-natives.

5734. It can be to natives of other tribes? – It can be done in some instances, but we are very careful about that.

5735. And does this lead to a landless section of the community? Are there any natives in Uganda who, as a result of this practice, do not possess land? – They all enjoy the advantage of having land. They can produce their crops and they buy land in any way they like.

5736. But are there any adults in Buganda who do not possess land? – As I have just pointed out, there are a very limited number of people who own land according to the terms of the agreement; so the other people do not possess land, but they have got the advantage of taking up any land they require of the land in possession of the Chiefs, and their liberty is safe-guarded by a law passed by the Kabaka and the Lukiko to see that they are safeguarded if they do occupy other people's land. . . .

Mr Hudson: 5770. You are concerned, are you not, if they charge you high freights for your goods? – About the high freights and charges, that has not been brought to our notice, and I think before Closer Union is made or Closer Union of economic services is made in that way, it should be left entirely in the hands of the natives to bring up any dissatis-faction they may have on such Closer Union of the services.

5771. Just let me return to that point about the freight of goods. Are you satisfied in Buganda about the management of that railway? Do you make any complaints about the charges that are made to you? – As far as I can remember, and as I have just pointed out, we are not at all concerned with the charges or whatever may be the rates on the railway. I know there may be some discontent which we happen to see in the paper, but as natives in general we are not very much concerned with it. If we were concerned with the management of the railways, we should have complained quite a long time ago of the treatment we get on the Kenya Railways when we are coming to countries like this. Of course, sometimes we want to pay for first class; we do not get it; we want to pay for second class sometimes; but the treatment we get there is not a treatment which is fit for human beings, unless you have got an official accompanying you. That is what I say, my Lord, that if we had a voice in other respects we would have made use of it in all these difficulties, but, of course, if it is put to us in that way, then we will be able to complain if we know that we have got the right to complain about these things. . . .

5781. Then the only other question I wanted to ask was a question from Chief Kulubya with regard to education. You are very clear indeed, I think, that you wish to have English as the principal language learnt; apart from the native language, English is the next language? – Serwano Kulubya: Yes.

5782. Are most of your people agreed upon that? – They are agreed, and there has been very serious complaint about it. They were very disappointed when they were told about Swahili; so all the people are agreed that English should be the language which is taught in all schools on account of books and several advantages which one can get through studying or learning English.

5783. I noticed what you said before about English giving access to certain things; could you tell me a little more about that? What sort of things do you mean? Are there many things that the people would like to have access to which they could get through English but which they could not get through Swahili? What sort of things do you mean? – What we want is the general education as it is known. We say that we should be given education which is not set aside particularly for us, because the tendency has always been that ways should be found to find a suitable system of education for the Africans. But what we want is education as it is known in this country, although it may not be to that extent. I do not say that we want to see it being sprung up in the country in two years' time, but what we say is that we should start from the bottom properly, and that we should be given the standard course of education which would enable those who can to come and join universities or certain colleges in this country. The present education which we get as it is in Buganda will take us nowhere. If we get young people who have finished their studies, for instance, at Makerere College,* they cannot come and join any class in this country. What we want is the general education as it

95

is known, that facilities should be extended to us in English for those purposes.

5784. I want to ask about Makerere College. You think the standard is not quite high enough; they ought to educate them up to a higher standard so that they could take advantage of the universities later? – Yes, because at the present time the boy finishes his education in Makerere and, if he wants to join any of the colleges and universities, I do not know what you call them in this country, there are so many schools, I cannot identify them properly, but he cannot go in any class in this country.

5785. I quite understand that. It was this point which I wanted to know your opinion upon because this is a very important question, and I know you have thought deeply about education. Many people say there should be a special kind of education for the African, that it should be chiefly technical education? – That I do not agree with because we require leaders for our people; I say that the principal system of education as it is known in this country should be extended to us.

5786. What we call a general or cultural education? – That is so. . . .

Sir J. S. Allen: 5795. Do a lot of natives use boots and shoes in Uganda? – We use boots and shoes and everything which is brought into Uganda.

5796. I asked the question because the impression created by some evidence was that all the boots and shoes of that kind that come through were for European use, and I understood myself, from information I had, that a great deal was used by the natives? – We use boots and shoes in Uganda, just like Europeans, not because we want them, but because we see the advantage of them. There are so many snakes in our countries, and they are very useful to us in protecting us from snakes and things like that, just as well as Europeans. . . .

5808. I take it that Uganda has benefited by having the railway. You are able to get your cotton out in a way you could not have done if there had not been a railway? – Undoubtedly it has benefited us in that way, if the railways are not going to be controlled by the Kenya settlers.

5809. In any question I have asked you I had in mind that the control would be a balanced control, and would not be under, as you say, Kenya settlers or any other particular party, but a control for the benefit of all parties interested? – That is what I say: that the control should be left in the hands of the Governors in all the respective Protectorates as it is at the present time.

5810. Therefore, you have not really studied it, and you do not look upon it as part of your evidence – any of these questions as to railway management, or finance or anything of that kind? – I have studied it, and I have given my views, although they may not be satisfactory views. We have studied it as far as the railways are concerned. To a certain extent we know it.

5811. I do not want to trouble you with anything beyond trying to get out, if I can, whether you had any experience. I know you have had experience and I know you have knowledge, but I want to know whether you would give us the benefit of your knowledge, or whether you would prefer not to say anything more on the subject? – I say that we do not want the railway to be united as it will interfere with our present rates on those railways if they are joined together in that way. We would rather be just on the present principles as the railways are run by the various Governors of the several Dependencies in East Africa.

5812. In fact, you are quite content as long as questions in dispute come before the Governor's Conference, or ultimately before the Secretary of State, and you feel that is what you want? – That is so, and we do not want to be cut off from the Colonial Office. . . .

Mr Ormsby-Gore: 5820. I would like to ask a few further questions regarding the constitution of the Lukikos and the appointment of chiefs. May I ask the Treasurer of the Kingdom of Uganda, when there is a vacancy for a Saza Chief what procedure is adopted to fill that vacancy? First, is any Gombolola Chief eligible for promotion? Is the new Chief appointed by the Kabaka on the advice of his Ministers and the other Saza Chiefs, and do the British officers interfere in the selection in any way? Could he answer that? How is a Saza Chief exactly appointed when there is a vacancy? – Serwano Kulubya: When there is a vacancy for a Saza Chief three or four names are put up. Letters are written to the Saza Chiefs asking them to put in their views, because they cannot be called in every time. They write to us suggesting certain names. We go through their lists; we take out names and we put in new names which we submit to the Kabaka, and we consider them together until we arrive at one decision, and then the matter is put in the regular form. A letter is written to His Excellency the Governor pointing out the name. Of course, this procedure varies. It all depends upon what type of Provincial Commissioner you have got, if I may say so. We get some difficult Commissioners, and some of the other type. The name is put forward and we just discuss it with the Provincial Commissioner, and if he agrees with our views, or even if he does not agree we can write directly to His Excellency the Governor whose decision is final, in accordance with the agreement. But now that attitude is changing very rapidly, and if there is any difficulty the views of the Lukiko are always taken into prior consideration.

5821. There are one or two points in that statement that I should like you to help me upon if you could. When you say 'we consider the list of names put up by the other Saza chiefs', does 'we' mean the Kabaka himself personally and the three Ministers? – The three Ministers, according to this agreement from the Government of Buganda; those people who may be lieutenants of the Saza Chiefs who may happen to be in town.

5822. That is to say, it is really a system of co-option by the leading chiefs in the native Government, and they, as it were, co-opt another man, when there is a vacancy, to fill that vacancy? – Yes.

5823. Subject to the subsequent approval of the Governor? – In accordance with the 1900 agreement. I have got the section here about these appointments.

5824. I think I have got it clear. Now can anybody be appointed first a Gombolola chief, then rise to be a Saza chief, and finally a Minister? Is there any qualification required before a man can get an appointment in a responsible position? Has he a standard of education or anything of that kind to pass? – The man who is supposed to be the best at that time is appointed after having been considered. It does not follow that he is going to be a Gombolola chief first. I remember the present Kangawo was acting as the Chief Householder to His Highness the Kabaka. He was appointed directly from that post to a Saza chieftainship; and there have been some instances of that kind, appointing the most suitable man for the post.

5825. In appointing a Saza chief or a Gombolola chief, you do not necessarily take a man who lives in that district or is a landowner in that district. He can be selected from anywhere in the Kingdom of Buganda? – Yes. . . .

Lord Ponsonby: 5934. Most of my points have been covered, but there is just one question I should like to ask the Treasurer of Buganda. On more than one occasion you have said very emphatically that your people did not want representation on the Legislative Council? – Serwano Kulubya: Yes.

5935. Would you say why that decision has been so emphatically made by them? – Because here we state that we would like to follow our old constitution; and then we have got our own agreement which sets out properly the constitution of our Lukiko. If we get a representative on the Legislative Council, it is quite possible, say with one representative, or two representatives, that he will be out-voted there by the majority, and when he has been out-voted in that way it will be very difficult for us to reopen the question, because we have got our representative there; so if you leave it as it is, we have got every chance of complaining on anything which may be passed by the Legislative Council, and we can always approach the Secretary of State if nothing is altered. . . .

– from *Report of Joint Committee on Closer Union in East Africa*, Vol. II, Minutes of Evidence, House of Commons Paper 156, 1931, pp. 550–52, 556–7, 560–61, 563–4, 565, 566, 567, 568–71, 577.

The Chairman of the Committee was Lord Stanley of Alderley.

Letter to The Uganda Herald, *26 August 1932, from 'A Muganda'.*

I should be very grateful if you could let your readers share with me this thought I am bringing to the notice of the public.

It goes without saying that it is one of, if not the foremost and primary work of any Government to educate its subjects. And I think it is also the work of the Government not merely to educate children in the primary stages only, but to see that the enterprises of some men or bodies of men to further the education thus started to higher and fuller development of man's activities receive the Government's encouragement and support; and that poverty is not in any way a complete bar to higher learning but that intellectual capacities, just like monetary privileges, fit a man for responsible places in one's country.

It is part of the history of this country that elementary schooling is in the hands of the Missions, and the higher one in the hands of the Government, and also that Government does subsidize the Missionary efforts, to a certain extent. But this reverse order of the responsibilities of the education creates problems peculiar to itself; such as making elementary education to be a paid-for proposition, and therefore making it difficult to a greater many to get a good and sound elementary schooling. And again, it puts into the hands of the Government the whole and absolute power to dominate education, a thing that has not proved to be beneficient to the educational system of Uganda. Although that of Germany is based on such grounds, yet, as there seems to be some drawbacks in it, there is a tendency now to discard this form, where high education is concerned. One is aware of the fact, however, that without a Government subsidy towards high education such attainments in education as we know them might have taken longer in being achieved.

If, again, this reverse order of responsibilities is viewed from another angle, one finds that it makes people in the country less able to demand educational facilities as, in the reverse order this is not the direct responsibility of the Missions. About this point I will like to say a few more words.

Was it time to enforce an educational rate? The answer would come without the slightest hesitation. I think the Government was not fully justified in introducing a new tax during such times of economic depression. Apart from that, one thinks that the Government knows and is aware of the fact that the African people in the Protectorate are not getting back sufficient return from the Government of what they pay in all kinds of taxes. The best part that the African peoples in the Protectorate get in the return from the Poll Tax is the salaries of the chiefs, in other words they get not more than 20%, as in the case of the Buganda Kingdom. It is wicked, I should venture to say, in some parts of the Protectorate, where the African people pay in direct taxes something like nearly half of what their actual earnings in the way of wages would be if they worked every month throughout the year, to have added on the top of that the educational rate! One admits, however, that in such areas the elementary school buildings are far better than the same in Buganda Kingdom, but is that enough?

Nowadays the Indian community are building a first rate educational institution in Kampala, and one hears that the Government is giving a shilling to each one the Indian community subscribers for the purpose. Apart from this, the Government is going to pay the emoluments in the personnel of the School, together with the general upkeep, etc. One therefore puts such questions to himself as whether the proportion the non-Africans pay in direct taxes highly exceeds that of the Africans in the Protectorate. The question now is, therefore, why has not the Government helped the Baganda in building the Junior Secondary School at Budo? Is it simply because they do not pay the educational rate? Of course the Indian community does not. On the other hand the Baganda started a long time ago, to pay what is known as a Development Tax, which was levied mainly for two purposes; one was for the hospitals and the other was for schools. True that Mulago and Makerere College* came into existence as the result, perhaps! But Mulago is now for the whole Protectorate, and the buildings of the Government dispensaries throughout Buganda Kingdom is the work of the Buganda Government.

And, again Makerere, too, is now for the whole Protectorate, and is tending towards becoming a University College for the whole of Eastern Africa. Although the Baganda do not pay the educational rate, they, by the contributions above referred to are entitled to such educational facilities as the other peoples in the Protectorate.

While on this question, I would like to touch upon one other point. Suspicions are being entertained that the hand of retrenchment in Government Departments might fall on the Education Staff. As I have been trying to point out above, it is obvious that the Government has yet a long way to go in giving mass education, and at this stage to curtail even the effort that is being put forth would be disastrous and by far, uneconomical, for just as one great educationalist said 'the wealth of a Nation is not in her battleships, her bridges etc. but in her people'. The required ends could, however, be made to meet if, instead of spending fresh sums of money on building a new Indian School, it could have utilized the money, if not on other things, but on the improvement of educational system at Makerere, because the building of the Indian School at once confronts Buganda and Uganda with the question of segregation in education.

In conclusion, therefore, it is only just to say that Buganda Kingdom, looking at the fortune that has come to the Indians, turns and looks up to the Government with appealing eyes, and says 'Is it ill-luck that similar help is not forthcoming from the Government when she is building up her Junior Secondary School in Budo?'

– from *Uganda Herald*, 2 September 1932.

Mulago: the main Government hospital.
Makerere College: founded in 1921, it was not at this time a University College.

31. THE IMPACT OF CHRISTIANITY, 1933

The death of Canon Apolo Kivebulaya in Mboga, Congo, as told by Rev. (later Bishop) Aberi Balya.

He stayed in his house at Kabarole, he was not at all well, his legs began to swell. He said to us, 'Carry me and take me back to Mboga.' I said to him, 'You are not going back to Mboga, we want you to stay here, and when you die we will bury you by the church here, we want your grave to be with us here.' He said, 'If you don't return me to Mboga, you will bury me badly.'

Then Russell*and I took counsel together and we decided to send him back to Mboga.* People carried him, and he bade farewell to Toro, to the people who came to say goodbye to him, with great joy . . . about 50 Christians from Mboga were waiting for him at the Semliki* to take over from the Toro carriers. When he arrived back at Mboga he got steadily worse. On 22 May I received a telephone message from Mboga (for some years a single telephone wire connected Irumu, Mboga and Fort Portal) that Apolo was dying. I went to see the Provincial Commissioner to ask permission to go Mboga. I had to pay 14 shillings and 50 cents for a wire to get permission. They granted me permission quickly. I set out on the 23 May and got there on the 25th. I found him very ill and very swollen. He was very pleased to see me. He drew me down to himself as he lay and greeted me with such a joyful embrace. His heart was not thinking about death, but about the work. He said, 'In the morning you will give Holy Communion to the teachers, and afterwards you will go into the forest and baptize those people whom I examined, whom I have not been able to baptize because of my illness.' I said to him, 'But I cannot, my feet are already cut and pricked with thorns from the journey to Mboga, anyway I have come to bury you.' He said nothing, but I could see he was not pleased. Then I told him that Omwami Yosiya Sewali, the Katikiro of Toro,* had sent him a bolt of cloth to bury him in. He said to me, 'In the morning I will send it to the teachers in the forest.' I was surprised. Other things I had to say I refrained from saying.

On 26 May the teachers came in for Holy Communion, it was an important day, Apolo was worse. The Rev. Russell and his wife arrived on the 27 May; he had come from Ankole* where he had been on a tour of the Deanery. Apolo was very pleased to see them.

On Sunday the 28th we took the bread and wine and gave Apolo Holy Communion as he lay on his bed. We bade farewell to him with the sacrament of the body and the blood of Jesus his Lord, for whom he had worked for 38 years, working for Him whom he dearly loved, even until death. He loved Him above anything on this earth. He was very happy indeed . . . I was watching with him in his house, others came too. In the morning I prayed and talked with him about all kinds of things, I asked his thoughts about a lot of things, about the work and who should carry on his work and he answered, 'Tomasi Ndahura, Nasani Kabarole, Yosiya Kaburwa, Yusufu Limenya, they will be able to help the church in Mboga, I have trained them.' I asked him if he had any money in the bank, he said, 'I have not even one shilling in the bank.' I asked him if he had any debts, he said, 'There are no debts, except some shillings of Tomasi Ndahura's, which he gave to me and put in the fund for paying the church teachers in the forest, 250 shillings. Sell my table and chairs and kettle and anything else to pay these shillings.' He then told me he had two cows at Butiti. 'Leave them,' he said, 'to the church at Mboga. There is nothing else left,' and truly there was just nothing else, anything he had had he had already given away. He did not die like other people, who have many possessions, anything he ever possessed he used in the service of God. He ate little and wore little and had few bedclothes, he had neither wife nor child, so he was able to please himself and do what he liked, knowing that when he died he had no one dependent upon him. He knew that God had given him many Christians and they were his children.

I found as I talked with him that he had been preparing for some time to leave this earth, he said, 'Let me go, to find those children of mine who have gone before me into Heaven, to be with my Lord, whom I have served from my youth to my old age.' Two things he asked before he died, first that there should be no wailing for him and secondly he wished to be buried with his head towards the forest (it is custom to bury a man with his head towards his home) 'to signify that I am still going towards the forest to preach the gospel, even now my spirit is towards my work'. He spoke in faith and hope. At that time he was very ill . . . and swollen from his feet to his head and he breathed with great difficulty, but all the time he was full of joy and peace, without fear or worry. He was a marvellous witness to all. To those who came to visit him, he led them in sickness as he had led them in health, and he led them too in death. To us the workers, he was a great example in life and in death – as St Paul worked so did Apolo, both were bond servants. I finished talking with Apolo on

29th, that was the last time I spoke with him. On the 30 May at 2.45 p.m.
Canon Apolo Kivebulaya died. He left this world to go to another which
has no poverty or sorrow. He rested with a quiet happy face as if asleep. I
was there, together with Damari Ngaju, a woman who was the first to be
baptized at Mboga. . . . So Apolo fell asleep in the midst of his people . . . I
sent for Canon and Mrs Russell. They came and found him gone. We knelt
and thanked God for all the good things He had enabled Apolo to do.
Then they went away, I and some others remained to prepare his body
for the burying, we placed it in a coffin which we had brought from Toro,
the gift of the Mukama George Rukidi. Then some of the Belgians came
to pay their respects. They were indeed all very sorry, for they had great
respect for him and the work he had done on their country. They helped
us a lot.

On the 31st May at 10 a.m. we buried Canon Apolo, we buried him
near the church at Mboga. . . .

> – from Anne Luck *African Saint: The Story of*
> *Apolo Kivebulaya*, London 1963, pp. 145–8.

Russell: The Reverend W. S. R. Russell, C.M.S. missionary.
Mboga: over the Uganda border in the Congo.
Semliki: the river Semliki.
Toro and Ankole: kingdoms to the west of Buganda.

32. ATTITUDE TO NON-AFRICANS, 1934

Some inhabitants of Kyadondo to Chief Secretary, Uganda, 22 January,
1934.

We are humbly writing introducing our complaints to you, after reading
the declaration prohibiting non-Africans to trade or carry on their jobs in
the African trading areas adjacent to Kampala township. This order is to
be effective next year in 1935. The places concerned are: 1. Wandegeya.
2. Katwe. 3. Mengo.

Sir, when this declaration from the D.C.s office came to our knowledge, prohibiting non-Africans from renting premises in the above named
places for trade or other purposes, we decided to write to you informing
you of our concern over this matter and the amount of loss it would inflict
on us. We, as African traders, have erected expensive buildings, and in

some cases loans have been taken, in the hope of providing ourselves and our children with some steady income. These houses were built to assist African trade by bringing it into contact with non-African trading. Non-Africans are our guides in trade, if they are removed from these places it will have an adverse effect on African trade. Erection of such buildings for hire to non-Africans is one of the major African trading activities. Trusting that Government is always for helping people, we pray that our case does receive a sympathetic consideration. Ever since non-Africans started trading among Africans, there have never been any complaints about them. They have only assisted in uplifting African trade, and to bring about good co-operation beteen Africans and non-Africans.

We appeal to the Protectorate Government to save us from such heavy losses. The Government always being our protector, we had already entered into agreements with the non-African tenants, and these agreements do not in any way contravene with any law.

> We are,
> Sir,
> Your obedient servants
> (Signed by 13 people)
> – from P. C. W. Gutkind *The Royal Capital of Buganda*, Hague 1963, p. 300.

33. THE IDEOLOGY OF BUGANDA

'Education, Civilization and "Foreignisation" in Buganda'. The Kabaka's pamphlet, 1935.

For some time past I have felt that it might be somewhat interesting to review Education and Civilization in Buganda, since the advent of the Europeans in this country. Quite recently my thoughts were suddenly turned towards quite a new element which I am very strongly of opinion is the outcome of Education and Civilization separately or both combined, and this element I have been compelled to call 'Foreignisation' for lack of a more appropriate or suitable word to express what is in my mind.

Every one knows that education and civilization were started simultaneously in this country in their respective rudimentary forms by the kind efforts of the members of the various Missionary Societies and have now been enhanced largely due to the assistance rendered by the Protectorate Government.

Naturally Education and Civilization gained tremendous favour among the Baganda, and as a consequence there are numerous Schools in remote villages in Buganda Kingdom for the Education of the young generation; while every facility and luxury which are the outcome of civilization are today being extended to all the Baganda, who can afford to avail themselves of the same, throughout the country.

Now my fears are that instead of the Baganda acquiring proper and legitimate education and civilization there is a possible danger that they may be drifting to 'foreignisation' I must apologize for this word which I cannot vouchsafe for its accuracy as it is my own invention. But I venture to submit that it is the nearest word which could adequately express my idea of the state of affairs of the present young generation of the Baganda. To be more explicit, what I mean by the word 'foreignisation' is that instead of the Baganda acquiring proper education at the various Schools and of availing themselves of the legitimate amenities of civilization, I am very much afraid the young generation of this country is merely drifting wholesale towards 'foreignization' of their natural instincts and is discarding its native and traditional customs, habits and good breedings. What is at present popularly termed as education and civilization of a Muganda may be nothing more nor less than mere affectation of the foreign customs and habits of the Western Countries which in some instances are only injurious to our own inherent morals and ideals of native life.

I am well aware that it has been said more than once that the Baganda have neither morals nor public opinion, but I very much regret I have always been very strongly opposed to this statement, or shall we say, false accusation brought against the Baganda as a nation. There has always been and shall always be 'black sheep' among all nations and tribes throughout the World and naturally I do not wish to be considered in this article to uphold the Baganda as a Nation of Angels – But what I do maintain is that prior to the advent of the Europeans the Baganda had a very strict moral code of their own which was always enforced by a constant and genuine fear of some evil or incurable or even fatal disease being suffered invariably by the breaker of this moral code. In fact I maintain the Baganda observed most strictly the doctrine of the Ten Commandments in spite of the fact that Christianity and the so-called Christian morals were absolutely unknown to the Baganda. For instance there was a very strong public opinion against the following offences, which are the fundamental principles of the doctrine of the Ten Commandments:

(a) Theft was always punished very severely, invariably by the loss of the right hand of the offender, so as to render him incapable of committing the same offence again.

(b) Adultery was almost unknown among the Baganda and any man found guilty of such offence was always ostracised from Society.

(c) Murder was invariably followed by a very severe vendetta between the members of the family or clan of the victim and those of the offender.

(d) Filial obedience was most honoured among the Baganda and disobedience or disrespect of one's parents was always supposed to be punished by some higher power by the infliction of some horrible or incurable disease upon the offender.

(e) False evidence was looked upon with contempt. The person who bore false evidence and the person against whom it was given were both subjected to a very severe test by forcing them to drink a certain kind of strong drug known as 'Madudu', which was supposed to result in making one of the parties who was in the wrong unconscious.

In this connection I should like to point out that although polygamy was universally recognized among the Baganda and was never considered as immoral yet prostitution was absolutely unheard of. Civilization, education and freedom are the direct causes of the appalling state of affairs as regards prostitution and promiscuous relationships between the Baganda men and women. For instance all female members of one's clan were always considered as his sisters or aunts, according to their degree of relationship in their respective lines of descent; and intermarriage among the members of the same clan was therefore never tolerated or countenanced and any illicit intercourse between any male and female member of the same clan was not only severely punished but was also supposed to be accompanied by some dreadful disease suffered by the offenders in this respect. As a further illustration of the strictness of the old moral code of the Baganda I should like to point out here one of the most important native custom of looking after the daughters in a Muganda's home. It was one of the worst filial offence for a daughter to become pregnant while living with her parents. As soon as she was discovered in that condition she was at once expelled from her parents' house, and was absolutely cut off from them. She could not eat with them nor would her parents touch her until the child was born and some rites had been gone through which necessitated a great deal of hardship and shame on the part of the girl and her seducer. This custom was intended to stimulate morality among the Baganda girls, since any girl who went astray before she was given in marriage suffered this indignity and was always looked upon with contempt by all her relatives and friends. Furthermore any girl who was given in marriage and was found not to be virgin merited unspeakable disfavour in the eyes of her parents, relations and friends. All this, however, is of course, no longer the case. The present so-called education and civilization prevailing in this country has completely destroyed this moral code by removing the constant fear just referred to above from the minds of the young generation of the Baganda by the freedom and liberty which are the natural consequences of the present World civilization.

I think it would not be out of place to state here definitely that it is my firm belief that prior to the introduction of Christianity in this country the Baganda could not be classified as the worst type of a heathen tribe of Africa since they never indulged in any of the worst heathen customs or rites such as human sacrifice or torture which are found in other parts of Africa. Whilst on the other hand apart from their ignorance of Christianity and their practice of polygamy I am strongly of opinion that most of the traditional customs and etiquette of the Baganda generally speaking were quite consistant with the principles of Christianity. In support of this argument it is only necessary to mention a few customs of the Baganda to show that they unconsciously possessed a sense of the modern Christian morality:

(a) It was one of the most important etiquette among the Baganda for one's neighbour to be considered as his own relative and to share with him in his happiness or unhappiness. For instance a Muganda would always invite his neighbour if he killed a chicken or goat to share it with him, whilst in case of any danger or misfortune it was always the duty of the nearest neighbour to render every assistance to the party in danger or distress.

(b) It was the recognized etiquette for a Muganda to salute every one that he met on the road, whether he knew him or not.

(c) When a Muganda was taking his meal and any one passed by, it was always the custom to invite him to share it with him.

(d) It was always the duty of every one who hears an alarm at any time of day or night or a cry for help to go at once and render assistance to the party in distress or danger. In fact, in case of a house being set on fire anyone who was supposed to have heard of the alarm and failed to respond to it was always held to be a suspect of the offence of having set fire to that house.

(e) It was the duty of every Muganda, when requested, to assist any traveller in directing him to his destination, or to give him food or water, and even to give him shelter from rain or for the night.

These are only a few of the Baganda customs and etiquettes which I consider are far from being repugnant to the doctrine of Christianity but which I am ashamed to say have been discarded and are no longer being observed owing to the so-called Education and Civilization of the present generation of the Baganda. This is what I call 'foreignisation' of our natural and a traditional instincts and good breeding.

My intention therefore in this article is to emphasize the fact that while boasting of having acquired Western education and civilization in an amazingly short period, we have entirely and completely ignored our native traditional customs. In other words we have 'foreignised' our native existence by acquiring the worst foreign habits and customs of the Western people. I am only too well aware that this is inevitable in all countries where Western civilization has reached, so I have considered it my duty in this article to warn very strongly all members of the young generation of the Baganda that while they are legitimately entitled to strive to acquire education and civilization they should also take a very great care that acquisition of Western Education and Civilization does not automatically destroy their best inherent traditions and customs which, in my own opinion, are quite as good as those found among the Western Civilized countries but which only require developing and remodelling where necessary on the lines and ideas of western civilization. In other words members of the young generation of Buganda should not 'foreignise' their native instincts, traditional customs and habits but should always endeavour to ameliorate them as well as the conditions of their life where possible. This is what I call proper education and civilization.

> – H. H. Kabaka Daudi Chwa *Education,*
> *Civilization and Foreignisation in Buganda,*
> 1935.

34. 'WHY BRITISH ADMINISTRATION FAILS', 1936

Newspaper article by J. Mukasa.

In the Uganda Herald, dated the 11th March, page 14, Column 4, Mr Winston Churchill tells us of the 'easy, hesitant, half-measures of the British Colonial Administration', probably the effect of 'apologetic diffidence', as he calls it.

Mr Churchill's words have come in time, just when I was thinking to write something about the present situation of the administration in this country, and are not more nor less than our conclusions arrived at of what is happening in this part of the world. As an African interested in the British rule and protection, during my travels as a private business man in Buganda, I have a good chance to see and hear many things.

On numerous instances, I have noted that Europeans and Africans are comparatively equally good, or bad, and so are their customs or manners. If it had not been for the existence of the slight influence of decent Europeans and Africans the whole country would have gone to pot, though it must be remembered that they are not the moving spirits. The moving spirits, now, in this country, are the bad ones, on either side.

Lately there has been an outcry about the lack of civility now apparent among the young generation and it is suggested that our old customs and manners should be encouraged to avert the danger of corruption. This gave rise to controversies in the local press, both in English and Luganda, with reference mainly to His Highness's Memorandum contained in a pamphlet and published in the Beacon, of October 1935, on Education, Civilization and Foreignization. This has called forth public criticism, to distinguish which customs of ours should be encouraged. Finally, we have held that His Highness and other writers meant good customs. I congratulate His Highness on bringing up a question before the people who undoubtedly have not failed to appreciate the situation.

It appears that in response to the outcry, Europeans or rather the Protectorate Administration have embraced the question, and are adopting a policy to conform to the customs demanded in the Education Department (as the Director of Education stated on the last Speech Day at Makerere that he would see that they were encouraged). In courts in recent cases judges have based their decision on our customs and our regulations. In Administration they have probably endeavoured to do so.

But when they do so, do they conform to the good customs? That remains to be seen. What customs do we wish to be encouraged? The good ones of course.

There is a common tendency among both Europeans and ourselves in this country, that when either side wants to follow the other, people take up the wrong customs or manners of their neighbours. Europeans are the ruling and leading race and they style themselves our trustees in everything. Therefore the blame lies mainly with them, but the Africans are at fault not to find out which is the correct manner or custom of the other that is worthy of adoption. Both good and bad customs or manners exist and are very common among Europeans and Africans. But they are not at all to be followed without discrimination. Any European adopting the corrupt customs of the African is no more than that African.

While the co-operation at which the British Government is now apt, is appreciated, it would be observed that in doing so they err to a large extent.

It has been our custom, if any one is entrusted with the upbringing of his son or daughter, to do so to his utmost, teaching his students the best social manners. At present, parents are ignored by all educational institutions. It is an appalling position. We demand to be given education to which we are entitled as the fruits of the taxes we contribute to the public revenues. The Government tries to hedge about its duty to give it. Why put off what you will have to do in the future? Why not do it earlier without being forced to do so? The result of obstruction is always unpleasant. We hear that they fear what happened in India as the result of education there. What has caused trouble in India is not education but obstruction. When people get it, they get it when it is too late and the situation has become disgusting instead of one of a happy co-operation. Is this the British diffidence to which Mr Churchill refers?

The Protectorate Government, on the administration side have received for quite a long time now our views on their policy with regard to our Lukiko that it should be a representative body for the country and not a group of Government servants. While I say so, was that not the customary form the Lukiko (parliament) took before the advent of the British Administration? The [form] which the Lukiko took in the past, prior to the existence of the British Administration and the introduction of the Uganda Agreement of 1900 was that it consisted of purely nobles and the landlords, who were not simply government servants, but free agents with fixed rights within the powers of the Kabaka and who represented the people. The Kabaka thereby followed the parliament with the wishes of the people. The parliament formed according to the Agreement coincides with the framework which was in existence when it was made. But instead of being an approved system, now we see that all the Kabaka's nobles are being actually turned into purely British Government servants, who do only what has been directed by their departmental officers. Who were the Government's servants in the past? Those who were under the nobles, who collected the Kabaka's tithes and also the warriors (military), and Batongole (heads of economic department of the Kabaka). These were responsible to the nobles and the nobles to the Kabaka.

Practically all the chiefs at the present time, could be styled government servants. They have no fixed salaries and depend entirely on the quantity of taxes collected and number of payers they have in their districts. The people in this country are therefore without a place to voice their views. The people have again and again appealed to the Kabaka and to the Government to be allowed representation in the parliament.

There are groups from which parties in parliament could be formed, such as landowners, agriculturists, or other private business people. In developing the system which has so long existed in addition to the County Heads there should be enough gombolola chiefs to provide magistrates and even a separate group of tax collectors (these would be government servants). The police and road supervisors exist at present but not the collectors. The county and gombolola chiefs combine all tax collection, magisterial work, road supervision, etc., with the result that instead of taking particular interest in actual administration work their attention is distracted.

They actually spend their time going from one house to the other demanding poll tax etc. Any of them who collects more tax is recommended by the D.C. and the P.C., for a reward. We do not care if they remain so, but we want other persons to represent the people in parliament. The parliament should meet four times a year, instead of the time wasting system of having them to sit everyday doing nothing; and nothing should be allowed to be done by the Ministers before it is passed through the Lukiko, the Kabaka then would have had a representative body from which he would receive the wishes of the people. Representatives from parties should be chosen by people, by votes.

It should be remembered that this is what the public have been asking for quite a long time. They do not ask for a new thing. The system has already existed and was confirmed by the Uganda Agreement, but is not being applied.

Appointments of Ministers, county chiefs and sub-chiefs take place in many cases, upon the British Government's recommendation and the very persons so chosen are unpopular, but the Government supports them and suffers together with them for their unpopularity.

There is a sort of 'cabinet' at Mengo which is only a meeting of government servants, carrying out what the P.C. wants them to do. A few weeks ago, the British Government wanted a site for an aerodrome and directed the Katikiro to ask the landowners at Kabowa, on the proposed site, as to whether they wish to sell their land to the government.

In other cases the Ministers and the Kabaka are required to go to the P.C.'s Office in Kampala.

A thing which has astonished people is the taking of Namirembe Bazaar and Nakivobo land on which trees have been planted which could be done by His Highness if he had been advised that that was required. The Lukiko was not consulted about these things. They should have been.

In the Uganda Agreement of 1900 it is stated that when resolutions have been passed by the parliament, the Kabaka should only take advice of His Majesty's representative (the Governor), but not before. It does not say that there will be any other official to give advice as in the present manner.

– from *Uganda Herald*, 15 April 1936.

35. MITCHELL'S SECRET MEMORANDUM, 1939

Sir Philip Mitchell's* 'Relations of the Protectorate Government in Uganda with the Native Government of Buganda, Note by the Governor', 15 April 1939.

The relations of Buganda with the Protectorate Government are based upon the Uganda Agreement of 1900, which is in fact a treaty.

There are eleven subsidiary Agreements, a list of which is attached [it has been omitted here] which modify or amplify the terms of the original Agreement.

2. At one time it was held that if an Agreement of this kind were to be found to conflict with an Order-in-Council or Ordinance, the Agreement would prevail.

This view is no longer maintained by the Protectorate Government. The Courts can only give effect to the law, and Agreements are not law.

But it is settled policy that effect is to be given to the Agreements in spirit and in letter. If, therefore, a law, or projected law, is found to conflict with them, it should be amended or altered as may be necessary to remove the conflict, unless modification of the relevant Agreement is negotiated with the Native Government.

3. The Agreement of 1900 is regarded by the Kabaka, the Ministers and Chiefs, and Baganda generally, as having an almost scriptural authority and inviolability. In their eyes it is a document covering the relations of the parties to it, and like a statute subject to strict verbal interpretation.

The Agreement, however, considered textually, is not a satisfactory document by which to regulate the relations of the parties to it; nor could a complex and constantly changing political and administrative situation, such as exists in Buganda, be exactly regulated in every respect by the terms of such a treaty, negotiated forty years ago in different circumstances.

It is important that there should not be on the part of officers of the British Government acquiescence, or the appearance of acquiescence, in the view that the Agreement is to be interpreted in a narrow textual manner as if it were a statute enforcible in a court of law, with the corollary that in matters in which it is silent there is no power of intervention.

4. The relationship between the British and Native Government is, in fact, that known to constitutional lawyers as 'protected rule', and it depends for its satisfactory operation on an assumption that in all important matters touching his government the Head of the Protected State must seek, and be guided by the advice of the King's representative, that is to say of the Governor.

It is usual for the instrument whereby this relationship is established to contain an express provision to this effect. At first sight this provision may appear to be absent from the Uganda Agreement; nevertheless it does contain provisions of a general nature in Article 6, which are a sufficiently, if not ideally, precise expression of the constitutional position, in the following terms:

'So long as the Kabaka, chiefs and people of Uganda shall conform to the laws and regulations instituted for their governance by Her Majesty's Government, and shall co-operate loyally with Her Majesty's Government in the organization and administration of the said Kingdom of

Uganda, Her Majesty's Government agrees to recognize the Kabaka of Uganda as the native ruler of the province of Uganda under Her Majesty's protection and over-rule.

'The name of the person chosen by the native council must be submitted to Her Majesty's Government for approval, and no person shall be recognized as Kabaka of Uganda whose election has not received the approval of Her Majesty's Government. The Kabaka of Uganda shall exercise direct rule over the natives of Uganda, to whom he shall administer justice through the Lukiko, or native council, and through others of his officers, in the manner approved by Her Majesty's Government.'

Subsequent Articles (for example Article 11) treat particular questions more precisely, but that does not detract from the force of the words quoted above.

It is a matter of first importance that the relations of the parties to the Agreement should be progressively developed on this assumption, but it should not be expressly asserted in any communication to the Native Government without authority to do so from the Governor.

5. It is on this constitutional theory of 'Advice' that depend the ultimate supervision and control exercised by the British over the Native Government. In an extreme case failure to accept the 'Advice' tendered by the Governor on behalf of the Crown might lead to the deposition of the Native Ruler and to the suspension or cancellation of the Agreement, and the substitution for it of alternative arrangements.

No such extreme case should be permitted to occur, if it can be avoided, and political officers must always have this in mind. It is especially necessary to exercise care in matters of secondary importance and in personal relationships lest avoidable difficulties should arise which might come to assume a significance disproportionate to their nature and origins. It is equally important that whenever a question arises which may raise a major issue with the Native Government, the Governor should be consulted as early as possible so that the line taken by his representative should be certain of his approval and support.

6. The main objectives and interests of the British and Native Governments are the same. They may be described as first and foremost the peace and good government of the country, the promotion of the moral and material welfare of the people, and the fullest development compatible with its capacity at any given time of the native political and administrative organization of Buganda.

By virtue of the Agreement, and as a matter of settled policy these objectives and interests are to be pursued first through the agency of the Native Government assisted, when necessary and practicable by British officers; secondly by direct British Government action in matters in which either the Native Government is not yet disposed, or fitted, to operate, or the special problems created by the presence of a considerable non-native public arise; or, as has been explained, as the final controlling and over-ruling authority.

7. The general administrative arrangements at present in force in Buganda are largely the result of historical causes and have served their purpose well enough hitherto.

In the early days of the Protectorate Buganda was divided into four British Administrative Districts. Among these Districts the twenty counties were distributed. The Kabaka was a child and the Native Government was in the hands of three regents. The country had been dis-organized by wars and rebellions.

British Administrative Officers were appointed to the District under the titles of District Commissioners and Assistant District Commissioners, and over them a Provincial Commissioner. There was thus in organiza-tion and nomenclature nothing to differentiate Buganda from any other area under direct British rule in East Africa.

To what extent in these circumstances the District Commissioners directly administered their Districts as they did elsewhere, e.g. in Kavi-rondo, to the practical, if not theoretical, exclusion of the Native Govern-ment at Mengo it is difficult to say at this date. It has to be remembered that the authority of the Native Government extended only to natives of Buganda (since 1917, as regards the Native Courts, to natives of the Protectorate), and that all administrative and judicial functions in respect of persons not under its jurisdiction had to be discharged by the British Administrative Officers, who had also, as they still have, a direct responsibility by virtue of the Agreements in the matter of the native poll tax.

8. In more recent times much attention has been given to the main-tenance of the authority of the Native Government and its subordinate authorities, for example by the extension of the jurisdiction of the Native Courts over all Africans in Buganda. As regards natives and the Native Government the District Commissioners are now, in theory at least and largely in practice, no more than advisers and inspectors. It is still neces-sary, however – and will continue to be for as long as can be foreseen at present – to maintain an administrative and judicial organization with British officials to deal with matters involving the non-native popula-tion. Moreover the geographical divisions of the British and Native Governments do not at present coincide, and although the Saza Chiefs receive their instructions from a single Native Government centre at Mengo, in their dealings with the British Administration they are distri-buted in three districts each under its commissioner.

Since the Provincial Commissioner (now the Resident), the Kabaka and the Ministers reside at or near Kampala it is inevitable, as long as these differences of geographical division remain, that the District Commis-sioners, in dealing with County Chiefs and other subordinate native officials as well as the natives of their districts, should at times find it impossible to avoid at least the appearance of executive intervention, particularly when the limitations and imperfections of the Native Government at this stage of its development are taken into account, as well as the necessity of protecting the weak from oppression or abuse and of ensuring the discharge of numerous technical functions in connection with public health, agriculture, veterinary control, and so on.

There is indeed a fundamental incompatibility between an organization under a Provincial and District Commissioners on the one hand, and the constitutional status of the Kabaka and his Government on the other. Unless appropriate measures are devised and put into effect this incompatibility must become more prominent as a result of the inevitable development which comes with education and a growing racial consciousness. The fact has to be faced that as the Native Government progresses in experience and confidence, and the people in education and interest in political questions, detailed intervention and control, whether in the judicial, administrative or technical field, is certain to become an increasingly difficult, and in time politically dangerous, method of discharging the responsibilities of the British Government.

9. It has accordingly been decided, with the authority of the Secretary of State that the policy to be gradually put into practice as circumstances permit should involve a readjustment of the British Administration on a functional in place of a geographical basis. As a first step indicative of the new orientation of policy the title of the Provincial Commissioner, Buganda, has been altered to Resident.

The effect of this readjustment will be to substitute for the detailed supervision through District Commissioners and their Assistants a less detailed but eventually more powerful and effective influence by means of a group of advisers at the centre under the Resident, through whom the Native Government may be guided and assisted in the pursuit of the objectives common to it and the British Government.

It will doubtless be found convenient, as and when each step in this readjustment is taken, to aim at a closer coincidence between the allocation of duties to British officers and the distribution of business between the Ministries of the Native Government, which will presumably increase in numbers in future. Thus the time may be anticipated when, for example, the Treasurer of the Native Government will deal with one British Officer on all departmental business, the Chief Justice with another (see below) and so on. This will not only ensure a convenient distribution of business but will make for continuity of personal contacts upon which, more than anything else, efficient and harmonious working will depend.

Personal contacts, indeed, are of the greatest importance at the present day, and should be continuously developed. Such contacts include of course private correspondence, by means of which, and of frequent personal interviews and the use of the telephone, it should be possible to keep formal official correspondence to the minimum. Misunderstanding and friction, to say nothing of delays, are probably more often due to the limitations of official correspondence or to premature recourse to it, than to any other single cause.

10. Such an arrangement has, in its main principles, been a familiar means of dealing with analogous situations elsewhere. In each case there are found particular local difficulties requiring special treatment.

In Buganda, for instance, the British Government and important European and Asiatic commercial and agricultural enterprises are situated within the Protected State, and mainly for historical reasons the functions of the British and Native Governments are distributed according to no settled plan. Moreover, Europeans and Asiatics, and even some Africans, are exempt from the authority and jurisdiction of the Native Government and enjoy in fact an extra-territorial status.

11. In one respect, indeed, the existing situation held such danger of serious difficulties or dispute that preliminary steps to meet it have already been taken by the appointment of a Judicial Adviser on the Residency staff.

The British Judiciary and a native judicial system with such extensive powers as are enjoyed by the Native Courts in Buganda could not continue to function indefinitely side by side, exercising in some cases a form of concurrent jurisdiction, evolving gradually divergent procedures and involving a number of matters in which the weaker (native) is incompatible with or unacceptable to the stronger, without eventually coming into serious conflict.

The Native Government and people are tenacious of the powers enjoyed by the Native Courts under the Agreement. Apart from the opposition to be expected from the Kabaka and his Ministers, a proposal seriously to curtail the judicial powers reserved by the Agreement to the Native Courts would be generally resented by the Baganda, and many would also resent a suggestion to diminish the authority of the High Court.

The time is not far distant when it is to be expected that there will be natives of Buganda who will take up the law as a profession and become barristers. There is only one system of law that they can take up in this way at present, and in which they can practise – the British. It is of great importance that steps should have been taken before that time comes to bring the British and Native systems into closer relation, one with another, for whatever opinion may be held about non-native barristers practising before native courts, it will manifestly not be possible to deny indefinitely to Baganda barristers the right of practice in the courts of their native land.

It was therefore necessary to provide a link between the two systems capable of interpreting them to each other, and of gradually bringing the Native system into closer accord with the British and with the basic principles of judicial practice and procedure upon which the supreme judicial authority must in the last resort insist. This link is the Judicial Adviser on the staff of the Residency in Buganda.

The relations of the British and Native Governments in judicial matters are two-fold. On the one hand there are certain purely judicial powers reserved to British judicial officers and on the other hand the drafting of legislation, the organization, staffing and procedure of the Courts, prison administration, and many other matters normally the responsibility of a Ministry of Justice. It follows that the Judicial Adviser must necessarily occupy a special position, for while in the exercise of his judicial functions he must be as independent of his official superiors as is the Chief Justice of the Governor, in other respects he is the legal adviser of the Resident, of whose staff he is a member.

It is likely that it will be necessary for a new Judicial Agreement to be negotiated, but for the present it has been decided that further steps should wait until the newly-appointed Judicial Adviser has had time to study the existing situation and to secure the confidence of the Chief Justice and other Ministers of the Native Government.

12. If the Native Government is to develop in capacity and authority it is essential that its activities should be gradually extended so as to include a wide range of functions and services, technical and social, as part of its normal responsibilities. Particularly in the field of public health and agriculture progress may only be attainable at the cost of opposition and odium and even organized agitation against some plainly necessary reform.

It is important that the Native Government, in its own interests and for political reasons, should learn to shoulder responsibilities of this kind and should not shelter itself behind the Protectorate Government because particular innovations and activities are not likely to be popular. In such cases there is a special value in maintaining direct consultation between the Heads of technical departments, or their representatives, and the Ministers of the Native Government. The Resident should give facilities for such special meetings as may be required for these purposes and where more extended explanations of specific measures are desirable the Administrative staff should be available to give them.

Developments of this nature will involve from time to time financial adjustments between the British and Native Governments. At present a payment amounting normally to about £30,000 is made to the Native Government as a rebate on the poll tax, and in addition a substantial subsidy (£15,000 in 1939) is paid towards the upkeep of roads. Further adjustments must be considered on their merits from time to time as occasion arises. They will normally, no doubt, be made on the basis of increasing the rebate from the Poll Tax pari passu with the assumption by the Native Government of services (and therefore of expenditure) previously provided by the British Government.

13. The Residency in Buganda is the agency through which the policy outlined in this note is to be put into effect. It has the dual function of

supervising and helping the Native Government and explaining the policy and actions of the British Government to it and to the Native people, so as to promote confidence, co-operation and understanding.

The Resident is a member of the Executive Council and thus one of the principal advisers of the Governor, with a special responsibility in respect of relations with the Native Government. In that capacity he has complete freedom, indeed it is his duty to make representations on any aspect of those relations whether in the actual or projected policy or actions of the British Government. He may make representations of this kind on his own initiative or at the request of the Native Government; and he will, in addition, often find himself in the position of adviser to the Native Government. It may happen, in these circumstances, that occasions will arise when his personal views do not coincide with those of the Government he serves. This dilemma is common to high office, especially to high political or administrative office, and there is no workable alternative to the general rule that an officer so placed must act without reserve in conformity with the general policy or particular decisions of his Government, or ask to be relieved of his office. Anything less than this would at once introduce an element of dangerous uncertainty into the relations between the British and Native Governments.

The matter may be summarized by saying that the Resident and Residency staff must be a continuously active agency of the British Government, that the advice tendered to the Native Government must correctly reflect the views of the British Government, and that anything short of complete and zealous support of Government is incompatible with office of this nature.

14. It is not proposed that the general policy which has been adopted, and which is discussed in this note, should be made the occasion of any drastic or immediate reorganization, nor that a public pronouncement should be made. Some steps have already been taken and are described above: others will be taken as and when circumstances seem to require them. The purpose of this note is to place on record the general policy which the British Government has adopted for the discharge of its responsibilities vis-à-vis the Government and people of Buganda. It is of necessity a secret document since its publication might lead to misunderstanding, but there need be no secret about the policy which it records, which ought to animate and indeed be plainly perceptible throughout the actions of the British Government and the agents through whom it functions. The text of the note is to be communicated (under secret cover) to the Resident and such senior officers serving under him as, in his discretion, he may decide; and to the members of the Executive Council.

It is important that the existence of the document itself should not become known to any except those to whom it is addressed under the authority given above, but the principles which it lays down should be communicated departmentally by appropriate means to all officers of the

Protectorate Government whose employment is likely to bring them into contact with the Native Government.

– from a copy in the editor's possession.

Sir Philip Mitchell was Governor of Uganda 1935–40. See his *African Afterthoughts*, London 1954, Ch. IX.

36. THREAT TO THE LAND, 1944

D. S. K. Musoke, Buganda Nyafe (*Buganda our Mother*),

My dear Child:

I have written to convey to you these ideas as happenings never forecast themselves; I have thought of bequeathing to you my ideas about our land – the land of your forefathers and your grandchildren: because since my birth I have known many people who have misbehaved by selling their lands: their misbehaviour has brought misfortune to them as they are miserably poor without any money and can never redeem the land back to us. I desire to emphasize it to you that it is your responsibility to preserve this land which should not be fragmented until you depart from it and bequeath it to your grandchildren. In the following pages I will endeavour to illustrate to you the bad luck which has befallen nations which sold their lands to Europeans. I beseech of you to learn and understand more of the Europeans than they can do to yourself; you should also appreciate the fact that Europeans have their own agents amongst our own selves who report to them matters: who are in receipt of large remunerations and who are promoted to respectable chieftainships in our country whereas they are actually the traitors of anything beneficial to the cause of the indigeneous population and who are always ready to transfer same to the Europeans: beware and avoid company of such people. Money is easily expended and exhausted whereas our native land remains permanently. . . .

. . . a case has recently come up regarding the land of Kangawo Samwiri Mukasa, when a certain Muganda told lies purporting to be the purchaser of that land in an auction sale; and when the time for resale came the Government purchased the land notwithstanding the fact that fraud had been committed by an Indian on the Abaganda land: but as the Government was interested in acquiring the land in question, the truth was dispensed with and they purchased the said land: the original proprietor lost it and the land so purchased totalled seventy acres.

The land purchased by Government adjoins the land requisitioned from Kakungulu by Government which means that it would be easy to extend the University buildings from where it is now up to the land which was privately purchased, up to Mulago, Kololo, Nagulu and Nakawa, an area which comprises twelve square miles. This land in their possession is being reserved and instead they are planning requisitioning the Baganda land on Makerere hill on the pretext that they are going to erect a University for our benefit. It is true, none of us is not in favour of such an institute of high learning; but the argument put forward that the University would only benefit the Baganda if erected on their land, and that it would not benefit them if erected on the land already acquired by Government – has made us appreciate the Englishman's veracity experienced in many other countries where he has dispossessed lands from the native peoples. We have therefore stubbornly refused to part with our land and have suggested that the University should be built on land within the 9000 square miles originally allocated to the Government for the purpose of such beneficial development schemes for our country. . . .

Recently, on the 14th of April, 1944, we the landowners at Makerere were invited to a meeting in Kampala Technical School by the Owekitibwa Katikiro who was deputized by Omwami Kintu and the Native Land Officer one Mr Dungu – who represented the Buganda Government while the Honourable the Resident was represented by Mr Bessell – the latter addressed us as follows:

'You of Makerere, I have come to talk to you about matters regarding your land which the Government intends acquiring by purchase for a beneficial development scheme in the country; I have come just to assist you in advancing the information so that you may be made aware of the forthcoming proposal. I should like you to understand that none of you will object: You have no power to value the land as you wish, except that the Owekitibwa Katikiro and the Resident will only come to pay you any sums which they will decide in their discretion. None of you may dispute as anyone who may attempt to do so will lose his land; anyone who may attempt to resist the sale, his land will be appropriated in terms of the law. Have you understood?'

After the above had been said, the landowners started to explain what they had in reply: Their first inquiry addressed to the Resident's representative was as to whether the law for compulsory acquisition of land existed at all. They also wanted to be clearly informed as to whether the Honourable Gentleman had come to take the land by way of robbery or by way of purchase, and as to whether the Kingdom of Great Britain, had law provisions for robbing people's property in their dependencies. They further explained to the Honourable Gentleman, that they deplored the habit of frightening natives on the question of land and asked him to abolish same and then discuss the transaction in a peaceful atmosphere;

the official soon realized his mistake for which he apologized, but still insisted in saying that the law for the compulsory acquisition of land existed. When he was asked to give the book and chapter and the year it was enacted, which he could not find, he suggested to some of our number to go and read of it in his office. Some of the landowners who were present pressed for the production of the law in question in order to avoid unnecessary conflicts by raising objections – or misrepresentations of something unknown – in face of the law. And they eventually asked Owesaza Kago to bring the law from the office of the Resident and read same out to them but up to now the law in question has never been brought. . . .

In the morning hours of the 26th April, 1944, the Lukiko was in a quiet session, the sun outside was not very bright and could not be felt burning anybody, while the people of Buganda were anxiously waiting to hear as to whether the Lukiko was going to decide the fate of selling Buganda to slavery as a result of what was going to be discussed: Some of us were so much worried that we left our homes without taking our morning tea as it would hardly be swallowed: others did not even wash their faces. We went up and entered the Lubiri where we had to wait for some time until the Katikiro arrived. He eventually arrived and the item rescinding article 15 of the 1900 Agreement was the one to be first announced by him and our hearts were all startlingly agitated.

After the Chairman had introduced the subject for discussion supporting the enactment of a law enabling Government to compulsorily acquire land from natives for the purpose of transferring same to companies intending to develop the country, and stressing that it was an important issue – the Owekitibwa the Omulamuzi, who had already lost his mind to the outside world in the same way as a child suckling his mother, rose up: we at first thought, he was going to oppose the motion and save us, but to our surprise he supported the motion, stressing that he was very much in favour of the motion which he recommended the Lukiko should immediately pass for the sake of our country's development. He further stated that unless the proposed law was enacted the country was doomed to progress. He spoke at length and then sat down, while some of us were perspiring because of indignation and our hearts were all anxiously restless. The Owekitibwa Omulamuzi had the confidence of the Abaganda for a long time and when he supported the motion we lost hope of successfully opposing same and thought we were doomed.

After the Owekitibwa had sat down, the Owesaza Kangawo rose up and strongly supported the motion, illustrating that the 9000 square miles allocated to the Government were unproductive desert lands and therefore we should pass the resolution supporting a law. When another member rose up, he opposed the motion and enumerated quite a number of miles owned by the Government and which were not desert lands and in which nothing had practically been done; discussions went on until the majority of the legislators realized that a lot of land was available within the hold of the Protectorate Government which could be utilized for such development schemes.

During the discussions and before voting, we visualized that we were doomed to lose all our country as there did not exist any piece of land which the European did not want. It was envisaged that as the country had an abundant rainfall, planters were very much fond of coming and settle herein and start developing plantations since the law would enable him to demand the acquisition of the best pieces of land for agricultural development. . . .

I should like to state that the British Government did not start ruling in our country and to further state that Europeans divide themselves into sections: the one of Government Officials or rulers and the other section is the one of settlers, which means that once a settler could later become a Government Official and when he gets in power he brings about measures to remedy what oppressed him for betterment while it is also easy to find once a Government Official becoming a settler, therefore while a Government Official, he plans the betterment of conditions in which he is going to settle in later years. Because of those reasons, they persuade the natives to give favourable facilities to Europeans.

By the year 1918, a law similar to the one suggested, which made provisions enabling companies to start development schemes in the country was enacted in Kenya. The natives were deprived of the privileges of owning land by this law, which lands were transferred to whites. The law in question is known as 'The Resident Native or Squatters Ordinance', which made provisions enabling Europeans to acquire any fertile land in Kenya while the natives were by the same law compelled by Government to work as slaves for their European landlords for 180 days a year while European landowners were prohibited from permitting Africans to settle on their land without the prior permission from a Magistrate; and that no African may settle on any European's land before first entering into a contract for rendering such landowner services for one hundred and eighty days a year; and that no contract may be entered into between the African and the landowner of any period less than three years.

Is that fair play on the part of the British Government to have enacted such a law, when it claims to defend the peace of the people? And as it was feasible for such Government to have committed an atrocity to the Africans of Kenya, is there any difference between the Africans of Kenya and us out here? What reasons have our fellow men like Lawuli Kiwanuka who supported the motion got to advance as conclusive proof to the effect that the Government will not treat us as has been done elsewhere? I challenge the other people who support such a law to be enacted in our country such as Chief Mulyanti and the Owekitibwa Kulubya: are they so clever who can predict without any doubt that we shall not become the victims of a similar catastrophe which befell our neighbours? The reason why I am challenging them, is to force them leave the question open in case their advanced knowledge has enabled them to give us convincing explanation and succeed in influencing us to support the enactment of such a law when it is brought up again for discussion as they have been endeavouring to inform the public. . . .

Before I end my argument in this chapter which treats European land laws, I should like to advise you that in case you do not take precautions about European wisdom and betrayal cunning laws, our country will ultimately suffer a terrible disaster; because as a result of laws similar to the one the Lukiko was asked to enact, thousands of people are now without homes:

Kenya	100,000
Tanganyika	200,000
Nyasaland	40,000
Northern Rhodesia	1,160
Southern Rhodesia	300,000

To which numbers we intend adding those of Uganda! . . . .

The European experienced much difficulty to manage subjecting the African in his bondage; and he consequently approached another African whom he employed as an agent or assistant. He associates with him for necessity otherwise he dislikes him. I should like to give you a descriptive illustration as to how Europeans treat an African ruler:

'The European employs an African in the way as a master treats his dog; you should appreciate the fact that the dog is an animal but as it resides in a man's house, it treats itself differently while under the impression that the rest of its kind against whom it barks, are the animals, while it thinks itself to be half of what a man is. Had the African rulers been possessed of sufficient wisdom, they should have considered this seriously, because a man is not permitted to use the same latrine as the dog just in the same way as the European will not permit an African ruler, however much he may feel esteem for him, to use the same latrine with him. It is all easy to feel so much for a dog and try to show much for it while playing with same alone but when your fellowmen arrive at the scene, you neglect it all together and only have in consideration your fellowmen. The European similarly employs our fellow Africans to enable him to learn much of us. Had he not employed Africans to learn much of us through them, it would not have been easy for him to place us into his bondage. That is the true illustration of how any European treats any native ruler, through whom he learns so much of us. The European gives him verbal orders of ideas not properly digested in the same way as a hunter instructs his dog.'

Any native ruler, which term does not only include those of Buganda, has as his main duties to see that orders are obeyed by his fellowmen or natives, to enforce European laws and to see that his wishes are carried out.

Notwithstanding the fact of bad laws or orders he might be given for people under his leadership to carry out. . . .

Britain at one time detested the trade of slaves who were bought or robbed and sold to America and to other countries which were in need of slaves. Because of such strong belief against slave trade, Britain worked hard to force other countries to abolish slave trade instead of which free trade was established between nations in any other commodities or merchandise exchangeable in a proper manner. . . .

Slave trade was abolished in one way while slave trade was again established in another form. The former slave trade was rather better as only few were transported from the country while their fellowmen who remained behind were left in peace; but the prevailing form of slavery includes children and women. Our necks are placed in the bondage of European laws even though we may have the impression that we are still in our birth-place homes.

The state of slavery in our nation of Buganda is not yet very acute but the time is not distant when we shall lose our land and become squatters on European estates, when the acute state of slavery shall be imposed on us in the same way as was done to our fellowmen in Kenya, South Africa and elsewhere. Our country is likely to suffer this fate of which our own people will be responsible: such people who are light hearted, who work for tribes and some of whom are already well known: beware of such men and more so when they are promoted to high ranks such as the Katikiroship.

The freedom which I enjoy within the British Empire has encouraged me to say what I know: What I say is the truth as I am also truthful. Anyone who may dare to misinterpret my words is not truthful and is a liar: so cunning that he can never rest until he has caused some evil, the one who deceives himself by thinking that his skin is the only thing black of his person while he is European in heart and blood.

– from a translation of Part I of D. S. K. Musoke
Buganda Nyafe, 1944.

37. THE RESIDENCY SYSTEM, 1944

Speech to the Lukiko by the Governor of Uganda, Sir Charles Dundas,*
2 October 1944.

Your Highness, I have requested you to summon your Lukiko Council to meet me in order that I might make to them a pronouncement on certain changes in the system of Administration in Buganda, which I have decided upon in agreement with yourself and consultation with your Ministers.

Under the terms of the Agreement of 1900, Buganda was to be a Province of the Protectorate and, for many years, the Senior Administrative Officer, was styled Provincial Commissioner. Some few years ago it was recognized that since his position and authority differed from that of a Provincial Commissioner in the other Provinces that style was unsuitable and it was changed to Resident, a style in common use in other parts of the Empire, where Native Rulers govern under the over-rule of His Majesty the King. The functions of such Residents are to give advice to the Native Ruler, to represent the Governor and to report to him on all matters.

Here in Buganda there are sundry affairs which are outside your sphere and solely the concern of the Protectorate Government, as for instance Townships, European and Asiatic affairs. There are thus two administrative spheres in both of which the Resident and the District Commissioners have hitherto been involved.

It is difficult for these officers to give close attention to both, to turn from one to the other, and yet keep in complete and constant touch with both. Moreover the interests of Your Highness's Government and People are sufficient in importance and volume to require the undivided attention of British Officers for that special purpose and free to devote their whole time thereto.

I have therefore decided to institute separate administration for those affairs which are the concern of the Government of Buganda and for those outside its scope. The Resident will in future devote himself to your affairs while those matters with which you are not concerned will be handled by two Administrative officers, who will be known as Protectorate Agents, one in Kampala, the other in Masaka. It will be quite easy to distinguish between these two sets of affairs but if at any time questions arise which affect both, they will be referred to the Resident as the Senior Administrative Officer and he will, of course, always be consulted by the Government and People, as for instance, taxation and other laws applied by the Government to Buganda, but otherwise I wish him and his staff to be relieved of all business in which the Buganda Government is not concerned.

In other parts of Uganda each Native Administration is supervised by one District Commissioner so that each area forms a single District Administration. In Buganda, the country has been divided into three District Administrations. I consider this is wrong because it may result in differences of practice and confuse the people, who may not know under whose authority they really live. In future the Resident and his Assistants, who will be known as Assistant Residents, will be centred at Kampala only and from there will tour the whole country. So far as concerns your affairs, it will be as though there were no districts, but only Sazas, the whole country being under a central Native Government advised by one centralized British staff. Thus affairs in the Masaka and Mubende areas will be dealt with in the same manner as affairs in Buruli or Bugerere have been handled in the past and the division into Districts will remain only for those affairs which are not your concern and which will be dealt with by the Protectorate Agents.

Together with this reorganization I desire to make the position and duties of the Resident more in accord with the intention of the Agreement than has been in the past. The Agreement stipulated that 'The Kabaka should exercise direct rule subject to the King's over-rule' which, of course, is delegated to the Governor. It is for this reason that a Resident cannot have the authority nor fill the functions of a Provincial Commissioner. His duty is not to direct affairs or to control your officials but to advise your Government and to advise me in the exercise of my authority. But since he cannot direct and control, he cannot assume responsibility for the actions of your Government and its servants. That responsibility lies with Your Highness acting on the advice of your Ministers and Council subject to the Governor's overriding powers. In the past it was necessary for British Administration to go beyond these limits and to take a direct part in detailed inspection of the work of your chiefs. That meant, however, that the Chiefs were under two masters and the people, particularly in the more distant parts of Buganda, looked to the District Commissioners as much as to your Government for adjustment of their affairs. In consequence there has been a dual administration within Buganda. As I say, such was perhaps necessary, but I consider that the stage has now been reached at which it should no longer be necessary for us to go beyond the scope set by the Agreement in the way of supervision of your administration, and I do not wish to perpetuate a system which I believe was not contemplated when the Agreement was concluded.

Accordingly I wish the Resident and his staff to confine themselves to advice and guidance, leaving inspection and control to your Government and its agents. In order to do so they will have to travel and acquaint themselves with all affairs and conditions and also satisfy themselves that the laws, rules and orders promulgated by Your Highness and the Protectorate Government are observed and not abused, as also that proper control and direction is exercised by the higher Authorities appointed by you and they will, of course, point out to your Chiefs and others any defects and abuses, that may come to your notice. They will report on their observations and the Resident will confer with your Ministers and, as may be necessary, submit report to me.

Ultimate responsibility for ensuring good and just Administration still rests with the Protectorate Government and this responsibility I may not in any circumstances relinquish. But I wish to intervene only to the extent necessary to the faithful discharge of that duty. Your Highness knows that such has been my practice and in the short time since you assumed the rulership of Buganda, our personal relationship and contact has been so agreeable that it has been easy to come to accord in many matters. In bringing about these changes of which I have been speaking I have reposed much trust in Your Highness, your Government and your officials. If, for causes beyond your control, it is shown that I have expected too much of you, that close and direct control by British Officers is still required, then the system heretofore obtaining must be restored. I am, however, confident that it will be the aim of all in office under Your Highness to prove that my trust was not misplaced. If you do this, Buganda will become an outstanding example and a model of governance of Africans by Africans, and that aim should be one to stir your pride and ambition. I open to you the opportunity, may you take it with resolve to prove yourselves capable of using it wisely and honourably.

> – from *Report of the Sub-Committee of the Lukiiko which was set up to examine the recommendations made by the Hancock Committee,* Mengo 1955.

Sir Charles Dundas was Governor of Uganda 1940–45. See his *African Crossroads*, London 1955.

38. THE MEANS TO PROGRESS, 1945

Article on 'Makerere College' by Ham Mukasa, ex-Sekibobo.

I would ask you to give careful consideration to my thoughts and ideas on this important matter, as I feel it deeply concerns all the Baganda people.

Let us suppose that you received at one time two urgent requests, one from a friend of yours saying that your father was dying, and had no one to help take him to hospital, and the other from another person saying that your great friend was also dying, and needed conveying to hospital, as he also had no one to assist him. What would you do under these circumstances? You could not very well help both people at the same time, and I think you would decide to help your father first, not only because you love him more, but also because he said he had great faith in the skill of the particular doctor in that hospital, who had cured him on other occasions of different diseases. So you took your father to the hospital and he was cured. It is only right that we should help our parents first in cases of illness, as we owe them so much for all they have done for us.

All of you who read this article quite naturally love your own nation more than any other, but this does not mean that we should totally disregard the needs of other nations. We all remember the parable of the Good Samaritan in the Bible, in which a foreigner was the one who felt he should help the man who had been attacked by robbers and left destitute and injured, and not those of his own race, who, in point of fact, passed him by, and didn't lift a finger to help him. It is sometimes rather similar with us, in our country. We have, in the past, often been helped by people of other nationalities and races, more than by our own people.

I am writing this article for all of you Baganda, whoever you may be, young or old, chiefs or peasants, and to you Your Highness, the Kabaka of Buganda. Do any of you feel that you would like to lose your Higher College, which belongs to you, and not to the Europeans? I myself would be extremely unhappy and upset if Makerere College was transferred to some other territory, since it was built in our own country, and the foundation stone laid by one of the Princes of England, from where our education first came. The late Kabaka of Buganda, His Highness Sir Daudi Chwa, who was present with the Duke of Gloucester, when the foundation stone was laid, worked very hard in order to obtain a Higher College in our country; and I am sure that the Duke of Gloucester would be very disappointed to think that the stone which he had laid in Uganda was going to be re-laid in some other territory, and he would doubt the wisdom of a Government which even considered this step. To all of you who realize the importance and position of this College in Uganda and its neighbouring countries I would ask you to consider whether the removal of it to another territory would not bring upon us all, Baganda, a sense of shame and disrespect. It would not be easy for us to explain to our friends, boldly and sincerely, the necessity for removing it somewhere else. It would be a confession of failure on our part if we allowed it to go, and instead of being praised and respected we should be despised and looked down upon by all. We should be like a man who was offered a light to help him to walk in the dark, but who refused it, saying that he preferred walking in the dark. Then when the light was taken away he fell into a deep pit, and lost his strength, his wisdom, and his honour, and was despised by all his friends. Only those who are still in darkness would think it desirable for Makerere College to be moved away from Uganda. I would like His Excellency the Governor and his advisers to know that we Baganda disagree most profoundly with this proposal.

Doubtless it is the aim of the authorities to do all in their power to raise the standard of education obtainable there up to the same standard as is found in similar institutions of higher learning in England. There are very many old schools and Colleges in England, founded hundreds of years ago, the sites of which were generously given by the landowners for the benefit of their country, and some of us in Buganda have also been very pleased to give up some of our land for a similar purpose. These people will always be remembered for their kindness and generosity. We could not possibly feel it was right to forego the chances of having a University for East Africa, situated in our own country of Buganda. The people who have been educated in the English Colleges and Universities and gone abroad to help more backward countries have done a tremendous amount to assist them on the road to prosperity, happiness, and freedom. Some English parents are prepared to spend about 4000/– a year on the education of one of their children, and this amount in East Africa would educate about 3 children. Those who have seen and experienced the best in education in England are anxious to provide similar facilities for us in this part of the world, without the additional cost of sending our children to England.

Those people who are not prepared to give up some of their land for the benefit of Makerere College, and East Africa as a whole, are taking up a very self-centred, and narrow point of view, and surely the day will come when they will regret the decision they made; and when they are the kind of people who eventually will have trained there, trained for the good of their own country, they will be forced to humble themselves and admit that they were wrong.

There was once a man who lived in India, at a place called Cherapunji, who had 15 children and was extremely wealthy. Two of his children went to England for higher education. They spent 10 years there, and each child cost the father 4000/– a year for his education. On their way back the boat in which they were travelling was sunk, and one of the children was drowned, and so the money the father had spent on him was completely wasted. Needless to say, the father was very upset and miserable about the whole matter, and, to make matters worse, the son who survived and reached home, later became very nearly mentally defective, and refused to obey his father, and cut himself off completely from his fellow Indians, assuming the status and position of a European. He was so proud and self-assertive that Europeans began to hate him, and he then became angry, and eventually mad, and lost all his friends. But I hope you will not misunderstand me. I am not suggesting that the father was wrong in sending his sons to England, because he was of the opinion that they would benefit a great deal, and become as capable as Europeans are, and he was prepared to sacrifice a great deal of his own money in order to give two of his sons the best chances they could get of a higher education. But pride always leads to a fall, and this has been proved again recently by the downfall of Hitler and Mussolini, who, as the years went by, assumed and exercised more and more power in their own countries, and others, but, in the end, had to suffer for it. If an African goes abroad to England for his education there is grave risk that he will come back to his country with a 'swollen head', and be very full of his own importance.

What I feel about it is this. If there are, as there truly are, people who are working hard to help forward our country and its people, they should not be hindered by a few selfish landowners, who refuse to hand over their plots to Makerere College, in order that its work and activities might be improved and extended.

There are a number of chiefs in Buganda who have very willingly handed over to the Government some of their land, and who have been repaid in other ways. Luzira was originally owned by Sir Apollo Kagwa, who gave it up to Government, and received compensation. Budo Hill was owned by the late Kabaka, who was prepared to give it up in order that a school might be built there. We all know that that hill is still used for the Coronation of the Kabaka. Then there is Namaliga, near Bombo, which was owned by the late Zakaliya Kizito Kisingiri, who handed it over when it was wanted, and received compensation. The island called Lujabwa, in the Sesse District, used to belong to Hamu Mukasa, but he gave it up when it was asked for, and in return was given another place which he wanted. All these plots of land were willingly given up by their landowners for the sake of furthering education in Buganda, and its neighbouring countries. It surely cannot be right to say that their landowners made a mistake in what they did.

Our late Kabaka Mutesa sent representatives to England to interview Queen Victoria and ask for her help; he asked Mr Stanley to go to England to find teachers to come and assist in the education of his people. These teachers settled in various places, which are still famous, e.g. Natete, Nalukolongo, Lubya, Kiwulve, and Kigungu. The son of Mutesa, Daudi Chwa, who succeeded his father, gave up many different parts of his land for the good of his country and people, e.g. Namirembe, Lubaga, Nsambya, and Old Kampala.

Twelve years after Kabaka Mutesa had sent representatives to England King Mwanga made an agreement with Captain Lugard, confirming the friendship of Buganda with England. Other agreements were also made, which resulted in peace and the abolition of slavery in Buganda. Kabaka Mwanga agreed to follow the thoughts and advice of the Europeans, and not allow himself to exercise too much authority and power without the consent of the protecting British Government.

It is now 68 years since the first teachers from England reached Uganda, and we can truly say that our country has progressed considerably in wisdom and knowledge during these years, thanks to the action of Kabaka Mutesa. But today what do we find? We find that some people are wanting to put obstacles in the way of our country's progress and prosperity. I would like to emphasize that these three kings I have mentioned, i.e. Mutesa, Mwanga, and Chwa, did not decide on their own to give up their land, but first consulted their chiefs, and discussed the whole matter with them, even though many of them were simple and comparatively uneducated people. It seems rather strange, therefore, that the people of today, who are much better educated than their forefathers, should take up this attitude of disapproval and selfishness.

If we Baganda carefully read and study our laws and agreements we shall understand that it is wrong for us to refuse to hand over our land if it is required for other purposes which will benefit our own country and help it to advance.

In conclusion, I would ask all of you Baganda to do all you can to help your country, and not to try to prevent or hinder your own people from going forward. As you will realize from what I have said, I myself feel strongly that Makerere College should remain in our own country, so that our people may have the honour and privilege of having it situated here, and that they may gain all they can from it.

– from *Uganda Herald*, 25 July 1945.

39. ANTIPATHY TO ASIANS, 1946

G. R. Kiẓẓa of Kalokwe, Gomboloa of the Musule, Busiro, in Gambuze, *26 April 1946.*

Ladies and gentlemen, the readers of this newspaper, *Gambuẓe*, I am greatly pleased to be in a position to write and to add to what Omw. Chr. Kawanawe Nsubuga wrote in *Gambuẓe* of the 15th March, 1946, on page 5. It gives me much pleasure to note that the gentleman mentioned above was able to look ahead and understand about those insects which he called 'parasites' which suckle at Uganda our Mother.

Omw. Nsubuga showed us one way by which the Indians mar us, together with our Mother Uganda, wishing thus to make it into one of the subject countries, and also where they can trade. Also that is the method of trading which they employ when they rob us and make us poor.

Whilst adding to what has been said about the Indian traders, I should say that they are a millstone weighing many pounds around the neck of the African, and which would destroy us the people of Uganda. I hope there will be a certain amount of reflection and a wish to know how they will efface us. My explanation of this is as follows:

My friends, if the Europeans were as many as the Indians who are in Uganda, on what plane would our civilization and state of learning be at this time? Regarding this remember that their trading community arrived via Mombasa a long time ago and it was the first one in this country. And now they have come to this country where they have given birth to numerous insects. In other words the number of this community merely continues to increase in this country.

(a) They trick us and they rob us saying that they are selling goods to us reasonably at proper prices whereas in fact they are profiteering.

(b) They employ our young children, boys and girls, at very low wages In fact, the Shs. 2/- which is given to them does not suffice to obtain a shirt or a frock to help them out of the difficulties which have induced them to work. As a result the boys learn pick-pocketing and the girls become prostitutes. Also the Indians are the instigators of these young girls in taking up the profession. For instance, look at the number of Mulattos or people with mixed colour and the majority of them belong to the Indians of Uganda. What causes this mixture of colour is their desire to enrich themselves. The result is nothing but misery because these Mulatto children have nothing to help them, neither do their fathers leave them anything when they go back to India, even though when they go back they have amassed a great amount of money from this country.

(c) The personal servants and the people who work for the Indians are people who are always found to be exceedingly dirty and untrustworthy. It is amongst them that we find ignorant people who speak in an obscene manner and who have not the manners of polite people. This, therefore, shows that they are low fellows and they copy this from their masters, the Indians. The personal servants and also the employees of some Europeans are found, however, to be paid good wages and are also clever and clean at the same time.

Leaving aside the trading community, let me speak about the members of the Indian community who work in the offices, and government departments, such as the S.A.S.'s in the Medical Department, Stationmasters in the Railway, Postmasters in the Post Office, clerks in the offices, guards and many others. They may be made into the deputies of our masters who direct employment, because of their white colour. These are the people who have mostly destroyed and taken away the trust which our masters had for us; and belittled our education.

(1) By carrying tales about us and talking about us in a very bad way to our masters, informing them how we are incapable of doing our work and also they have a way of convincing our superiors so that they listen to them.

(2) When an Indian is left as the deputy of the master on any job:

(a) He cannot respect the people working under him. I think you have all seen something of this.

(b) He will not speak well about any person or recommend him if he is asked about that person's work. Yet many Africans have shown themselves capable of duties which do not any longer require Indians. Also it is apparent that they intend to belittle the African because they wish to obtain employment for their fellow Indians and their children in such work. For example, when an Indian child in Uganda goes to India for his education but afterwards he returns here to look for work in Uganda. My friends, in what condition is India? Is it full to capacity? Our masters are blinded and accept the tales which are carried to them.

These days it shames the Indians, who call themselves superior, to see that today the Africans are capable of competing with them in work and even surpassing them, yet they receive high wages. They think that if they recommend an African they will see that their jobs are taken from them by us. When you think a little you will see that the time has come when the Indians should not take our places and keep us down, as if there was no work in India.

I hereby ask anyone who may know the reason why we should wait for them to increase and spread in this country to explain to me and I shall be very pleased to hear it. Also I shall be very pleased if our native Government and also the Protectorate Government would endeavour to diminish the number of Indians in this country.

These are my ideas which I would give to our guardians, native and white, in order to decrease these people in our country.

It appears that all cannot return at the same time; but the Government could do as follows:

1. Regarding the Traders and Tailors: one whose agreement expires would just go to India; and every Indian who has more than three children will have the surplus children sent back to India; also they will not continue to build other shops, and those people who are in the villages are to be returned to the important townships, such as Kampala and Jinja etc.

2. Regarding the doctors and the workers in the Offices: they are asked to return and sell their medicines in India, or in another country; or if not that not to sell their medicines here. About the workers in other trades: they are asked to make their applications in India and other places, but not here.

Remember that the Jews were driven away from the countries which were not theirs as they brought wars and poverty to the countries in which they had settled. I should be glad if both Governments would combine to remove this danger.

– from a translation: *Gambuze*, 26 April 1946.

E. M. K. Mulira and J. W. Kiwanuka to the Editor, Uganda Herald, *30 April 1947.*

In 1927, when closer union loomed high in East Africa, the late Kabaka and his Ministers took the lead in voicing African opinion. Then Kenya and Tanganyika followed the lead which Buganda had set. So did the neighbouring tribes of Uganda. We are afraid we have lost that leadership now.

Last year when White Paper 191 was introduced, Kenya African leaders of opinion sent their delegates to Uganda to consult with the leaders here. They actually flew, to mark their mission as of a spectacular importance. They saw the Regents and Ministers of Buganda and one or two other prominent Africans here. How were they received? According to their report very poorly indeed, and they went back not only disappointed but puzzled whether this was the Buganda which was supposed to be the leading country in East Africa. Not only that, even we, the inhabitants of Uganda, looked up and waited to see what our own leaders were going to say about this Paper 191, for in a country like Buganda, where there are no political bodies, people naturally look to their Central Government for guidance in such matters, but nothing was said to guide the public opinion of this country.

Now there is this revised Inter-Territorial Organization, Paper 210. We fear the same lack of response is going to take place.

In view of this fear we wish to propose what should be done and done quickly. Let our Ministers rouse themselves and appoint a Commission to advise them on this important document. This committee should be given specific terms of reference and in the end report to the Ministers. These recommendations may or may not be debated in the Lukiko. If they approved of them, then they would, in their capacity as the Regents of Buganda, sign that report and submit it to the Protectorate Government as containing the Buganda view of Paper 210.

1. Let not the Ministers trust their own judgment that they can do it by themselves: for one thing they cannot that way assess what the public thinks of the Paper: for another, to do that would be to assume infallibility.

2. Let not the criterion for forming the Committee be chieftainship. Chiefs may be appointed to it by virtue of their ability to understand what the Paper contains and not merely for their position. Therefore, we should recommend a formation of a Committee on the lines that the Luganda Orthography Committee was formed, i.e. membership by those who are most capable of understanding the issue. They can be Chiefs, Ababaka

b'Abantu, teachers, business men, Journalists, etc. – but not Chiefs by themselves.

If we do this, perhaps we can restore our leadership in East Africa, and what is more we should have helped to shape the future of our countries. To keep quiet is to fail in our duty to our generation and to the generations to come.

– from *Uganda Herald*, 30 April 1947.

Paper 191: *Inter-Territorial Organization in East Africa*, Colonial No. 191 London, Her Majesty's Stationery Office, 1945.
Paper 210: *Inter-Territorial Organization in East Africa: Revised Proposals*, Colonial No. 210, London, H.M.S.O., 1947.

41. THE COTTON GRIEVANCES, 1948-9

Resolutions of a general meeting of the African Produce Growers held under the auspices of the Uganda African Farmers' Union, at Makerere, 18 May 1948.

That a deputation wait on His Excellency the Governor with a view to receive His Excellency's approval, support and guidance to our petition that will be presented to His Excellency by our deputation.

(2) That next year's, i.e. 1948-9 cotton crop be collected by the African Produce Growers and request the Governor to help us in arranging the ginning of our raw cotton on the nearest ginneries to every buying post on reasonable charges.

(3) The African Produce Growers be authorized by the Governor to sell direct their cotton lint to United Kingdom or British Commonwealth or through the Government Agent.

(4) That His Excellency be requested to grant us good sites for erecting our own ginneries in Uganda which should be ready to handle the crop of 1949–50.

(5) That the Government be requested to allow us to open buying stores for raw cotton at all principal centres which will be open at any time for inspection by Government officials.

(6) That next year's seed cotton price as published in *Mawulire* (we believe to be the official organ in the Department of Public Relations and Social Welfare) on Monday, 5th April 1948, is viewed as unsatisfactory

after having learnt that the latest local price of lint cotton has gone up. The price of Americani* which in pre-war days cost a few cents per yard and today the price has increased by four hundred per cent, we say nothing of the price of beef which is essential to agricultural labourers. Any future increased price should be published in the *Uganda Herald* and vernacular papers as well as local headquarters of Native Administrations.

(7) That every grower should take great pains to see that his produce is free from foreign material before it is sold so as to raise and maintain his commercial honesty, e.g. if a grower is selling cotton 'A' quality it should be 'A' quality only.

> — from Uganda Protectorate, *Report of the Commission of Inquiry into the Disturbances in Uganda during April, 1949*, Entebbe 1950, pp. 74–5.

Americani: the cheapest kind of cotton cloth.

42. THE ONSET OF THE 1949 DISTURBANCES

Report of an audience by Kabaka Mutesa II to 'eight peoples' representatives', 25 April 1949.

Present:

Owekitibwa Katikiro
Owekitibwa Omulamuzi
Owekitibwa Omuwanika

Representatives:

Samwiri Male, Bugerere
Mikaeri Kirima, Busiro
Yake Kyazze, Kyadondo
Paul Mukasa, Kyadondo
Kulanima Musoke, Busiro
Eryeza Bwete, Kyadondo
Sedulaka K. K. Katongole, Kyadondo
Gomeri Lwere, Kyadondo

The Katikiro introduced the representatives as above. Then a representative read their representations whilst all were standing. They came to present five grievances of the people. The people were pleased with His Highness's letter, which has helped them in getting an opportunity of approaching him. The memorandum was read by Male of Bugerere.

'Their Representations:

(1) That His Highness inaugurates "Democracy", whereby people elect their own chiefs.
(2) That the number of Lukiko representatives be raised to sixty.
(3) That the present Government resigns.
(4) That they gin their own cotton.
(5) That they sell their agricultural products directly wherever they like.'

Male stated that they had been sent by the people and by all elders of Buganda. The following are the other representatives who signed the memorandum but who did not come: Lwanyaga, Sonko, Nalwanga, Lutete, Mukasa, Bate, Nambi.

Yake: (1) – We have been sent by the people to present their grievances so that you may settle them. The people require democracy, to select their own rulers. We have every hope that if this was granted all trouble will disappear, because the elected chiefs will be interested in the welfare of their people. Such kind of rule exists in England. All the people would have been here but they are prevented by the chiefs from coming here.

P. Mukasa: (2) – The Sixty Representatives. Though this matter is included in our memorandum we know that Your Highness promised that this will be given your due consideration. If your subjects were granted sixty representatives there would be no trouble, and there would be understanding between people and rulers. We want to fulfil the 1900 Agreement. It was by your own goodwill that the thirty-one representatives were granted to us during 1946 which number was thereafter increased to thirty-six. It is our desire to keep the Agreement wholly. If the number of representatives was raised to sixty, public matters would receive due consideration and not be kept in the background.

Kulanima Musoke: (3) – That the present Government resigns. People want to elect their own rulers. As long as the present rulers remain there will be no betterment in the present condition. You rendered great assistance to the Omulamuzi's department when you appointed more junior judges to it. Your present rulers are after their own peace and not peace for the general public. We have neither intrigues nor jealousies. Your Highness will not be able to grant peace to the public whilst retaining the present rulers.

Eryeza Bwete: (4) – Cotton Affairs. I am a representative of the growers, we have twenty-four societies. The people are poor, they have sent me with four matters to be put before the present government. The Government realized £200,000,000 – the Protectorate Government returned a part of it. The Katikiro asked for proposals from the general public. We were astonished to find out that we were merely bluffed. Nothing has come out from their proposals ever since. We proposed that a Committee of four people be appointed to find out ways of enriching people. The Chiefs are just playing with the money – they make roads and roads made are not to be seen. They use the money to meet their own and their children's ends. People wanted to acquire ploughs and tractors for agriculture. This Government was not interested in African farmers, what they do is help the middlemen. The people asked for agricultural tractors, coffee hulling machines, ginneries and a bank. The Government itself just played about with these matters. Membership in Agricultural Societies number some thirty-five thousand.

The people outside there are in agony. Why should Co-operative Societies be registered in Kampala. This Government could appoint its own Registrar to register such societies.

As regards cotton: We went to Matuga to arrest cheaters; then the Katikiro circularized chiefs saying that we were extorting money from growers – Shs. 5/– from each grower. Every Indian ginner regards his ginnery site as a royal palace, because the Ordinance allows them such a privilege. We, therefore, need our own ginnery in order to help ourselves; the growers are dying from hunger. Of course the Indians lend us money to help us cultivate plantain gardens, but they do this demanding a very big rate of interest.

The people asked me to approach the Roman Bishop and ask him to keep our money; this was forbidden us.

The transport in respect of our propaganda campaign teaching the people the sense of *ownership* cost us Shs. 20,000/–. The chiefs chased us wherever we went to explain to people.

Governor Sir John Hall gave us permission to gin our cotton. The Katikiro and Government stated that the ginning of cotton was not profitable. The growers sent you a letter hoping to be able to gin their cotton. The Uganda Company have refused to gin our cotton and the growers have refused to part with their cotton in the same way as the Nigerians did with their cocoa. The Government, to save face, has enacted laws with the intention of convicting growers. We, the growers, are angry because of Katikiro Kawalya. These chiefs receive money from the Indians as a return for the assistance given to them. The Supply Board has prevented growers from selling their grams. There is a growers' banner outside bearing a picture of a man tied with ropes, which means that we are willing to be imprisoned. The present Government is not helpful because the people are too poor and they will not pay taxes. We are in possession of three and a half million pounds of cotton. The Indians send their men to set fire to houses and thirty thousand pounds of cotton have been destroyed. Chiefs are not helpful to us since no Committee has been appointed to help us in this matter.

Gomere Lwere: (5) – Our Agricultural Products. We came here to tell the truth: Kawalya's Government may kill us, let us die. All the people say that it was better to die.

All imported materials arrive here already bought by Indian millionaires, who sell them to other Indians, who sell them to a third party – Indians; the latter then sell them to Africans, with no profit allowed, and the result is thieving. We have been lied to for long that Government could not be expected to take part in trade. Cannot Government import goods for sale to us?

In a book written by Canon Grace it is said that 'coffee at 30 cents a lb. in Buganda is sold at Shs. 3/– in England, and the profit goes to the middleman'. People were undernourished, they eat bad food because they have no money. Buganda is now like Hitler's Germany. We have come before Your Highness ready for imprisonment but we have spoken the truth. Co-operative Societies are hypocritical. Co-operative Societies are for European enrichment. Europeans instruct Co-operative Societies to keep their coffee berries clean – these great ones pay poor people 2 cents only, over which they rejoice. After the coffee is bought it is mixed with other European coffee and sold at Shs. 3/–, thereby receiving much profit.

Kirima: We bring these matters as unofficial representatives.

Sedulaka Katongole: Your Highness, I am a Mutaka; these matters are brought to us by your subjects and they have intimated to us that the present Government is harsh. We have also noticed that secret affairs concerning the Baganda were being communicated to the aliens. These children of ours (the chiefs) have failed us. Matters which would only be settled by you and ourselves are referred to aliens. For example, they say that in Buganda there are no Bataka. The Bataka are the crown of the nation and owing to them the Kabaka enjoys the title of Sabataka (head of the Bataka).

His Highness: I have heard your statements properly. Will you tell me how many of you like the 1900 Agreement?

The People: We all like it.

His Highness: Your first three matters concern the 1900 Agreement. In my recent speech to the Lukiko I explained the question of the number of unofficial representatives.

Reply: The unofficial representatives did not convey these statements to us. The people would not have come here today had they conveyed the statements to us.

His Highness: The representatives are elected by you; it was up to you to ask them about these matters.

Reply: The way of election is not good, some of them are not allowed to explain to us unless they belonged to our constituency. Unofficial representatives sometimes resemble chiefs. They do not carry out our instructions. They should be selected from the well known.

His Highness: You should give people in the villages an opportunity of being elected and approaching His Highness in the same way as other people. However, you must remember that the appointment of chiefs and election of representatives were both provided for in the Agreement, and I have already mentioned about them in the Lukiko.

Reply: We want an immediate increase of their number, since the standard of education of the chiefs and the people were the same.

His Highness: You neither support nor respect them.

Reply: This, Your Highness, is because we are overwhelmed by their majority in the Lukiko and consequently our views are disregarded because the chiefs were in the majority.

His Highness: You have given me no opportunity to be able to help you. Why could not you interview your representatives?

Reply: When we send representatives the chiefs say they were expressing their own views and not popular opinion, and this is why we brought the people here – to make it understood that we were expressing popular opinions.

His Highness: You want to cause an uprising? You seem as if you want to tie my hands.

Reply: Your Highness, the people say we are weak and that their representations are never conveyed to you.

His Highness: You should have told the people that you would yourselves convey their representations to me.

Reply: The people came here so that we may be able to explain to them when we leave here since we generally have the opportunity to explain to all of our people.

His Highness: Do you expect me to reply to you instantly? I will go into the matters concerning agriculture and, in the first instance, seek the advice of my advisers. But you must report truthfully what I have said.

His Highness to Katongole: It appears that you, the Bataka, send your representations anywhere directly, instead of passing them through myself, as you sent Mulumba. I wish to see you with a view to coming to a proper understanding.

Katongole: Your Highness, that was a mistake on our part. I will go back and explain to the Bataka.

His Highness: How many of them have sent you?

Katongole: Five Bataka of the first rank and other representatives of the Bataka.

A Representative: Your Highness, the law forbidding people not to keep cotton in unlicensed premises will lead all of us to prison. Your Highness, they will imprison us.

Gomeri Lwere: Your Highness, the people will not believe us when we convey your message since the present chiefs contradict your orders. For instance when the Kabaka ordered the election of cotton buying observers the Katikiro immediately sent letters forbidding the trial of cotton cheating cases detected by us. Whereas normally it is the complainant in theft cases himself who lodges his complaint before court, producing the stolen property as an exhibit.

His Highness: Go and tell your people to return to their homes.

His Highness arose and retired.

The Kabaka gave the Katikiro a written reply of which the following is a translation:

'With reference to the three matters which you have spoken of, they are laid down in the 1900 Agreement. I myself have a great duty to keep the 1900 Agreement and I believe that you also agree with the Agreement.

All answered willingly that they accept the Agreement.

With regard to the ginning of cotton and selling of your produce direct I will go into the matter after having received the advice of my advisers.

Tell your people to return to their homes.'

> – from Uganda Protectorate, *Report of the Commission of Inquiry into the Disturbances in Uganda during April, 1949.* Entebbe 1950, pp. 21–5.

43. ALIENATION, 1948–9

Semukula Mulumba's* telegram, 18 August 1948, to the Commissioner of Police, Kampala (copies to United Nations Organization, Prime Minister, Colonial Secretary, Governor, Bakabaka, Bataka, Uganda Press).

Hell Hall bills display his stupidity and idiocy. He is a Tory reactionary who needs refresher course Labour Policy U(nited) N(ations) charter. The Progressive Bataka elders have made him feel the need of harsh legislation to crush democracy Uganda state to cause to continue idiotic quislings. Aristocratic Uganda Government's Hall is a wild dog longing for black blood. You have read letters Stuart matter and news of the British Government in Uganda. I hope you are amused to know what you are like, you white swine the dung in which you wallow is our wealth which you stole by Agreement. Let us not talk of sedition; the law of the English thieves is for frightening people in order to hide your misdeeds. You should at once drop action against the Bataka Sebbanja and Kibuka;

they are guiltless of any offence. The English judges in Uganda have no justice for the black people; you yourselves the Governor Legco Police Missionaries deserve jail shooting the atomic bomb the gallows the guillotine because of your humbug and lies. Fierceness and force do nothing to diminish your misdeeds – they always merely show up more clearly your idiocy and stupidity and savagery. We scorn you like the droppings in a privy; rage, you English thieves, white swine, burst if you want; even if you were to kill me a thousand times I would revive, rejoicing, and tell you too that you English are liars, thieves, drunkards, idlers, who drain away the money of the black folk. Your heart is as hard as the hide of a hippopotamus; go and be hanged you beasts/animals/cattle it couldn't matter less.

'Message from the Governor', 27 April 1949

A comparatively few evil and self-seeking men have brought great trouble and disgrace upon Buganda. Acting on Communist inspiration from their so-called representatives in Britain, they are seeking to oppose by violence, intimidation, arson and murderous assault all constituted authority, the authority of H.H. the Kabaka's Government, the authority of the Protectorate Government and of the King's forces of law and order. In so doing they are following the usual pattern of Communist penetration, with which people in Europe and the Far East are already familiar. Their attempt was prefaced by a long campaign of foul lies and slander aimed at deceiving the people and shaking their confidence in His Highness's Government and the Government of the Protectorate. This too follows the usual Communist pattern.

The great mass of the Baganda, conscious of how much has been done for their welfare by their own Government and by the Protectorate Government, were too sensible to be deceived by these lies and slanders, so failing in this part of their campaign these wicked people have had to resort to violence. In this they will surely also fail, because their dupes and supporters are few and the forces of law and order are strong and will be still further strengthened until the evil-doers are crushed and peace and security restored.

The two bodies responsible for organizing and inciting this disturbance of the public peace – although their self-appointed leaders invariably withdraw when physical danger threatens – are the so-called Bataka Party and the African Farmers' Union (which latter have deceived a number of credulous cultivators by promises which they knew to be false and unfounded). Both these bodies have now been declared to be unlawful societies, and from now membership of those bodies will constitute an offence under the law.

Many disgraceful crimes of savagery have been committed. Innocent people have been attacked and beaten nearly to death. Public property and the property of law-abiding persons have been destroyed by fire, and peaceful passengers on the roads have been assaulted by hooligans. Most of those responsible will no doubt be brought to book and condignly punished through the processes of justice. But all Africans in the areas of disturbance will suffer for the crimes of the comparatively few because Section 67 of the Police Ordinance gives power to the Government to recover from the community the full cost of compensation for damage to persons and property; that power will be exercised, and I fear that the cost of compensation will be high and the communal penalty imposed will be heavy.

J. Hathorn Hall, Governor.

– the first item is from Uganda Government *Report of the Communism of Inquiry into the Disturbances in Uganda during April 1949,* Entebbe 1950, pp. 88–9; the second from a Protectorate Government printed handbill in the editors' possession.

Mulumba: Semakula Mulumba, formerly known as Brother Francis, acted as representative at this time of the 'Butaka Union' in London.

44. THE 1949 DISTURBANCES

Two letters from Buganda to Semakula Mulumba in England.

I

My friend Semakula Mulumba:

I am writing at the time when your country, Buganda, is facing great adversities. The country is bathed in tears. Kabazi, Sebanja, Mponye, Luule Spire Mukasa, Nkalubo, and about 700 people are arrested and imprisoned without reason.

They were beaten with sticks and tortured in a manner you cannot imagine. All this is brought about by the Governor – Katikiro.

Sir, there is no longer a way of communicating with you. Whenever anyone is heard mentioning your name. or seen writing to you, they arrest him at once.

The white people of Kampala have agreed to write to the Governor to ask him to recall you, or to get you returned to Uganda to be tried. They allege that it is you and Mr Musazi* who have caused all this trouble in Buganda.

Sir, assistance can only come from you, before you get to know all the details. We are in great danger. There is no possibility of sending you anything. The white people want you to starve in Britain.

It was very difficult to have this letter reach you. But I cannot tell you from where I am writing these sorrowful words, with tears in my eyes. But you will excuse me because I am frightened.

I am hoping to be able to let you know further details if God wills it.

Inform Mr Musazi that Lwere and company are arrested. Good-bye, I had little time. All is in your hands.

II

On 25th April we all went to demand democracy from the king and to ask him to allow us to gin our cotton. On April 26th the troops of the Protectorate Government assaulted the people, some of whom were shot. From that time to this, war is unleashed against us. The Protectorate Government is killing the people with impunity and malice. Nobody can dare protest. An average of eight to ten bodies are buried every day. Other bodies are dumped in the same pit. Nobody is allowed to see them.

[The letter further alleges that since April 26, more than 300 people have been killed and more than 1,000 arrested, and declares] the beating and every kind of torture inflicted on them exceeds Christ's sufferings.

Your uncle Sebanja, J. Miti Kabazzi, Luule, and all the active progressive Butaka whom you know, are in jail. They are continually flogged, and no food is given them. [The British authorities, the letter alleges, brought in troops with trucks and armoured cars, full of petrol, with which they burned the houses of the chiefs, of the employees of the Protectorate Government and the Baganda Government.] This was used as a pretext for arresting the Bataka. They were to allege that it was the Bataka who did it.

– *The Daily Worker*, 11, 17 May 1949.

Musazi: Ignatius Musazi, President of the Uganda African Farmers' Union at this time.

Extracts from E. M. K. Mulira Troubled Uganda.

Years of unrest (1939–49)

King Daudi Chwa died in November 1939, and he was greatly mourned by his people. Mutesa II succeeded him. But Mutesa was only 15 when he came to the throne and was still at school. Therefore, a regency was formed, consisting of three Ministers; the Prime Minister, the Chief Justice and the Minister of Finance. By now there was war and the Regents' first job was to persuade the people to join the ranks of the British Army. It was a very difficult task, and it made them unpopular at once. In the end, however, they managed to bring the people round to see their point of view.

In the army, the Baganda gave some trouble to start with, for the officers did not know how to handle them. The Baganda resented the white man's approach of regarding all Africans as primitives, who must conform to one rule. They are a proud and intelligent race and have never thought of themselves as primitive. After the officers had learnt how to handle them they gave very good service, and they ended the war with a fine record.

In 1941, Buganda faced a storm, perhaps the greatest in this century. A very sad thing happened to the Queen-Mother, which, since then, has been known as the 'Nnamasole Affair'. It was a palace-matter connected with the re-marriage of the Queen-Mother (Nnamasole) to a commoner. There were strong divisions of opinion, and when the church allowed her to marry under a licence many people lost confidence in the church as a whole. The Prime Minister, who had attended the wedding service, was severely criticized, and stones were actually thrown at him; he was forced to resign against his will, as British officials supported the opposing chiefs. The fact of chiefs forcing the resignation of a Minister had never been heard of in Buganda before. Naturally the Kabaka appoints his ministers, but this time the chiefs selected the new Prime Minister from among themselves. Samwiri Wamala was elected, and he was approved by the Governor.

The country was now divided into two parties. There was a minority who supported the Queen-Mother's marriage and a majority who opposed it. A period of slander, rumours and propaganda now followed, such as Buganda had never known. One sad result of these rumours was that they killed confidence. There was no more confidence between African and European, between people and the Church, between one section of people and another. We were all like sheep without a shepherd. For the first time in the history of Buganda authority lost its hold over the people, as the chiefs now courted the people's favours to support them in office. Hence the intense propaganda by some chiefs about themselves and the slander against their rivals.

There were a number of other unhappy incidents in these years. The creation of a religious sect, the Abalokole* (or 'saved'), who believed they heard the voice of God directly, all but caused a schism in the Church. Less significant, but still important, was an incident at King's College, Budo, in 1942. A series of misunderstandings ended in a schoolboys' insurrection. A Commission of Enquiry investigated, but its Report was never published. This incident was almost turned into a political issue.

The year 1944 was also a disturbed one. The Government wanted to get land for the extension of Makerere and for the Empire Cotton Experimental Station. The way they went about it caused great misunderstanding. In the same year, 1944, the British Government granted a greater measure of independence to the Kabaka. The District Commissioners were withdrawn and more financial control was allowed to the Buganda Government. But, it had one sad result. In his ceremonial speech, the Governor had said that complaints had come to him that in the Kabaka's Government, educated people were not being promoted to responsible posts, and he advised him very strongly to see that the educated talent of his country was utilized. In this statement, the educated people saw chances of a rise to power. There followed a period of scheming and plotting. Some of the old chiefs saw at once that their survival lay in being on good terms with the young educated class. This led to the crisis of 1945.

The rising of 1945 was caused by many factors, but in the end it centred round one person, Mr S. W. Kulubya, the Finance Minister. Mr Kulubya was the most outstanding man in public life in Uganda. He is well educated, cultured, highly intelligent, dignified, wealthy, progressive, respected by all communities but envied by many of his own people, especially by his contemporaries. It was he who had represented Uganda in 1931, at the Joint Select Parliamentary Committee in London, where he made a wonderful impression. But he lacked one quality indispensable to a politician – the courage to come out in the open and influence public opinion. He left it to his opponents to slander and damage his name without uttering any word in self-defence.

Fourteen Ssaza Chiefs raised a complaint against him. They said that he was spending the money of the country irrespective of the wishes of the Government. They signed a document and sent it to the Kabaka. The Kabaka went into this question with his advisers and found no fault with him. He wrote to the fourteen signatories that he saw no cause for his resignation. But the chiefs set on foot a vigorous propaganda that this minister, together with a few other chiefs, were selling the country to the British secretly. What Kulubya had done was to support the Bill for the acquisition of land for Makerere College and the Empire Cotton Experimental Station.

The rising first took the form of an economic strike, and was directed against the British Government Officers, but after two days it swung over to the Buganda Government headquarters and to the Kabaka's palace. The reason for this was that a rumour went round that the British Government had agreed to raise the salary of all the Government employees and of the labourers and had also agreed to raise the price of cotton from 10s. per 100 lbs. to 40s., but when Mr Kulubya was asked by the Government for his advice he had answered that the Baganda were like soup made of peanut; they swell but after a while 'they'll go down', and that because of this advice the British had withheld the increase.

The people demanded an immediate withdrawal of Mr Kulubya or else they would burn the capital and kill the Finance Minister. When Mr Kulubya, who was surrounded by the mob outside the Palace, heard this he sent in his resignation at once. When the mob received the news they said they had got what they wanted, and dispersed.

In the enquiry that followed some of the leading chiefs were found guilty of treason; many were deported and a new set of chiefs appointed to take their place. Unfortunately they, together with other prominent people in the rising, were deported by the order of the Governor without trial and this caused a fresh set of difficulties.

Martin Luther Nsibirwa was now returned to the Premiership. At once he got busy, under pressure of the British Government, to pass the Bill empowering the Kabaka to acquire land for public purposes, which his predecessor had resisted, and which had made him as popular with the Baganda as it had made him undesirable to the British. Martin Luther passed the Bill. But the people would not let him triumph. He was assassinated. More chiefs were found guilty and were deported, also without trial.

Mr Michael Kawalya Kaggwa, son of the late Sir Apolo Kaggwa, then became Prime Minister. Some of us had great hopes of him. He was the first educated Muganda to reach that position. He had a long experience in the war, and his origin encouraged such hopes. Unfortunately, he has not satisfied the people.

The year 1946 saw the appearance of the Abataka to champion the cause of the people. They sent appeal after appeal to the Governor that their complaints must be taken seriously. Then they sent their representative – Semakula Mulumba – to the Secretary of State for the Colonies in London with a host of complaints, but he was not received. So Mr Mulumba forwarded a petition to UNO through the Soviet representative.

The submitting of their grievances to UNO was enormously popular with the Baganda but bitterly resented by the Protectorate Government. The result was more misunderstandings, especially as seditious propaganda became rife throughout the country. This propaganda caused some concern, and the chiefs thought it their duty to take action. They sent a document signed by 14 Ssaza Chiefs to the Protectorate Government advising them that the so-called Bataka were not the genuine traditional Bataka but a semi-political party which was misleading the country and that the Government should arrest Semakula Mulumba and send him back to Uganda for trial.

The followers of Mulumba took revenge and pleaded with the Kabaka that these chiefs should be removed as not representing the true interests of the people. When the Kabaka could not grant their request, they took the law into their own hands, and, now being joined by the members of the Uganda Farmers' Union, they were a very strong force. A reign of terror, looting, arson and beating followed. Uganda had now been flung into a more terrible uprising than ever before. As in 1945, so now, an armoured force of the British army from Kenya was employed to put down riots. But the harm had been done.

We may conclude this part by saying that the past 25 years have seen immense material and intellectual advances in Uganda, but these advances have not been accompanied by true progress, which expresses itself in love, understanding and fair play. Perhaps it is not only Uganda that is lacking in these qualities? They are lamentably absent throughout the world.

The causes of unrest

The fact that I am going to point out some of the causes of the troubles in our country of Uganda is not an indication that I am blind to the desire on the part of the British Government to develop the country. On the contrary, I believe that the British Government, and especially of late years, is trying genuinely to improve conditions. . . .

(a) Is it Communism?

The first question is – is it Communism? We are told by the Governor of Uganda that the so-called Bataka Party is in contact with Communism from outside. He is in a position to know. But there are two warnings. The Bataka Movement did not primarily start as just another branch of the Communist movement. They set out to fight for certain reforms, and it was only after they were disappointed by the Buganda Government and the Protectorate Government that they decided to send a representative – Semakula Mulumba – to London. When he failed, too, he turned to UNO and to the Soviet delegate to help him. It was then that a number of chiefs disowned Mulumba, and his supporters tried to force them to resign, and resorted to force and intimidation when they failed to secure their resignation. Thus the story is something much more complicated than the simple explanation 'Communism' would suggest.

The second warning is this – it is very easy nowadays to make Communism fit any given context of facts, instead of making the facts fit

Communism. It is easy to see, in these troubles in Uganda, only the traces of Communism and shut one's eyes to the causes that made it possible for such a large section of the people to resort to Communism, for it is a well-known fact that Communism feeds on grievances.

Let me, then, describe some of the fundamental causes:

(b) The Whole System of Chieftainship

Indirect Rule was a very good system at one time. Unfortunately it was inherently static, and as such it has not moved with the progress that has been brought about by education.

In 1900, those who had accepted Christianity were the most highly educated people in the country, and their education was twofold: on the one hand, they had been trained in leadership in the old school of the Palace (which was their university), in war and in the other methods by which the people of old taught their young and initiated them into responsibility. On the other hand, they had learnt to read, and as readers they had an added advantage of having met the white man and having befriended him. Therefore, when the British Government decided to work through such people it was doing the best thing, for they were not only the natural leaders but also the people who had been already tested in the hard school of life. Naturally the rest of the population listened to them.

In addition, the 1900 Agreement had given them land, and they became at the same time the propertied class. They had enough, and they did not have to spend sleepless nights trying to make ends meet. These men had yet another advantage – they had not gone through the system known as bureaucracy with all its restrictions and dependence on the next man above. No wonder that that generation produced such men as Sir Apolo Kaggwa, Sitanisirasi Mugwanya, Ham Mukasa, Kakungulu etc.

But once education was allowed to extend to the sons of the peasants, Indirect Rule was doomed, as now the more educated class shifted from the so-called leaders to the led, and the led did not see why they should not become the leaders even without becoming chiefs. Hence their clamour for a more democratic form of government, in which they too could have a say. That is the position today. But the chiefs are still looked upon as the leaders, whereas in education the professional men are, generally speaking, their superiors.

Let us see how the modern chief is created. He is promoted, for the most part, from the ranks of the clerks of Government offices, of the commercial shops, from Mmengo Lukiko, from Ssaza headquarters, or even from amongst the clerks of private individuals. So long as such candidates have someone of great influence to support their application behind the scenes (very often this involves great gifts), a definitely inferior man may get the higher post; whereas the man with the better qualities takes a worse one simply because he has no financial support or because he is not liked by one of the chiefs above. In other words, favouritism is the rule.

The posts of clerks are for the most part filled by men who have failed to achieve scholastic attainments. But when they become chiefs, they are regarded as being above the people, and as leaders. As clerks their chief asset is to execute orders willingly, but not to lead. Therefore, when they become chiefs, they are very good at passing on the orders from above, but when the 'hungry sheep look up' for leadership, 'they are not fed'. The chief, as a paid official of the Government, has become a tool of the Government, to carry out its orders. Therefore, he cannot represent the interests of the people.

This state of affairs is not the fault of the chiefs, but the fault of the system. But when Indirect Rule is criticized, misunderstanding is likely, for many people at once assume that one is preaching the opposite of Indirect Rule which is Direct Rule. But that is not the case, and it is not what we are advocating here. What we are after is to find a democratic way of government which will bring in more people of the educated class.

Not only does the present-day chieftainship not give the country the leadership it requires, but the chiefs are out of touch with the common man. The better educated people are in the professions and are usually Government employees, which prevents their taking an active part in politics. They could serve on committees, but even this they are not invited to do for only chiefs are regarded as responsible beings.

(c) Undue importance put on Chiefs

In spite of the shortcomings of the modern chief, it is surprising with what undue importance he is regarded. Both the Protectorate and the Buganda Governments are to blame in this respect. It is the chief who is put on this committee; it is the chief who is asked for that advice; even when he is the least fitted to give it; it is the chief who must attend functions, etc.

. . . It is time to realize that the chief is not the only leader now. The educated man is just as much a leader in his particular sphere as is the chief. The chief is a civil servant whose main job is to execute the business of Government. He should be regarded as a leader only on his personal merit, when his personal qualities warrant it, and not simply by virtue of his office.

Through the practice that prevails today, the Protectorate Government cannot reach the heart of the people, for the chief in whom they have put their reliance is not the person to open the door for them.

(d) Absence of the District Commissioner

In 1944 the Kabaka was given a greater measure of self-government which put an end to the office of District Commissioners in Buganda. This was very much welcomed by all the Baganda, but it was a pity that this desirable step should have been taken without first preparing the would-be successors to these District Commissioners. As it happened, the offices of these District Commissioners were never wholly filled by another body of men. Many of their responsibilities fell on the shoulders of the Ssaza Chiefs, who had already been over-worked, and who, in many cases, could not command the same kind of influence as the District Commissioners had done. Special clerks were appointed to shoulder the other responsibilities. The District Commissioners had been university men, but most of the Ssaza Chiefs had only the rudiments of education. The measure was an excellent one, but there ought to have been some training of people who would replace those university men. I am of the opinion that the troubles in the past four years in Uganda have much to do with this lack and I believe the unrest of 1949 was only the continuance of 1945.

(e) The Social Set-up of the Country

The social set-up of Buganda favours the spread of rumours and is not favourable for disseminating the truth. We do not live in villages and towns as other people do, but on farms. When the landlord was the chief of the area as well (from 1900 onwards) he silenced subversive rumours and not much damage was done. When these chiefs died their successors either sold out to smaller landlords, who do not automatically become chiefs of the areas, or they themselves are employed by the Government and the Missions, and therefore do not live in their home districts. Therefore, today, the peasant and anyone with a piece of strange news is regarded as one of the people-in-the-know, especially if he happens to belong to the educated class who do not work. Formerly the landlord-chief would have corrected such rumours, but today there is no such person in many districts, on the contrary, the landed man without any work may be the author of such rumours.

Even when the news is true news, by the time it reaches from one end of the country to the other, it has become distorted with many additions and subtractions.

With people who live in villages and towns this danger is not prevalent, as it is possible to disseminate information in the form of public speeches, by writing or posters, by the cinema, or radio.

Broadcasting would be one of the best ways of combating rumours. In 1938 a successful experiment in broadcasting was made, but the war broke out and since then nothing more has been heard of the idea. If this scheme could be revived, it would be a great help. Instead of spending money on the social entertainment teams, if that money were diverted to broadcasting, it would be better spent. Radio-receiving stations could be constructed on every Gombolola.

. . . .Perhaps more results of the mistake are yet to come. The great thing to remember is that a wild tare was sown in Buganda, the offshoots of which are now trying to outgrow the good wheat, and the eradication of which needs the efforts of all men of goodwill. When all the people, who tried in one way or another to have their own way, failed to gain their ends, they became malcontents, and since in every case the white man was or is the final judge, they lost confidence in him. Since their number went on increasing, their sympathies overlapped and they had the same target of attack as a common enemy – the white man. That is why loyalty by an African to the white man is now looked down upon as unpatriotic. Hence the appeal to the more intimate sentiments of the people, and the introduction or rebirth of the idea of Abataka – for by that name the whole of Buganda is included, for all of us spring from one Mutaka or another. According to their way of looking at things, if you are not in sympathy with the Bataka, then you are not a lover of your country, for how could you love your country without feeling at one with your ancestors as represented by the Abataka? Many listened to the appeal of Abataka without understanding the issues. All the people who were involved in making the demands at one time or another are not active members of the Abataka Party. But it is true to say that those who call themselves Bataka have many sympathisers in the country.

(g) The Deportees of 1945

As a result of the 1945 disturbances many people, including high-ranking chiefs, were deported and deported without trial. Whether it was right or wrong is not the question; I want to talk about the after-effects.

The relatives of these people never forgave the Governor for this act, and in very large measure it was responsible for the re-emergence of the Bataka Party. Governments do not listen so much to isolated voices, they listen to influential groups. Individual wives weeping for their husbands, and relatives lamenting their kinsmen, lacked both collective security and moral influence. So they congregated round a few genuine Bataka (who seemed to number only about three at the start). By 1946, however, they were sufficiently vocal to make the Government feel some concern. They sent letters to the Secretary of State, asking to have their people tried, and for a revision of the law empowering the Kabaka to acquire land. They began to collect money for the purpose of sending some of their number to England to interview the Secretary of State. That was early in 1946.

In the autumn of 1946, Ssemukula Mulumba (as Brother Francis) returned to the country from Great Britain. He did not join the Bataka until early 1947, but by the middle of that year, enough money had been collected to send him again to England to petition the Secretary of State.

Those who called themselves Bataka regarded the deportees as martyrs. It was this motive force behind them that gave such incentive. They seemed to believe that they were waging a semi-holy war, and they soon became the collecting bag for all those who had complaints either against the Church or the Government.

(h) Land Questions

In 1944, the expansion of Makerere College required that more land should be secured from neighbouring landowners. Land was also needed for the important Empire Cotton Corporation which was to be stationed in Uganda. The approach of the Government to the landowners was, in some way, unfortunate, as they departed from the normal procedure which was through the Kabaka and the chiefs, and this time made a direct approach to the landlords themselves; tempers rose, and the landowners refused to sell. The Regents were asked to intervene, but they had to bring the matter to the Lukiiko. The Lukiiko turned down the proposal because, although under the Uganda Agreement of 1900 the Government had the right to acquire land for *public service*, neither Makerere nor the Corporation came under this title. They did, however, come under the title of *public purposes*, and an attempt was made by the British Government to amend the clause in the Agreement to include land for public purposes. This caused great tension in the country. The fact that the Government was bent on acquiring this land by what was tantamount to force, caused the greatest distrust both of the British, and of the chiefs who supported the measure in the Lukiiko. The suspicion aroused in this way brought many recruits to the Bataka.

The Bill was never passed, and its opponents became national heroes. But after Martin Luther Nsibirwa was returned to power, the question of the Land Bill was raised afresh, and this time it went through. But Nsibirwa answered it with his life. He was assassinated. Many of the chiefs connected with the matter were deported without trial.

(i) Closer Union in East Africa

From 1924–31 the proposal for closer union of the East African Territories, initiated by the Kenya settlers was bitterly opposed by the Kabaka and the people of Uganda, whether African, European or Indian. The great fear of this idea was caused by the belief that the Kenya white settlers would have the lion's share in such a Union, and would turn East Africa into another South Africa. In 1946, the Secretary of State for the Colonies issued Paper 191, in which he showed how necessary it was to have a unification of Public Services. In it he proposed an equal representation of the three races in East Africa on a Central East African Assembly: 6 Africans, 6 Europeans and 6 Indians.

This Paper was supported by the Europeans, the Africans and the Indians in Uganda; by many Europeans, the Africans and the Indians in Tanganyika; and by the Africans and Indians in Kenya, as was evinced by newspaper comments, and only opposed by the white settlers in Kenya, who objected to the equality in racial representation. When Paper 191 was replaced by Paper 210 we were greatly disappointed to see that the Secretary of State had listened to the minority of the Kenya settlers rather than to the majority of all the rest of the races and had changed his first proposals. The races would no longer receive equal representation. Our former fears were revived, and we saw again the danger of the Kenya sett-ler looming over us.

When Mr Creech-Jones* flew to East Africa in 1947, we were warned beforehand that we should not mention the question of the White Paper to him, as he was on a different mission. But the white settlers discussed it with him in full. Again, the African's trust in the good faith of the British Government was undermined.

Paper 210 appeared on the Agenda of the Legislative Councils of the three territories almost simultaneously. In spite of representations to the Katikkiro that the people should be consulted, it was passed in the Legislative Council of Uganda, where there is an official majority, without the Native Administrations having discussed the Paper. The African members of the Legislative Council could not be considered as represen-tative as they were nominated by the Government.

Then the matter fell into the hands of the Bataka, because they saw that their country was being associated with Kenya, and their Government made no protest. It was argued that in 1931, when the East African Union was discussed the Kabaka's opinion was sought, and he had sent his representative with a memorandum containing the country's views. Why not now, except that since the action on the land question, the British Government had decided to take away both their land and country by force and cunning?

(j) The Social Transition

In general, Uganda is feeling the growing pains always connected with a social transition. For one reason there are many unemployed. Some are sons of landlords who were given land by the 1900 Agreement and then empowered to collect rent, on which they now live without working. There are those who have failed in business, and those who lost their positions in the 1945 disturbances. Many of these men are intelligent and command great respect. Society in Uganda is harbouring within itself a core of people with education, influence, grievances and jealousies – but without work.

(k) The Colour Question in East Africa

Dr Malan, the Prime Minister of South Africa, has been speaking about a United States of Africa, and his words have been eagerly caught up as far north as Kenya and Tanganyika. Many extraordinary speeches have been made by spokesmen in East Africa. In Central Africa they are talking of a Federation of these same territories into a Central African Dominion, and there is talk of an East African Dominion. Mr Bouwers, of the Kenya Legislative Council, said a few months ago that it was absolutely necessary that they dropped all prejudice against fellow Europeans in Africa and got together on a 'common colour platform'.

This policy, which is being influenced by the white settler element in East Africa (and many Government officials, including some of high rank, have already bought land in Kenya) is making it very difficult for Africans who would like to support British policy in East Africa before their countries are ready for self-government. However much they may like to work with the British Government (as directed from Whitehall, for that is the only Government they approve of) they cannot support a policy that is directed against their well-being. Many Africans would wish to be on friendly terms with the British, only it is being made increasingly dangerous for them. It is not clear how Great Britain can fulfil her pledge that she is training us for the eventual self-government, when, at the same time, a strong white public opinion in East Africa is definitely aimed not only at our domination, but also at our suppression!

It is this common colour platform which is disturbing the minds of Africans in East Africa today. It has been developing for quite a long time and now because of the Malan Government in South Africa it has become more urgent. And one can understand the African's fear and suspicion when he sees that vital measures that affect his very existence are taken without his being given a chance to take part in them. Two examples will suffice to show what we mean.

First, a new Makerere Council has just been formed. This council of twelve members includes no single African on it. The councils governing other British Colonial University Colleges have both the members of the indigenous population and white people. We fail to see why the Makerere College Council should be solely a white body.

Secondly, there is growing in East Africa the false idea that the African cannot do what the white man does. In West Africa more and more responsible posts are being filled by our brothers. In East Africa they tell us that we have not the necessary qualifications. When we demand the opportunities of securing the necessary qualifications they accuse us of being too fond of letters after our names and then add that degrees are not necessary. Then they offer us scholarship to the United Kingdom, they send us to do short courses in most cases, and in insufficient numbers, as is shown by comparison with the Gold Coast, which has an equal population, or Sierra Leone, with less than half the population of Uganda. For the year 1948-9 Uganda had in the United Kingdom 23 Government scholarship-holders, the Gold Coast 233, and Sierra Leone 34. When some of us obtain the qualifications they tell us that we lack character and experience, and so on. . . .

(l) Popular misconceptions

Much suffering and suspicion is caused in Uganda by simple misunderstandings – often through the failure of the authorities to explain things clearly. The law empowering the Kabaka to acquire land is a case in point. The people including those members of the Lukiiko who passed the law, thought that the Kabaka had been given full power to dispossess landowners, and could even hand over land to foreigners. But when a simple explanation is given to the people that, without such a law, the selfishness of a few landlords could prevent, say, a school being built, and that the Kabaka cannot act without the consent of the Lukiiko where the people are represented, the fears are dispelled. It is only while people misunderstand, and cling to *their* interpretation of the law, that they imagine their tenure of the land to be dangerously insecure. This misinterpretation has been responsible for the death of a Prime Minister, and contributed to the riotings of 1945 and 1949.

Another misunderstanding concerns the appointment of chiefs. People, hearing that in England people elect their leaders, believe that they should elect their chiefs – confusing chiefs with leaders. I, and others, have tried to explain that the representatives to the different councils and to Lukiiko should be elected and that there should be Ministers chosen in a more popular way, but that the chiefs, as well as fulfilling traditional activities were civil servants, and could not be elected. But the position is still not understood, and the election of chiefs remained one of their claims to the Kabaka before the 1949 riots.

Many people in Buganda seem to think that there are three important people in the world: the Prime Minister of England, the Secretary of State for the Colonies and Ssemakula Mulumba, and they believe that the three see each other at any time and that what the last man tells the other two becomes law, and if it does not, he simply walks to UNO and reports there; and because Mr Gromkyo supports his case, then a very wonderful thing has happened, and it is a day of jubilation throughout the land, and if you do not join in the mirth you are a traitor! The greatest importance is attached to Mr Mulumba's words by very large numbers of people. Finally, the Uganda Agreement of 1900. Very few people in Uganda have either seen or read this Agreement. And yet such mystical importance is put to it for weal or woe. Any new scheme which people do not understand is feared, since it is not in the 1900 Agreement. Anything that is in the Agreement which no longer meets the present needs will not be amended, because that would disturb the whole Agreement. For instance, whenever it is proposed that we should have at least two more Ministers, one of them as Minister of Agriculture, the answer is, 'the Agreement only mentions three Ministers, therefore, we cannot add to them.' The Agreement should be published for wide circulation and should be studied in schools as part of history.

– from E. M. K. Mulira *Troubled Uganda*
Fabian Colonial Bureau, Colonial Controversy Series, No. 6, London 1950.

Abalokole: the 'saved ones', members of the protestant evangelical revival movement.

Creech-Jones: Colonial Secretary in the post-war British Labour Government.

46. CONSTITUTIONAL REFORM IN BUGANDA, 1953

Memorandum on Constitutional Development and Reform in Buganda, 17 March 1953.

His Excellency the Governor and His Highness the Kabaka, with their Principal Advisers, have recently held a series of discussions about constitutional and local government development in Buganda, with a view to giving increased responsibilities to the Buganda Government and a greater part in the system of government to the people of Buganda. The purpose of this statement, which is issued jointly by His Excellency and His Highness, is to set out for the information of the Great Lukiko and of the general public the decisions which they have jointly reached with the full approval of the Secretary of State for the Colonies. In brief these decisions are as follows:

(i) responsibility at the Provincial level and below for the operation of certain departmental services will be transferred from the Protectorate Government to the Buganda Government;

(ii) there will in consequence have to be financial adjustments;

(iii) His Highness the Kabaka has decided that there will have to be an increase in the Senior Officers of the Buganda Government;

(iv) he has also decided to increase the number of elected members of the Great Lukiko;

(v) he will consult members of the Lukiko before appointing the Ministers;

(vi) he will put forward to the Lukiko proposals for a system of local government to be established at Saza* level to which the Buganda Government will devolve certain of its functions.

2. The intention is that the Protectorate Government should hand over to the Buganda Government responsibility for running the following services: in education primary and junior secondary schools; in medicine and health rural hospitals (at Bombo, Mityana and Mubende), dispensaries, sub-dispensaries, aid posts and rural health services; in

agriculture the field service for the improvement of farming methods and soil conservation; in animal health the field service for the improvement of livestock breeding and keeping and disease control. The Buganda Government for its part will continue, in the spirit of the Uganda Agreement of 1900, to carry on these services in accordance with the general policy laid down by the Protectorate Government and in conformity with the laws governing these services, e.g. in relation to the control of human, animal and plant diseases. The Protectorate Government through the departments concerned will be entitled to inspect the services transferred so as to ensure that all necessary steps are taken to carry them on efficiently. . . .

7. His Highness the Kabaka has decided that, when his Government takes over responsibility for additional services, it will be necessary to make further appointments of officers of Ministerial status who will provide political direction for the executive officers at the head of these services and will speak for the services concerned in the Lukiko. The new officers will be known as Ministers but will not rank as Officers of State for the purpose of carrying out the functions set out in the Uganda Agreement, 1900; in order to differentiate them from the existing Ministers, the latter will in future be known as Ministers of State or Senior Ministers. It is proposed in the first place to appoint three additional ministers who might deal respectively with Health, Education and Natural Resources (Agriculture and Veterinary Services). The Katikiro's position as Prime Minister will not be impaired. The new Ministers will be members of the Great Lukiko, being included among the six nominees of His Highness the Kabaka, if they do not already hold seats as elected members. In these decisions His Highness has the support of the Governor and the approval of the Secretary of State.

8. His Highness the Kabaka has decided, with the full approval of the Governor and the Secretary of State, to increase to 60 the number of elected representatives in the Great Lukiko. In accordance with Article 11 of the Agreement, three of these will be elected from each Saza for appointment by His Highness the Kabaka. One from each Saza will, as at present, be a person of educational standing or prominent in trade or agriculture elected by the full Saza Council. The other 40 (two for each Saza) will be elected from the muluka* level through a single electoral college. It is proposed that elected representatives one from each muluka, should meet at the Saza Headquarters and together elect the two Saza representatives directly to the Great Lukiko. Legislation to provide for these elections will be submitted to the Lukiko later in the year. . . .

10. Under Article 10 of the Agreement, it is the prerogative of His Highness the Kabaka to appoint the Ministers with the sanction and approval of the Governor; but His Highness recognizes that it will be to the advantage of his country, and in accordance with the democratic practice which he has chosen to follow, if members of the Lukiko are con-

sulted as to the appointments and the Lukiko itself is given an opportunity to pledge its support for the appointments. He has therefore decided to make use of the following arrangement:

(a) In any new Lukiko when the sixty elected representatives have been appointed, they and the twenty Saza Chiefs will meet together under the Chairmanship of the retiring Katikiro and select a delegation of twelve or sixteen persons whom the Kabaka will be able to consult about the appointment of new Ministers.

(b) The delegation will be composed in accordance with the composition of the Lukiko itself. It will consist as to one quarter of Saza Chiefs elected from among their number by the 20 Saza Chiefs; as to another quarter of representatives of the Saza Councils elected by the 20 Saza Council representatives in the Lukiko; and as to the remaining half of miruka representatives elected by the 40 miruka representatives in the Lukiko.

(c) His Highness will inform the delegation of those persons he has in mind to appoint as Ministers, and it will be the duty of the delegates to tell the Kabaka if any of them is likely to be unacceptable to the Lukiko.

(d) When a mutually acceptable list of Ministers has been prepared and has been found to be acceptable to the Governor, the retiring Katikiro will read out the list to the Lukiko and request them, without debate, to vote in favour of the list or against it.

11. This arrangement made by His Highness the Kabaka does not affect Article 10 of the Agreement and, should the process of consultation described above break down or should the Lukiko unreasonably refuse to accept the list of Ministers put forward by the Kabaka, it would naturally be open to His Highness, in accordance with his constitutional right under the Agreement, to proceed to the appointment of the Ministers himself, subject only to the approval of the Governor.

12. Circumstances might arise, although it is to be hoped that they will be avoided, in which there were continuing differences of opinion between the Ministers and the Lukiko amounting to a deadlock. In such a situation it would be open to the Kabaka to exercise the rights which he has under the Agreement, subject to the consent of the Governor, of dismissing the Ministers, or any one of them, or dissolving the Lukiko. Should it be necessary to replace a single Minister, His Highness would consult the delegation of the Lukiko but would not submit the appointment for ratification to a vote of the whole Lukiko.

13. It has been suggested in certain quarters in Buganda that Chiefs should be elected. In the case of the Ministers His Highness is prepared, as has been stated above, to consult with the members of the Lukiko before making the appointments; but Chiefs are in a different position from Ministers. Whereas the latter are the chief political advisers of the

Kabaka and the political leaders in the Lukiko for a fixed period only, the Chiefs are the permanent executive agents of the Buganda Government. Chiefs are in fact civil servants, and it is therefore necessary that their appointment and dismissal should not be subject to any political considerations, but should be vested in the Kabaka in accordance with the standard practice in other countries, subject only in the case of Saza and Gombolola* Chiefs to the approval of the Governor in accordance with the Agreement. It would be inappropriate for the members of the Lukiko to be given a say in the appointment of Chiefs and still more inappropriate for Chiefs to be elected. The Kabaka, the Governor and the Secretary of State are in full agreement on this matter.

15. By these decisions, the responsibilities of the Buganda Government will be much enhanced and the say of the people of Buganda in their government will be greatly increased; but the position under the Agreement will not be altered. The Governor and his advisers will continue to advise His Highness the Kabaka and his Ministers; in particular the Resident and his Assistants will continue to interpret the policy of the Protectorate Government to the Buganda Government and will be ready at all times to offer advice on the development of the country and its institutions. For their part, the Kabaka, his Government and his people will continue to co-operate loyally with the Protectorate Government in the organization and administration of Buganda in accordance with the terms of the Agreement, and will conform to the laws and regulations of the Uganda Protectorate so long as these do not conflict with the Agreement.

16. The Uganda Protectorate has been and will continue to be developed as a unitary state. The Kingdom of Buganda will continue to go forward under the government of His Highness the Kabaka and play its part, in accordance with Clause 3 of the Agreement, as a Province and a component part of the Protectorate.

– from Uganda Protectorate, *Memorandum on Constitutional Development and Reform in Buganda*, Entebbe 1953.

Saza: county.
Gombolola: sub-county.
Muluka: parish.

47. THE DEPORTATION
OF KABAKA MUTESA II, 1953

The Ministers of Buganda to the Governor of Uganda, Sir Andrew Cohen, 6 July 1953.

We have the honour to beg Your Excellency to be excused for addressing Your Excellency direct, a step which is unusual, but which has to be taken by us in His Highness's absence, on his own behalf and that of the people of Buganda, on the strength of the urgency of the matter in question.

Sir, the article which has appeared on the front page of the *East African Standard* issue of Friday of the 3rd July, 1953, is noted with misgivings* and has confused this Government and our people as to the value of the assurances given to us in the name of Her Majesty's Government, on every occasion in the past, when the question of the Federation of the three British East African Territories was proposed, and when the setting up of the East African High Commission was suspected by Africans in Uganda as a stepping-stone towards the realization of a political fusion in the three territories.

Sir, the statement quoted in the article, as made by Her Majesty's Minister, the Secretary of State for the Colonies can not be taken lightly and for that reason we are compelled to state that it is bound not only to shake the foundations of trust among our people, but will also badly damage the good relations which hitherto obtains between the Baganda and the British. Representing His Highness's Government and the people of Buganda, we have to state once again that our attitude towards any such contemplated political fusion is firm, and that it should be communicated to Her Majesty's Government.

Sir Andrew Cohen to Kabaka Mutesa II, 27 July 1953.

Your Highness, I have the honour to refer to the Ministers' letter of the 6th July, addressed to me in Your Highness's absence, on the subject of the remarks made by the Secretary of State recently at the East African Dinner in London regarding the relations of Uganda with the other East African territories. That letter referred to an article which appeared in the *East African Standard* of the 3rd July and I must point out that that article contained not the text of the Secretary of State's speech, but an

---

* This referred to a statement in a speech on 30 July 1953 in which Mr Oliver Lyttelton, Britain's Colonial Secretary, referred to the possibility (at a time when a European dominated Federation was being imposed on Central Africa) 'as time goes on of still larger measures of unification and possibly still larger measures of federation of the whole East African territories'.

interpretation of it by the *East African Standard.* The text of the relevant passage of the Secretary of State's speech appeared in the *East African Standard* of the 2nd July.

As the Resident informed the Ministers on my instructions, I referred their letter to the Colonial Office immediately I received it and I have now been authorized to assure you and the Ministers that you need have no fears in this matter. What will ultimately happen in the future is something which no one can foresee at the present time, and the purpose of the Ministers' letter was no doubt to ascertain the present intentions of Her Majesty's Government. I have been authorized to inform you, as regards the present intentions of Her Majesty's Government, that the Secretary of State's speech did not indicate any change of policy on the part of Her Majesty's Government; that the future development of Uganda and the other East African territories must be largely guided by local public opinion; and that the assurance which I gave to the Great Lukiko in my speech of the 23rd April, 1952, still holds good.

The text of that assurance is:

'Ministers of his late Majesty's Government in London assured you on several occasions that the establishment of the East African High Commission and Assembly was not to be regarded as involving the political fusion or federation of the East African territories. Your Ministers have recently drawn my attention to these assurances and I have informed them that the assurances still hold good.'

I have no doubt that you will regard what I have said above as satisfactory.

Sir Andrew Cohen's Statement in the Legislative Council of Uganda, 11 August 1953.

.... A good deal of interest has been aroused among the public by interpretations placed in the press on some remarks recently made by the Secretary of State in London on the subject of the relations of Uganda with the other East African territories. It is evident that much more has been read into these remarks by the public here than was ever said, much less intended. I have been authorized by the Secretary of State to say that any fears which there may have been in this matter are groundless. What may ultimately happen in the future no one can foresee at the present time; but, as regards the present intentions of Her Majesty's Government, I have been authorized to say that the Secretary of State's speech did not indicate any change of policy in this matter on the part of Her Majesty's Government; that future developments will take local public opinion fully into account; and that the assurance previously given by Her Majesty's Government, which I repeated to the Great Lukiko of Buganda last year, that the establishment of the East Africa High Commission and Assembly is not to be regarded as involving the political fusion or federation of the East African territories, still holds good. In fact there should not be read into the Secretary of State's speech any intention on the part of Her Majesty's Government at the present time to raise the issue of East African Federation.

Kabaka Mutesa II to Sir Andrew Cohen, 6 August 1953.

Your Excellency, I have the honour to acknowledge receipt of your letter dated the 27th July, 1953, in reply to my Ministers' letter on the grave matters in relation to the Federation of the British East African territories, for which letter I thank Your Excellency.

2. My Government has very carefully examined in great detail the assurances embodied in your letter, and have the following comments and claim to make.

3. For some years past, dating from 1922 up to the present the contemplation, and eventually the proposal of bringing the three East African territories into a political federation has, as Your Excellency knows, been causing much anxiety, trepidation, and forebodings to the people of Uganda, and more so perhaps those of Buganda. When the proposal for a federation was sponsored by the Kenya settlers who commanded racially the least proportion of the population in East Africa, a strong opposition, supported with convincing reasons, was put up by the late Kabaka, jointly with his Government in 1930. In fact, a deputation was sent to the United Kingdom to state, before the Parliamentary Committee set up on the Closer Union of East Africa, the reasons against the desirability of such a proposal. Since then many assurances have been given to us by Her Majesty's Government, whenever the proposal arises, through the Secretary of State, among which the following given in the Chief Secretary's letter No. 7153 dated the 18th March, 1922, is typical and sufficient for our present consideration:

'... The Secretary of State for the Colonies has requested that you may be informed that, if it should be decided to make any arrangements for effecting closer co-ordination between the Administrations in East Africa, whether by federation or other means, you may rest assured that no action will be taken involving infringement of the Uganda Agreement of 1900, and that in any event it is not contemplated that the Kingdom of Buganda or the Uganda Protectorate generally should be placed under the jurisdiction of any external legislative body in Eastern Africa, or that the Secretary of State's responsibility for the administration of the Protectorate should be reduced in any way.'

4. All these past assurances leave no shadow of doubt as to the intentions of Her Majesty's Government and, when examined alongside the

assurance given in your letter, at once a conspicuous difference between the past and the current assurances emerges. To be precise, former assurances made by the previous Secretaries of State were never limited to the present, but committed themselves to the future too and definitely excluded the Kingdom of Buganda from any possibility of any future inclusion into such a union, and even went asfar as saying:

'... It is not contemplated that the Kingdom of Buganda or the Uganda Protectorate generally should be placed under the jurisdiction of any external legislative body in Eastern Africa.'

5. By the course of recent events in Central Africa, coupled with an apparent lack of security in the future as portrayed in the latest statements, it is crystal clear that our future has ceased to be guaranteed as had been previously, thus the more our fears and forebodings about the future, for Her Majesty's Government seems to have ceased to embody the element of certainty in the path of our political development, it being apparently concerned only with the present. On a recent visit which I paid to the Colonial Office the Permanent Under-Secretary of State himself, in conversation, stated to me words very much to the effect that the ultimate political future of Uganda was unknown to Government! It is conceded that the future is not easily foreseeable but that is hardly a bar to making plans for that future and working for an objective, however distant that may be. You will, Your Excellency, no doubt appreciate the fact that our fears are not groundless.

6. As it is well known, and according to the framing of the 1900 Agreement, and all other Agreements prior to it, the Kingdom of Buganda is a protected state under Her Majesty's Government and consequently, the said Agreements were ratified by the Foreign Office under whose jurisdiction the affairs of Uganda lay since it was clear from the beginning that Uganda could not be treated as a Colony. But it was in 1902, for reasons not appreciated by the people of Uganda, that its affairs were transferred to the Colonial Office. Thus the status which is now accorded to Buganda is an indication of the direct result of Uganda's transfer to the Colonial Office. This transfer unmistakably reduced the status of the Kingdom of Buganda, in spite of its being a treaty state, to that of a colonial dependence, and Buganda came to be administered and recognized as not different from a colony. The reduction in status was so severe that the Kingdom of Buganda has reached a precarious degree of uncertainty and even insecurity.

7. Your Excellency, as regards the statement which has appeared in your letter, setting out a condition in the event of a political union of the three territories namely that such a union can only come about by the desire and the express of public opinion of the majority of local peoples, my people and Government have this to comment that as stated elsewhere in the foregoing paragraphs, recent happenings in the neighbouring

territories, i.e. Central Africa, have shown that however many there may be Africans opposing a proposal, the wishes of the minority who are generally non-Africans must necessarily prevail, no matter what petitions, deputations and representations are sent to the highest authorities by the Africans. Some African deputations from Central Africa were recently not even shown the courtesy of being received in London, and the federation has merely been imposed upon them however much it goes against their will. It will not be unreasonable to compare the destiny of Uganda to that which has overtaken Nyasaland, both countries being Treaty states, and Protectorates, but Nyasaland has been forced into the Central African Federation. This evidently suggests that local opinion seems to mean the opinion of the least section of the population as long as that section happens to be the most vocal.

8. The White Paper 210 which set up the East African High Commission is another case in point for when it was desirable to sound local opinion, it was the opinion of the Uganda Legislative Council which was sought but the native councils were ignored completely: in fact, the Great Lukiko was forbidden to discuss the proposal at all. What has happened before and elsewhere may happen here: thus the profundity of our present fears.

9. It is hardly necessary to remind Your Excellency that from history we learn that the Kingdom of Buganda was a self-governing Sovereign State, and record at the time of the advent of Europeans, almost 100 years ago testifies to this that they found Buganda an established kingdom, independent, and with its own dependencies. Her Majesty Queen Victoria's Government when requested to protect this country two major Agreements were completed, namely the 1894 Agreement and the 1900 Agreement, the latter amplifying the former and being designed to provide for land settlement, taxation, defence and detailed administration. These Agreements read together are a testimony to what has just been described.

10. No better evidence of the entirety of the Kingdom of Buganda could be produced than that found in those two Agreements. But as soon as the affairs of Uganda were removed from the Foreign Office and transferred to the Colonial Office, the act of transfer simply reduced Buganda's character and subjected it to policies affecting the administration of Crown Colonies. For this reason and in view of the fact that the future of our country is insecure, I am moved to state our immediate and strong desire that the affairs of our country be managed by the Foreign Office as was originally done, and no longer by the Colonial Office. This step will give stronger assurance to us against the possibility of a political union with the adjoining colony and territory.

11. At the same time I must bring to Your Excellency's notice the fact that as it is the policy of Her Majesty's Government to lead countries under its protection to ultimate political independence within the

Commonwealth, we ask Her Majesty's Government to prepare and put into effect a plan designed to achieve our independence and if possible within a short stated space of time. It might be pointed out that the generally accepted colonial theory of partnership will be unacceptable in the plan for Uganda, as has been indirectly refuted by Her Majesty's Government in the declaration of land policy in Uganda by the Governor in 1950, ruling out the possibility of non-African settlement in Uganda. In Uganda, as a Protectorate, co-operation with non-Africans should be the aim.

12. In conclusion, Your Excellency, I beg to state that the views set forth in this memorandum are supported by my Government and my people, and it is my ardent request that they are put before the Secretary of State and therefore to Her Majesty's Government for consideration.

These views are hereunder endorsed by my Ministers. . . .

Sir Andrew Cohen to Kabaka Mutesa II, 27 October 1953.

I have the honour to refer to your letter of the 6th August regarding the relations of the Uganda Protectorate with the other East African territories and to inform you that I duly referred this letter to the Secretary of State for the Colonies as soon as it was received. I subsequently discussed the contents of the letter with Your Highness and your Ministers and during my recent visit to London I discussed the matter with the Secretary of State.

2. The Secretary of State has instructed me to inform you that he has considered your letter with the greatest care and that he fully realizes from its contents and from what I have myself told him the strength of feeling on the part of the people of Buganda on the subject of Federation. Your letter and recent expressions of public opinion in Buganda reveal fears and suspicions about the intentions of Her Majesty's Government in this matter; the purpose of this reply which the Secretary of State has instructed me to convey to Your Highness is to dispel these fears and suspicions and to convince Your Highness and your Ministers, and the people of Buganda, that they are groundless. The Secretary of State attaches the greatest importance to removing these fears and suspicions and he has asked me, as Governor, to do everything in my power to achieve this object.

3. The reply which the Secretary of State has instructed me to make, on behalf of Her Majesty's Government to the points raised in Your Highness' letter falls into four parts. It deals first with past statements on the subject of federation; secondly it contains a further statement by Her Majesty's Government on this subject: while the third and fourth parts of the reply comment on your request that responsibility for Buganda affairs should be transferred from the Colonial Office to the Foreign Office and

your request for the separation of Buganda from the rest of the Protectorate.

4. Past statements on the subject of federation made by or on the instructions of Ministers of Her Majesty's Government have been examined and it has been found that no statement has been made in the past ruling out the possibility of federation for all time. The statement in the letter of the 18th March, 1922, quoted by Your Highness, which was repeated in 1924, specifically referred to the possibility of federation of the East African territories, and it is clear from all the discussions which followed up to 1931, when H.M. Government decided on the advice of the Joint Select Committee of the two Houses of Parliament not to proceed with the matter at that time, that this possibility included the Uganda Protectorate. East African federation, including Uganda, was being actively discussed in 1931, when a deputation from Uganda, including Mr S. W. Kulubya, went to London to give evidence on this subject to the Joint Select Committee.

5. No further statements on the subject are on record until 1945, when proposals were put forward, in paper Colonial 191, for the establishment of an East Africa High Commission and Assembly to deal with certain common services of interest to all three East African territories, in the spheres particularly of communications and research. Colonial 191 stated in paragraph 9 that the proposals then made involved 'neither political closer union nor the fusion of the East African Governments', and gave as the reason for this in paragraph 10 that 'H.M. Government in the United Kingdom have accordingly come to the conclusion after taking the advice of the East African Governors that political federation or fusion in any of the various forms which have been discussed in the last twenty years is not practical politics under existing conditions'. In his statement to Parliament of the 28th July, 1947, Mr Creech-Jones, in announcing that it had been decided to implement the proposals in the subsequent paper Colonial 210, said: 'The scheme is not to be regarded as a step towards political union or the fusion of the East African Governments.' Mr. Griffiths in his statement to the Great Lukiko on the 15th May, 1951, said that the statement that the present inter-territorial organization did not involve the political union of the East African territories still held good. Your Highness will observe that none of these statements ruled out federation for all time and I am instructed in particular to draw your attention to the use of the phrase 'not practical politics under existing conditions' in paragraph 10 of the Colonial 191.

6. In my letter of the 27th July, I informed Your Highness, on instructions from the Secretary of State, that as regards the present intentions of Her Majesty's Government the Secretary of State's speech did not indicate any change of policy on the part of Her Majesty's Government; that the future development of Uganda and the other East African territories must be largely guided by local public opinion; and that the assurance

which I gave to the Great Lukiko in my speech of the 23rd April, 1952, still holds good. I also said in my public statement of the 11th August, again on the instructions of the Secretary of State, that 'there should not be read into the Secretary of State's speech any intention on the part of H.M. Government at the present time to raise the issue of East African federation'. In the view of the Secretary of State this assurance, so far from falling short of past assurances, in fact went somewhat further in that, in addition to ruling out federation at the present time, it stated that future developments must be largely guided by local opinion. It appears to the Secretary of State that you may not have fully appreciated the importance of this part of the statement in my letter of the 27th July. But, in view of the terms of Your Highness's letter, the Secretary of State has decided that it is necessary to amplify the statement and make it more definite. I am accordingly instructed to inform you as follows.

7. Her Majesty's Government has no intention whatsoever of raising the issue of East African federation either at the present time or while local public opinion on this issue remains as it is at the present time. Her Majesty's Government fully recognizes that public opinion in Buganda and the rest of the Protectorate would be opposed to the inclusion of the Uganda Protectorate in any such federation; Her Majesty's Government has no intention whatsoever of disregarding this opinion either now or at any time, and recognizes accordingly that the inclusion of the Uganda Protectorate in any such federation is outside the realm of practical politics at the present time or while local public opinion remains as it is at the present time. As regards the more distant future, Her Majesty's Government clearly cannot state now that the issue of East African federation will never be raised, since public opinion in the Protectorate, including that of the Baganda, might change, and it would not in any case be proper for Her Majesty's Government to make any statement now which might be used at some time in the future to prevent effect being given to the wishes of the people of the Protectorate at that time. But Her Majesty's Government can and does say that unless there is a substantial change in public opinion in the Protectorate, including that of the Baganda, the inclusion of the Protectorate in an East African federation will remain outside the realm of practical politics even in the more distant future. The Secretary of State is confident that you will agree that in this statement he has gone as far as he possibly can and has given you safeguards which cannot fail to be regarded as satisfactory.

8. Having given the firm assurances contained in the preceding paragraph, the Secretary of State feels sure that you need have no further fears on the question of federation. Nevertheless he thinks that you will wish him to comment on the suggestions put forward in paragraphs 10 and 11 of your letter. He does not propose to comment on the remarks about Central Africa in paragraph 7 of your letter, but this must not be taken as meaning that he accepts these remarks.

9. The Secretary of State has asked me to say that your request for transfer of responsibility for the affairs of Buganda to the Foreign Office is evidently based on a misunderstanding. The Foreign Office is responsible for the relations of Her Majesty's Government with foreign countries outside the British Commonwealth. The Colonial Office deals with the affairs of territories inside the British Commonwealth for which Her Majesty's Government is responsible, whether they be Colonies, Protectorates, Protected States or Trust Territories. Your Highness has suggested in paragraph 6 of your letter that Buganda is a Protected State under Her Majesty's Government; but this is not correct in the accepted constitutional sense of the term. Under the terms of the 1900 Agreement Buganda is clearly stated to rank as a province forming part of the Uganda Protectorate (Article 3), a position which has recently been reaffirmed in the joint statement on reforms in Buganda issued by Your Highness and myself last March. Not only Article 3 but other articles made it clear that Buganda was to be merged both fiscally and legislatively into the Protectorate as a whole, and this in fact has been done. The whole tenor of the Agreement made it clear that Buganda was to be part of the Protectorate. Your Highness has referred in paragraph 9 of your letter to the 1894 Agreement as well as the 1900 Agreement. The Secretary of State is advised that it is the 1900 Agreement which must be regarded as the prevailing document and the instrument regulating the relations between Her Majesty's Government and Buganda. The Agreement was freely entered into and has ever since its signature been accepted both by H.M. Government, and by the Buganda Government and people as the document defining their relations with each other.

10. Even were Buganda a Protected State, which constitutionally it is not, its affairs would still be dealt with on behalf of Her Majesty's Government by the Colonial Office, as those of other Protected States within the British Commonwealth are. Your Highness has claimed in paragraph 6 of your letter that the transfer of responsibility for Buganda from the Foreign Office to the Colonial Office in 1902 involved a reduction of status; but this is not correct. As has already been stated, the 1900 Agreement clearly laid it down that Buganda should be administered as part of the Uganda Protectorate. In these circumstances there could have been no alternative but to transfer responsibility to the Colonial Office, a step which in any case logically followed once Buganda came under the protection of H.M. Government.

11. Furthermore the Secretary of State has asked me to point out that, even if it were appropriate to transfer responsibility for Buganda to the Foreign Office, which constitutionally it is not, this would not alter the position regarding federation at all. As far as Her Majesty's Government is concerned it is not any particular Government department or Minister who decides major constitutional issues of the importance of federation in the territories for which Her Majesty's Government is responsible,

whether in East Africa or elsewhere; such major decisions can only be taken by Her Majesty's Government in the United Kingdom as a whole, where necessary with the approval of Parliament. It follows that, since Buganda is under the protection of Her Majesty's Government, it would make no difference as regards federation whether it were dealt with by the Colonial Office or some other department, since the ultimate decision on this matter could only be taken by Her Majesty's Government as a whole. Therefore it is clear first that this request cannot constitutionally be acceded to and secondly that even if it could be this would not achieve what Your Highness has in mind.

12. In paragraph 11 of your letter Your Highness has asked that a plan should be put into effect designed to achieve the independence of Buganda. It is not clear to the Secretary of State from your letter exactly what is meant by 'independence'; but I reported the subsequent discussions which I had with yourself and your Ministers and the Secretary of State understands that you are not asking to go outside the Commonwealth – the wording of the first sentence of paragraph 11 indeed implies that you are not asking this. The Secretary of State also understands that you have informed me during the course of the discussions that Buganda has no wish to leave the protection of Britain. The Secretary of State in fact understands that you were seeking, without leaving the protection of Her Majesty's Government, to safeguard Buganda against the possibility of East African federation in the future, either by separating Buganda now from the rest of the Protectorate or at any rate by removing Buganda from the jurisdiction of the Protectorate Legislative Council.

13. The Secretary of State asks me to say that he is glad that Your Highness does not wish Buganda to leave the protection of Britain because he is sure that this would not be to the advantage of the people of Buganda. Your Highness will no doubt agree that the Baganda have received many benefits from British protection and that the association between the Baganda and the British people has been fruitful over the years and continues to be so. You will also, the Secretary of State is sure, agree that, apart from the many benefits received by the Baganda in the past, there have recently been very significant advances. In the political field there are the reforms announced earlier in the year, under which the people of Buganda will play a greater part in their system of government and the Buganda Government will be given substantial increased responsibilities for the operation of certain services in Buganda. In the economic field important benefits have been brought to the Baganda by the work of the Protectorate Agricultural and Veterinary Departments for the improvement of agriculture and cattle-keeping; by the expansion of the co-operative movement through the efforts of the Protectorate Department of Co-operative Development; and by the cotton and coffee reorganization schemes. In the field of education, to which so much importance is rightly attached by your people, the Protectorate has embarked on a

great programme of expansion both of general and technical education which will greatly benefit the Baganda, while Makerere College is continuing to expand, again to their great advantage. All these are benefits which have been brought to Buganda through its association with Britain and through action on a Protectorate-wide basis. The Secretary of State is therefore sure that Your Highness is right both from the point of view of the present interests of the Baganda and their future interests not to wish to leave British protection.

14. The points which require to be considered, therefore, are whether it would be possible or desirable in the interests of Buganda and its people, and whether it would affect the position regarding federation, either to separate Buganda from the rest of the Protectorate or to remove it from the jurisdiction of the Legislative Council. I have informed the Secretary of State that in discussion with me Your Highness has recognized that both these steps would involve amendment of the 1900 Agreement, since the Agreement lays down in Article 3 that Buganda ranks as a province of the Protectorate and in Article 5 that the laws made for the general government of the Protectorate are applicable to Buganda except in so far as they may be in conflict with the Agreement. Before discussing these suggestions in detail, the Secretary of State feels bound to say that he is surprised that they should have been put forward so soon after you had joined with me in stating at the end of our joint statement on the reforms in Buganda that 'the Uganda Protectorate has been and will continue to be developed as a unitary state. The Kingdom of Buganda will continue to go forward under the government of His Highness the Kabaka and play its part, in accordance with Clause 3 of the Agreement, as a Province and a component part of the Protectorate.'

15. As regards separation from the Protectorate, the Secretary of State seriously doubts whether this would be practicable, even if it were desirable in the interests of your people. Buganda geographically lies at the centre of the Protectorate and economically and in other ways its affairs are completely bound up with those of the Protectorate as a whole. These economic and general ties, reinforced by Buganda's geographical position, have been built up over many years and, in the Secretary of State's view, it would be virtually impossible now to break them down.

16. Nor does he consider that this would be in the interests of the Baganda. In recent years they have been playing an increasing part in the economic life of the country as a whole and they are now entering industries which are established on a Protectorate-wide basis. Your people, with a longer experience of organized government than many of the rest of the people of the Protectorate, are well fitted to play an increaseing part in public life on a Protectorate-wide basis and are in fact doing so. If Buganda, while remaining under British protection, were to be separated from the rest of the Protectorate, Her Majesty's Government would of course continue to do its best to help the Baganda develop in the

political, economic and social spheres. But this would be infinitely more difficult if Buganda were separated from the rest of the Protectorate than it is now. The Secretary of State is convinced that such a separation would gravely upset the economic stability of the country; would seriously interfere with schemes for the economic development of the Baganda and other Africans in the Protectorate which are now being actively carried forward; would reduce the amounts of money available for development and for the advancement of the people; and in a word would completely disrupt all that is now being done to help the Baganda forward. The Secretary of State is certain, therefore, that such a separation would be prejudicial to the present and future interests of the Baganda. Moreover the separation of Buganda from the rest of the Protectorate might well be objected to by some sections of the public in Buganda and particularly the minorities, and might even lead in the case of the minorities to requests for separation from Buganda.

17. On the question of taking Buganda out of the purview of the Legislative Council, while retaining it within the Protectorate, this, in the Secretary of State's view, would be seriously damaging to Buganda's interests. There are many laws of great and sometimes of vital importance to the Baganda which could not be passed by the Lukiko because they affect not only the Baganda but also Europeans and Asians. Notable examples of these are the cotton and coffee reorganization laws; but there are many other examples. If Buganda were taken out of the purview of the Legislative Council laws such as these would have to be applied to Buganda by the Governor by proclamation, and there would be no opportunity, such as is provided by the Legislative Council, for members representing Buganda to take part in the discussion of them, speaking for the interests of the Baganda. Such a situation would be detrimental to the interests of Buganda and would give the Baganda legitimate grounds for complaint that their views were not being properly put forward. In the Secretary of State's view, therefore, it would be wrong to take Buganda out of the purview of the Legislative Council. Indeed the Secretary of State would go further than that and say that the members from Buganda ought to be selected by the Lukiko rather than nominated, seeing that this would link the members with the people whom they represent.

18. It remains to discuss how the separation of Buganda from the Protectorate, or its removal from the purview of the Legislative Council, would affect the position regarding federation. It is evident from what Your Highness has said to myself in discussing this matter that you fear that the Legislative Council could of its own act bring Buganda into a federation; but the Secretary of State has asked me to point out that this is not so. So long as Her Majesty's Government in the United Kingdom is ultimately responsible for the administration of the East African territories, any scheme of federation which might be put forward could only

come into force with the approval of Her Majesty's Government; with Buganda under British protection this would apply whether Buganda was separated from the Protectorate or not. Her Majesty's Government would of course take into account the views of the Legislative Council of the Protectorate, but would also take into account the views of the Buganda Government. Separating Buganda from the rest of the Protectorate or taking it outside the purview of the Legislative Council would not therefore alter the position regarding federation – a position that is in any case safeguarded by the assurances conveyed to Your Highness in paragraph 7 of this letter. In so far as it would affect the situation at all, taking Buganda outside the purview of the Legislative Council would weaken rather than strengthen the position of the Baganda in this matter; for the Legislative Council, with its substantial number of African members, would provide an important mouthpiece for the expression of African opinion should this matter ever be raised. With Buganda members on the Legislative Council, these would have full opportunity to express the views held by the Baganda on this subject; but if they were not on the Legislative Council this opportunity would be lost.

19. For all these reasons the Secretary of State does not agree that the separation of Buganda from the rest of the Protectorate or its removal from the purview of the Legislative Council would be in the interests, either present or future, of the Baganda; nor would either of these steps alter the position regarding federation. The Secretary of State has instructed me strongly to advise Your Highness that the proper course is not to suggest breaking up the Protectorate into separate parts, but to strengthen its unity and to work for its future political, economic and social development. If the Protectorate were to be divided into separate parts, each of these parts would be much weaker economically and in every other way than the Protectorate as a whole; and not only much weaker, but much less able to hold its own in dealings with the neighbouring territories. A strong and united Protectorate rather than weak separate units must therefore be the aim of all our efforts in the interests both present and future of the people of the Protectorate.

Draft telegram from Kabaka Mutesa II to Britain's Colonial Secretary (Mr Oliver Lyttelton), [30 November 1953].

Attended Governor Uganda at his request with my ministers stop presented with document being an excerpt from your communication to Governor demanding my signature certain undertaking as follows:

(1) An undertaking by the Kabaka to accept the decisions of Her Majesty's Government conveyed to him by the Governor in his letter of the 27th October in reply to the Kabaka's letter of the 6th August and confirmed in the statement handed to him by the Governor on the 27th

November in reply to the Lukiko resolution and memorandum of September on the subject of federation. As part of the above, an undertaking by the Kabaka that he will not make any statement opposing these decisions, that he will not by word or deed encourage other persons to oppose them, and that he will inform the Great Lukiiko publicly at the opening of its next meeting that these decisions of Her Majesty's Government must be accepted.

(2) An undertaking that the Kabaka will positively co-operate in the future progress of Buganda as an integral part of the Uganda Protectorate; and a reaffirmation by him of paragraph 16 of the memorandum on Constitutional Development and Reform in Buganda issued jointly by the Governor and him in March, 1953, which reads as follows:

'The Uganda Protectorate has been and will continue to be developed as a unitary state. The Kingdom of Buganda will continue to go forward under the government of His Highness the Kabaka and play its part, in accordance with Clause 3 of the Agreement, as a Province and a component part of the Protectorate.'

As part of this general undertaking, a particular undertaking by the Kabaka to submit names of Baganda members for appointment to the Legislative Council and to inform the Great Lukiiko publicly at the opening of its next meeting that he will submit these names, since he realizes that the Great Lukiiko does not wish to do this itself.

(3) An undertaking by the Kabaka that he will co-operate loyally with Her Majesty's Government and the Protectorate Government in the organization and administration of Buganda in accordance with the terms of the 1900 Agreement and will conform to the laws and regulations of the Protectorate so long as these do not conflict with that Agreement.

Have replied Governor unable to affix signature without consultation with Great Lukiiko stop informed Governor affixing signature nullifying my position with my people and contrary to democratic principles stop grateful early reply as Lukiiko meets shortly.

– from Uganda Protectorate. *Withdrawal of Recognition from Kabaka Mutesa II of Buganda, Cmd. 9028,* H.M.S.O. London 1953.

The British withdrew 'recognition' from Kabaka Mutesa II on 30 November 1953 and deported him by air to London.

48. THE NAMIREMBE
CONSTITUTIONAL CONFERENCE, 1954

Statement by Bishop J. Kiwanuka to the second meeting of the Conference attended by the Governor, Sir Andrew Cohen, 3 August 1954.

Salient features in our Joint Talks with H.E. the Governor

I should like to inform your Excellency of the inner feelings and thoughts of the Buganda nation so that there may be no misunderstandings in the future.

Firstly under the 1900 Agreement Act 5 contemplated Buganda as autonomous in her internal affairs. The principle of repugnancy therein enunciated would otherwise make no sense. The powers of the Buganda Kingdom were to be left unimpaired except where such powers had been expressly surrendered or limited by the terms of the Agreement.

We demand observance of the spirit of the Agreement and the right to make our own mistakes in our own affairs.

Secondly, Buganda is anxious to place the Kabaka outside the storm centre of politics which caused the present crisis.

Lastly, she seeks a solution to the present crisis.

If these three points are settled we shall be able to give to the people a satisfactory account of our work on the Committee.

A Short Historical Review

1. Buganda was never conquered. She asked Britain to protect her until her 'coming of age'. She did not ask to be ruled as a colonial protectorate, but as a unit guided and assisted by the British and as a consideration for this protection the Kabaka and chiefs of Buganda expressly agreed to renounce in favour of Her Majesty the Queen tribute which they formerly exacted from neighbouring territories.

2. As regards her relations with other parts of Uganda, the Baganda would submit that the fact that they ceded their ascendancy over those territories does not mean that they should be placed on the same level with them. In fact in many respects the Baganda are more advanced. I may mention a general fear among the people that in matters of Education there is a deliberate policy to keep the Baganda waiting until the other countries in Uganda shall have reached their present level.

While we agree with Her Majesty's Government over the long-term objectives we submit that the short-term aims should be viewed in the light of the foregoing premises. If the above facts are borne in mind then plainly our requests are not favours or privileges but rather we are asking for what we had before the 1900 Agreement and what falls within the purview of the Agreement. It is time for us to assume full responsibility over our rights.

The Council of Muluka Mutuba I Kabowa, Gombolola of Omukulu we Kibuga, Kyaddondo, to Professor Sir Keith Hancock, Chairman, Buganda Constitutional Committee, 10 August 1954.

We, the undersigned, Members of Muluka Council of Mt: I, in the Gombolola of Omukulu we Kibuga, Kyaddondo, beg to lay before you our submissions as follows:

1. That, our Great Lukiiko's representatives, who had been sent out to the United Kingdom on matters affecting the return of the Kabaka, reported back to the Lukiiko that your coming out here would be the means for the Kabaka's return. On your part, however, you have told us that you had no intention whatsoever of touching on any subject or subjects affecting the Kabaka. We, however, would like to tell you that whatever you and your Committee do, is bound to prove fruitless, unless and until His Highness Kabaka Mutesa II has been returned to us and to his throne of the Buganda Kingdom; because we ourselves do not find him guilty of any crime warranting his deportation. In fact, all of us do still recognize him now as being our only Kabaka. The circumstances under which the Kabaka was deported were no other than his submission of our wishes to the Governor, which is and was one of the former's duties to do, and which he has been doing previously. Still more should you be convinced that whatsoever constitutional changes, that your Committee and yourself, are engaged on can neither be in themselves, nor be recognized, as right, without both the approval and the presence of the Kabaka here in this country. It will be only through the return of the Kabaka that our confidence in the Protectorate Government may be restored.

2. We should like to remind you that the two Agreements of 1894 and 1900, entered into between Great Britain and the Kingdom of Buganda, were negotiated and concluded merely out of mutual friendship, but not as Buganda being the conquered; between a great Nation and a young one, so that Buganda should be given peaceful protection and education. Because of this, Great Britain is not at liberty to deprive us of our rulers by sheer force and against our own consent. Should she resort to such a line of action, Great Britain would not be discharging her obligations to us, as undertaken by her. We therefore do urge for the abolition of whatever sections in the 1900 Agreement, whereby the Protectorate Government is, or may be, vested with any high-handed powers for the dismissal and/or

deportation of Native Rulers and for the usurpation of powers of Native Rulers by direct access to their people.

3. The present two-Government system should be done away with, and be substituted by a single power policy only, assisted by the Protectorate Government, because, it is only by this way that we can learn the ways and means of taking charge of our own Government ourselves. Responsibilities, in as much as they affect Buganda alone, such as over land, hospitals, schools, etc., should, therefore, be transferred to Mengo.

4. We are most strongly opposed to our Kabaka's being made a mere supreme Figurehead for the purpose of imitating European ways and customs, so far as it is within the power of the Great Lukiiko alone to elect and/or depose the Kabaka, should he prove useless to us.

5. We do urge that the ministers be elected in the Great Lukiiko and merely be approved by the Kabaka, similarly, that the matter affecting the Sixty (60) Representatives does remain as it is at present.

6. The present procedure, impoverishing our Government and the Country, should be abolished, inasmuch as it is being deprived of sources of taxation revenues, and since it is by the same procedure that we are denied free access to trade facilities.

7. The Uganda Legislative Assembly should draw its powers from Provincial Administrations. Therefore people from various provinces in Uganda should meet and decide how they want that Assembly to be conducted.

8. We most strongly protest against being annexed to Kenya and Tanganyika and we do not accept in any way that European and Asian immigrants into Uganda, should either be regarded as 'Settlers', nor that they should compete for seats on the Legislative Council, as if they were Africans.

9. We do urge for self-government with the least delay, by reasons of the fact that the British were invited here merely to protect and educate us, but not to assume the powers of conquerors over us.

> – from the minutes and papers of the Buganda Constitutional Committee 1954 in the possession of various of its members.

The Buganda Constitutional Committee met in part of the Anglican Bishop's lodgings on Namirembe Hill, Kampala, from which the subsequent Conference took its name. Sir Keith Hancock, the chairman, was at this time Professor of Commonwealth Studies in the University of London. Bishop Kiwanuka was Catholic Bishop of Masaka – see also No. 58 below.

49. PROPOSED CONSTITUTIONAL REFORMS, 1954

Explanatory Memorandum* issued by the Namirembe Constitutional Conference, 1954, concerning its Agreed Recommendations.

. . . 5. In recent years political development has been going forward in Buganda and the Great Lukiko now has a majority of elected members. The Conference has had to consider how to safeguard the dignity of the Kabaka's office in these circumstances. The Buganda Constitutional Committee decided to recommend that this should be done by placing responsibility for the conduct of public affairs in the hands of the Kabaka's Ministers, so that, if mistakes are made, the Ministers and not the Kabaka himself will bear the responsibility for them. Articles 8 to 11 lay down the methods and procedures by which this purpose is achieved. Each Minister will be individually responsible for the conduct of policy in his own department and the Ministry will together be responsible for the acts of the Kabaka's Government.

6. The Kabaka will formally appoint the Ministry by handing the Ddamula to the Katikiro, in accordance with custom, and by handing to each Minister the seal of his office. Before formal appointment takes place, however, certain things must be done to ensure that the Ministers will be men who possess the confidence of the country. Article 13 establishes a procedure which may appear at first sight to be rather complicated, but in practice the procedure will prove easy to understand and to work. The Lukiko elects, the Governor approves, the Kabaka appoints the Ministry.

7. The arrangements recommended in Article 13 for the formation of a Ministry suit the conditions of the present time, in which political parties are still unformed or in a very early stage of formation. But the arrangements will also remain workable when political parties have been firmly established. However, if and when that time comes, it will be open to the Protectorate and Buganda Governments to consider together whether a different system should be established of finding a Ministry which possesses the confidence of the Lukiko.

8. Great care has been taken to ensure stability of Government. Under the recommendations, a Ministry, like the Lukiko itself, will be appointed for five years. During this period an individual Minister can be dismissed by the Kabaka or the Katikiro only in exceptional cases. Only in exceptional cases (Articles 15 and 16) can a Ministry be obliged to tender its resignation to the Kabaka or be dismissible by the Governor in Council. The former contingency would arise if the Ministry were defeated on a motion of no confidence in an important matter by a two-thirds majority of the whole Lukiko. The latter contingency would arise if a Ministry

failed to accept or to act upon formal advice tendered to it by the Governor in Council, thereby endangering peace, order or good government. The Articles in Chapter II establish a new system of consultation between the Protectorate and Buganda Governments, which will in practice enable them to iron out any difficulties and differences, thus making it unlikely that a situation could arise in which the Governor in Council would have to consider tendering formal advice.

9. The Ministers, in assuming responsibility for the conduct of policy of the Buganda Government, will require the support of a strong civil service; and each of the Ministers will be assisted by a Permanent Secretary (Article 19). Permanent Secretaries and all other civil servants must have both security of tenure and the freedom to carry out their administrative duties without political interference, subject of course to the control of Ministers in matters of policy. It is most important that the appointment, transfer, dismissal and disciplinary control of civil servants should be free from all danger or suspicion of political pressure or influence. For this reason these matters are put into the hands of an Appointments Board, to be appointed by the Kabaka on the advice of the Katikiro and with the approval of the Governor (Articles 21 to 23). The Appointments Board will act in accordance with Regulations drawn up by agreement between the Protectorate and Buganda Governments and will have the power to make decisions on appointments and the other matters concerned. The Appointments Board will be under the chairmanship of the Permanent Secretary to the Katikiro, who will be the Head of the Buganda Civil Service. It will have four other members experienced in public affairs, but not actively engaged in politics. Appointments of Chiefs and Permanent Secretaries to departments will be made by the Kabaka in accordance with the decisions of the Appointments Board, the Governor's approval being required only in the case of Permanent Secretaries, although such approval will not be withheld save in exceptional circumstances.

10. These arrangements for public administration in Buganda will ensure continuity with the past. The Saza, Gombolola and Miruka Chiefs will remain the backbone of public administration and will be given the support of the Protectorate Police which they require for the fulfilment of their responsibilities (Article 24). At the same time the departments of the Kabaka's government at Mengo (including the three new ones that will be set up in fulfilment of the policy agreed upon in March, 1953) will have the reliable staff which they need for the performance of their responsibilities in the future. In Article 42 in Chapter II the Protectorate Government recognizes the need for adequate remuneration of Buganda Government servants in order that officers of the right calibre may be attracted.

11. The Kabaka's Government needs to be efficient. It needs also to keep in close touch with the Lukiko which has elected it and whose confidence it must strive to retain. Members of the Lukiko themselves have a

contribution to make in the formation of policy on such important subjects as finance, education, health, local government, etc. For this reason, Article 27 makes provision for committees of the Lukiko which will meet under the chairmanship of the appropriate Minister and have attached to them the administrative and technical officers who are required for their efficient working. These committees will be advisory. They will in no way detract from the individual responsibility of Ministers for the conduct of policy in their departments or from the general responsibility of the Ministry as a whole. At the same time they will be an effective means both of keeping Ministers in touch with the needs and wishes of the people and of giving elected members of the Lukiko practical knowledge of the business of government. . . .

13. No alteration at all is made in the traditional dignities and ceremonies of the Kingdom of Buganda. The effect of the Articles in Chapter I is to reconcile the high status of the Kabaka with the conduct of a Ministry answerable to a mainly elected Lukiko. Article 4 recognizes the Kabaka as the symbol of unity of the people of Buganda and of continuity between their past, present and future. The other Articles which have been explained above raise the Kabaka above the turmoil and danger of political conflict. New conditions are established which bring the principles of monarchy and democracy into harmony. . . .

23. [In a Statement attached to our Recommendation] the Governor first refers to the declaration by the Secretary of State for the Colonies in the House of Commons on the 23rd February, 1954, that 'the long-term aim of H.M. Government is to build the Protectorate into a self-governing state' and that 'when self-government is achieved the government of the country will be mainly in the hands of Africans'. The Governor then describes the ultimate aim of constitutional development in Uganda as a responsible Government answerable to an elected Leglislature of the whole Protectorate, with proper safeguards in the constitution for the rights of the minority communities resident in Uganda. . . .

25. With regard to the Executive the Governor proposes that a Ministerial system should be introduced; and that seven members of the public, of whom five would be Africans, should be invited to join the Government and to sit on the Government side of the Legislative Council. . . .

26. The Legislative Council [of the Uganda Protectorate] was enlarged early in 1954 and now has fifty-six instead of thirty-two members in addition to the Governor as President. There are twenty African members on the Council as against eight in the previous Council. The Governor now proposes to increase the membership of the Legislative Council to sixty, of whom half would be Africans.

27. On the representative side of the Council the Governor proposes that instead of fourteen Africans, seven Asians and seven Europeans, there should be eighteen Africans, six Asians and six Europeans. Of the four

new African seats two should go to Buganda, provided that the Great Lukiko agrees that Buganda should participate fully in the Legislative Council through elected members. This would increase the number of representative members from Buganda from three to five. . . .

30. The Buganda Constitutional Committee has studied the Governor's Statement carefully and, in the light of the Governor's recommendations to Her Majesty's Government and of the pledge on East African federation referred to in the Statement, has recommended in Article 43 that the Great Lukiko should agree to the representation of Buganda on the Legislative Council of the Protectorate. The Committee has also recommended that the representatives of Buganda should be elected by the Lukiko by secret ballot.

> – from the *Explanatory Memorandum issued by the Namirembe Conference* [*1954*].

This Memorandum was explanatory of the Conference's *Agreed Recommendations* which were published at the same time. These formed the basis for the Buganda Agreement 1955.

50. MANIFESTOES OF THE POLITICAL PARTIES
1950s

Freedom Charter and Manifesto of the Uganda National Congress by the President-General, I. K. Musazi [*1952*].

The rising tide of nationalism and the will and struggle for freedom has, during the last fifteen years, resulted in the creation of some Asian and African Countries into independent nationhood.

Uganda, today, is marching towards that goal of freedom which has been achieved by more fortunate nations. It is, therefore, incumbent that the peoples of Uganda must display the same loyalty in the fight for freedom as the other nations did. Petty bickerings and personal aggrandizement are elements which are ultimately capable of dynamiting the will and struggle for independence.

This independence cannot be achieved either by words or violence, but must be achieved by deeds and negotiations on parliamentary basis. Independence and freedom are not slogan words, but are conditions of Nationhood that should bring Peace and Plenty. Freedom must bring with it the realization of national responsibility to one and all of Uganda's peoples and the desire for hard work in order to maintain it on a progressive level in this fast moving civilization of the Atomic Age.

Freedom is the birthright of all peoples irrespective of colour or Race; a right to choose their own Government which would guarantee the human rights of peoples to choose and practice any religion, trade or occupation, to protect the sanctity of the Home and to respect individual liberty and parliamentary opposition. In short, a Government which will seek to do the greatest good for the greatest numbers, irrespective of Race, Colour or Creed.

In order that Uganda may be blessed with an atmosphere conducive to the formation of such a Government (of the people, by the people and for the people) that the Uganda National Congress enters its political arena with a will to instil the spirit of the equality of man and to seek, by democratic methods of negotiation, the independence for the peoples of Uganda; so that Uganda may achieve its goal of independent nationhood and at the same time, may contribute her strength and support to the larger struggle for world peace, tolerance and understanding between nations.

It is hoped that the peoples of Uganda will become more alive to the needs of the nation in the struggle for independence and contribute their support to the efforts of the Uganda National Congress in the achievement of freedom which is the greater glory of the nation.

Aims and Objects of 'Uganda National Congress'

The primary object of this Congress is to devise ways and means to foster goodwill, understanding and unity among the peoples of Uganda with the ultimate aim of obtaining a democratic self-government for its peoples.

The Congress will serve to unite all democratic forces against dangers of undemocratic ideologies foreign to the nature of its peoples; and at the same time will enable members to demonstrate in a practical and peaceful manner its policy for the solution of the problems of the country.

This Congress believes:

(a) That Uganda belongs to all its peoples irrespective of caste, colour, creed or tribe; and that no Government can justly claim authority unless it is dependent on the will of its peoples from whom it draws its authority to govern.

(b) That liberty, peace and unity must be restored to the peoples of Uganda in order to enable the Country to evolve a Government of the people, by the people and for the people; which alone can secure peace and plenty for its peoples.

(c) That the country cannot be free and prosperous until such time as all our peoples decide to live in a spirit of brotherhood and enjoy equal rights and opportunities.

(d) That peaceful transference of power from the Colonial Office to the peoples of Uganda is of paramount importance and it is, therefore, essential that a system of such peaceful transference should be worked out.

In view of the democratic beliefs of this Congress, we the peoples of Uganda, through this Congress, pledge ourselves to strive together, irrespective of caste, colour, creed or tribe; for the welfare and political independence of Uganda in a spirit of brotherhood and equality.

This Congress is further pledged to contribute towards creating peaceful conditions for the achievement of independence and peaceful transference of power; and to work and contribute towards the creation of a democratic Government which will:

1. Recognize the rights of adult men and women to vote.

2. Entitle all peoples to take part in the administration of the country on the qualification of ability alone.

3. Guarantee equal status in the bodies of state, Judiciary, Educational and other Institutions for all peoples, irrespective of caste, colour, creed or tribe.

4. Protect individual lives and property.

5. Defend and safeguard the sanctity of the Home and individual liberty and practice any religion, trade or profession without fear or favour.

6. Recognize equality of man before the law.

7. Recognize rights of individuals and parties to democratic Parliamentary opposition.

8. Encourage trade, agriculture, mining and industry and recognize rights of free enterprise.

9. Recognize rights of working men and women to form Trade Unions.

10. Recognize the necessity of and provide free medical aid and primary education.

11. Encourage activities for the discovery and development of national talents in the realms of Science, Art and Culture.

12. Prohibit Child Labour and set up Model Schools for the teaching of trades.

13. Maintain the Judiciary free from any political or administrative influences.

14. Recognize the freedom of all nations, the aspirations of Subject nations and work for the furtherance of the human rights as outlined in the United Nations Charter.

The Progressive Party Manifesto 1955.

When King Mutesa I was asking the explorer H. M. Stanley to send him missionaries to teach him and his people, he said that he was in darkness and that he was like a blind man and what he needed most was to get light.

It was that light which King Mutesa I invited which became a torch to Uganda. But Uganda will not be contented with only a torch light; she needs the full lumination from within. It is the greatest aim of the Progressive Party to see that Uganda gets the full light:

> The Light of knowledge;
> The Light of trade;
> The Light of progress.

Anyone who bothers to read what follows in this memorandum, will find that we have no other objective except to fulfil that longing which Mutesa I had for his country – full development.

It is now 80 years since Mutesa I said those words. But Buganda had existed for generations long before him as a sovereign state. It had never known any foreign rule, and when Mutesa I invited missionaries he never realized that in the end it would mean surrender of his and his neighbours sovereignty. It was left to his descendants to discover rather too late that they were under colonial rule.

Mutesa I asked for light for a sovereign state. No state can attain the full light under a foreign domination. Consequently, unless we overthrow colonialism first, we can never hope to comprehend that light fully. That is why the PP is determined to lead Uganda to self-government at an early date. . . .

The New Uganda

I: The Kabaka's Deportation

The past two years have been for Buganda, and indeed for the whole of Uganda, her greatest hour. The Kabaka was deported by the British without trial and without his country knowing the cause for such humiliation. The decision was 'final'.

The Country reacted as any self-respecting country would react – the people spoke with one loud and firm voice that this they would not allow and that return he must. Many also believed that God would not allow injustice to prevail. In the end the Kabaka *returned*.

In this situation three things stood out prominently:

(1) Unity
(2) Faith in ourselves
(3) The traditional spirit of 'Obuntubulamu' (the most respected behaviour of a human being) of the Baganda which won them universal praise throughout the world.

These three things are important in the struggle for self-government of any country.

2. What we have learnt

We have learnt three great lessons:

(1) Dignity is more rewarding than mere shouting (Obubambaavu).

(2) Violence is not the best means of getting what you want.

(3) We ourselves can solve our problems provided we respond to leadership. These are great lessons.

The Kabaka's sacrifice has given us, too, a new agreement which will determine the pattern of our constitutional progress during the next six years.

3. The next stage

The next stage is all important. What happens now sets the pace of achieving self-government. This is time for hard work. The effort we put in fighting for the return of the Kabaka must not be allowed to flag; the lessons learnt must spur us to further effort for the building of a new Uganda.

But to build a new Uganda we need new methods. A party system throughout the country is one of the answers. Democracy, which all of us want and must have, cannot function except by means of organized parties.

Political parties are based on differences of temperament and habit of mind. Some people by nature are fond of affecting change by shouting and violence; others prefer working in a different way.

4. The Government of the People

We give this Memorandum to the public from the belief that if people are to be saved from whatever danger that threatens them, whether it be the degrading evils of colonialism or the social scourge of poverty, ignorance and disease, they will in the last analysis save themselves through their own indigenous power, pride and responsibility. If outsiders are to be helpful, their help must take the form of friendly and unobtrusive support.

We will see Uganda run by 'a government of the people for the people' (Gavumenti y'abantu erwana okuyamba abantu baayo).

II: The Progressive Party

A party working for progress toward the building of a new self-governing Uganda.

Progress towards self-government in Uganda can only be achieved if three things obtain namely: leadership in self-help, education and economic development of the African. By education is not merely meant schooling, but the wider sense of the word, which the Baganda called 'Okugunjula'. It is the aim of the Progressive Party to give the country these things.

A. *Self-Government*
1. To achieve and maintain the Independence of Uganda as an African State, under a federal Government.
2. To be the vanguard of action in influencing affairs of national survival (e.g. the return of the Kabaka).

B. *Progress for the African*
1. To serve our people to serve themselves.
2. To secure political responsibility for the African to guarantee his economic and other freedom.
3. To raise the standard of living of the African by providing for him means of access to knowledge, wealth and health.
4. To keep the best in African culture and the traditional rights of the African.
5. To gain women a vote and to see that they stand for election to the Lukiko and the different councils and to the Legislative Council.

C. *Greater Uganda*
1. To safeguard the liberties of all the inhabitants of Uganda.
2. To ensure that Federation with the other East African territories is not imposed on Uganda.
3. To work with other progressive movements in Africa and other countries with the view to putting to an end imperialism and colonialism and to support all measures for world peace. . . .

Our Philosophy

Our philosophy is progress through directed self-help. The progressive aim at giving their country their utmost for the highest improvement of their lot and the lot of the society they live in. Action not words.

All progress is the result of sustained action, either by an individual or by a group. Where people work and work hard there is progress; where they idle or simply enjoy life, society is dead. Work, therefore, is the key to progress, knowledge and wealth.

In man there are two voices: the voice that tells him to languish; and the voice that urges him to action, to getting on in life by sacrificing easy pleasures and easy time and giving his life to doing something worth while. The latter is the voice of progress. In losing his life by giving it away to some useful purpose man finds his true existence and happiness. Knowledge and wealth are never gained except through hard work. Knowledge and wealth coupled with sacrifice are prerequisites of progress both individual and social.

Secondly, there is in man a spirit that revolts against outside fetters. The progressive rebel against outside interference with their freedom. Their aim in life is to be independent. Knowledge and wealth are means to this end. And this is true independence, to do to each man as you would each man to you.

But the man is free from outside fetters only, within him there is a Higher Authority, the obedience of whom is the beginning of true freedom.

Thirdly, self-government starts with the freedom of the individual. Until men are free with themselves, they cannot be stewards of the freedom of others.

Self-government is the expression of the will of the free. Those who would participate in the running of the affairs of their country must needs aim at achieving their individual freedom first; that way they can guarantee best the freedom of the state.

To help propagate these ideas the Progressive Party came into being.

Our Motto

'Ffenna ku lwa Uganda' (all for the good of Uganda). . . .

V: Political Organization

One of the distinguishing marks of the people of Uganda was the idea of co-operation. People co-operated to do work for the common good in every walk of life. In agriculture, they co-operated to plant together and to harvest together. In business, they made bark-cloth and blacksmith work together. In social life, they made wells and roads together and they married their sons and daughters in this spirit of co-operative effort. We could produce many other examples but these are enough to show how people were accustomed to do things in this magnificent way. Even defence was done co-operatively. An alarm was enough to summon all the people in the neighbourhood and passers-by to come to the rescue of any one in need. There were social sanctions against people who did not respond to the community need of this kind.

With the introduction of Western ideas, this fine spirit died until today people are helplessly suffering social and economic uncertainties which were not known in the old days.

What is required is to revive this idea by the interplay of social, political and economic thinking. This can be done by a new orientation of power. Instead of imposing power from above let us have it originate from below from the people themselves, from each individual in his locality.

The Kiganda proverb, 'Kamu-kamu gwe muganda' (one by one makes a bundle) is very fitting here. We want each individual contribution to the progress of our different localities. We wish each person to feel the pride of being useful to the community in which he lives. It is these isolated local prides when put together that constitute community spirit and the sense of belonging. Isolated local communities make society, and the different societies with one idea running through them make a country.

'One by one makes a bundle' – several small bundles of sticks make a bundle of firewood and bundles of firewood make a heap. We need to base our social, political and economic thinking on this idea. . .

The following is the plan which the Progressive Party is prepared to put into effect as soon as they come into power. They are prepared to decentralise power and take it to the smallest unit. Here is the plan:

1. The Unit – the Omuluka

The unit of political organization shall be the Omuluka.

There will be local government, with limited powers, for each Muluka so that each individual can have the chance to play a part in the running of his immediate affairs, the idea being to revive the old custom of working together for the common good.

There will be a Muluka Council to which the people of the Muluka will elect their representatives to run the affairs of that Muluka according to the powers that will be granted by law to such council. The Muluka Chief will only be the executive head who carries out the decisions of the Council and who links the Muluka with the outside world.

2. The Bundle – the Ssaza

The Ssaza will be the next step above in local government. The Gombolola will remain for administrative purposes, but without a political set-up. Each Ssaza will have its local government as practised at the present time in the districts. Each Ssaza will have a Council of elected members from the Ssaza. By law each Ssaza will be designated what powers it must exercise and what functions it must do for the good of their Ssaza.

3. The Bigger Bundle – the State

To start with there will be twelve states: Buganda, Bunyoro, Ankole, Toro, Busoga, Kigezi, Bugishu, Teso, Lango, Acholi, Arua and Karamoja. Later we believe there will be more than 12 states in what will be known as 'the Great Uganda'.

Each state will have its own Lukiko, Rukurato, Isingiro, etc., as the case may be. By a written agreement each state will carry out certain responsibilities as a state and leave the rest to the Central Government (see below). Each state will be independent of the other states. The meeting ground will be the Central Government.

4. The Great Bundle – the United States of Uganda

Size in this matter does not matter; what matters is identity. The different states will be united under a Central Government. The Central Government will replace what is generally called the Protectorate Government or the British Government. This will be a government of the people of Uganda, by the people of Uganda for the people of Uganda. That is self-government.

The Central Government will have a Parliament and a Senate or a Lower House and an Upper House. The Parliament (Lower House) will be the House of Representatives from each state, elected on a strict population basis. The Senate (Upper House) will be on the basis of equality of the different states. As to the nature of the members of the Senate it will be left to the states to decide. But this second chamber will be necessary as a protection for smaller states, since all the states are varying in size.

There will be a Council of Ministers or a Cabinet, with a Prime Minister as head of the Government. . . .

VII: Epilogue

1. That then is the new Uganda as we invisage it and what we propose to do to bring it about. But it is the people themselves, you and I and he and she, who can determine all this. If you take part in solving problems of your destiny you will be able to achieve these things.

Hence the need of decentralizing power and spreading it to the people themselves. It is this which has done wonders in other countries.

2. We wish to appeal to our people to develop the spirit of love of country, which alone is the first requirement and not to think of themselves first and what they can get. The true test is not what you can get out of your country but what you can give to it. That is what has made our countries great. But here in Uganda, people are often heard saying that so and so joined such and such a party or is doing public service because he wants to become the Katikkiro or a big chief. That is the wrong attitude altogether to take. We must join public service because we want to serve our country and people; because we want to give some of the gifts which God has given to us back to Him through service to our fellowmen, to whom in turn we owe so much for our existence. Our existence is inter-dependent. We exist as a result of the work of other people. We need to do the same to them. The more we are given the more is required of us.

We want those who are prepared to serve their country and their fellowmen. If it is necessary for some people to get into important positions let it be because these important positions offer greater opportunities of service; let no one aspire to such positions for gain.

3. In ending we wish to emphasize that this, the contents of this memorandum, is what we of the Progressive Party have to offer to the country if we are voted into power; it is our set policy. Such ideals cannot be realized by any party unless it is in power and no party can get into power unless all the people who hold the same beliefs of ideals support it.

After reading this memorandum, if you find that what it has to offer is what you would like this country to have, your first duty is to join the Progressive Party at once and add to its strength to determine the acquisition of these things. The Party depends on your support, and your support means that Uganda gets the government of its own choice, gets more schools for her children, more food for her population, more wealth, more knowledge, more jobs for her citizens and above all more freedom. These are things which all countries need. They are yours and your children's if you join the Progressive Party.

> – the first item is from I. K. Musazi, *Uganda National Congress – Freedom Charter and Manifesto* [no date], and the second from *Self-Government for Uganda: An African State Manifesto by the Progressive Party*, 1955.

51. ATTITUDE TO ASIANS, 1955

Statement by Mr S. M. Sekabanja, Chairman of the Executive of the Uganda National Congress, 5 July 1955.

Mr Sekabanja said that the congress had affirmed that Uganda was an African state. They believed it not to be enough for an immigrant simply to make his home here without identifying himself with the country. Identification meant abandoning political allegiance to the country of origin and abandoning its culture, as well as the intention of returning to it. Put positively, it meant that Asians and Europeans who intended to stay must associate themselves in a fusion of life and customs with Africans and become in a sense white Africans and brown Africans.

Africans already had rights in Uganda; Asians and Europeans had yet to be granted them. Therefore the congress demanded that the representative side of the Legislative Council should now be wholly African and that they should then consider the qualifications for citizenship required of members of other races. Mr Sekabanja said he was not in a position to state what, in the view of congress, these qualifications might be, but his personal opinion was that, though communal rights in schools, hospitals, and politics should be abolished immediately, special African rights in land should be maintained for 15 or 20 years.

The congress demanded that the principle of the common roll should be granted now, though they recognized that it would not be drawn up until the question of citizenship had been settled, as they demanded by African representatives. Mr Sekabanja said that, though the Asians and Europeans had each given up one seat on the Legislative Council and, apparently, one seat each on the Executive Council, as they had no right to these seats on communal grounds, the changes were of no significance and Africans were not impressed. He saw no objection to the election on their merits of European and Asian Citizens, but he thought that Europeans would adapt themselves more easily than Asians.

– from *The Times*, 6 July 1955.

52. BUGANDA ALONE

Letter from K. Nagawa to the Uganda Argus, *9 July 1957.*

The present controversy about the position of the Supreme Ruler for Uganda and the position of the African Rulers would have been funny were it not a revelation of the mental infancy of some of the writers.

Buganda is always playing a lone game in the field of Uganda development in all spheres. It is the Baganda who have striven to broaden the outlook of all Uganda natives about the possibility of self-government and eventual independence for Uganda. All or nearly all, the other tribes simply look on; they are always the 'good boys', the spectators of the game!

One does not wish to blow one's trumpet but I am sure no one would argue that were it not for the labours, imagination and ambition of the Baganda, the economic position of East Africa would have been so low that there would be no substantial revenue to run any of the ungrateful tribes for one year.

What the Baganda get from their neighbours are simply sneers and abuse. If the Baganda had not been sensible and far-seeing enough to make friends with the pioneer Europeans, where would the other tribes in Uganda be? Which of any Native Rulers had such sense as our Kabaka Mutesa I to invite the British when he realized that his people needed it? Did not the other Kings only choose to fight the pioneer Europeans?

All the people who now have nothing for Buganda but abuse and ingratitude would only open the eyes of some Baganda who are still blind to the fact that Buganda should and can stand on her own feet. It appears to me, and it will appear so to many Baganda now, that the newly formed political party known as the Baganda Party, which advocates independence for Buganda alone, has come in the right time. Let Buganda forge ahead alone. When she achieves her independence, perhaps the other tribes will realize their dilemma. If any of the other tribes feel that Buganda is a hindrance to their growth, they can please themselves. They can fight for their independence without our interference.

Buganda has carried on alone for the last thousand years and can carry on alone for the next thousand years . . .

. . . Our Kabakas and their people have made considerable contribution to the well-being of Uganda and yet even some Baganda have the cheek to suggest that the Kabaka will have to share their position with the other rulers in the so-called 'Council of State'. If other rulers and their people do not want to share the pains and burdens of achieving self-government, why should they be willing to share the fruits of other people's labours?

– from *Uganda Argus*, 9 July 1957.

53. CROSSING THE RUBICON

Letter from Abu Mayanja to the Uganda Argus [*6 March 1958*].

The threat by the Kabaka's Government to sabotage direct elections for Legislative Council in Buganda is so full of ugly possibilities for the future that it is high time somebody did some very straight talking to the reactionary elements in Buganda who seem to imagine that somehow Buganda can contract out of the 20th century, and revert to a system of administration when the efficiency of guns used to be tested on human beings.

These elements are seeking to block the development of democracy in Buganda whilst pretending to pay lip-service to its principles. An example of this was the attempted intimidation of Makerere students by the Lukiko speaker when the former demonstrated against the reject of direct elections to the Lukiko. The Katikiro's admonition of those who dared to criticize the speech from the Throne is another pointer in the same direction. So, too, is the recent statement by the clan leaders threatening those joining political parties with expulsion from the clans. Nor is it purely coincidental that leaders of the political parties have been subjected to a spate of denigration and prosecutions – only to be acquitted after their reputations had been tarnished. Sir, it is not at all fanciful to see in these and other instances the presence of a plan not only to sabotage democracy within Buganda, but also to seek to entrench the anti-democratic system by cutting Buganda from the rest of Uganda where it might be subjected to democratic influences. I am not saying that it is wrong for anyone to be against democracy; the world is only too full of examples of anti-democratic regimes. What I am pleading for is that we should recognize these facts for what they are. I am also appealing to those who think in this way to come out in the open and tell the country exactly what they believe in.

If they want Buganda to go back to the 18th century, with the Kabaka ruling through hand-picked men and clan heads, let them say so – they owe it to the country to speak the truth. I also think that the notion that the Kabaka's Government – which is but part of the Government of Uganda – can defy the latter is a matter so grave that it must be clarified and the correct position authoritatively stated.

There is grave responsibility which these events cast on the Protectorate Government. There is obviously a clash of objectives between those who want to see a democratic system developing in Buganda, and those who do not.

It would be dangerously tempting for the Protectorate Government either to observe a benevolent neutrality, or to play off one faction against the other. I hope the Protectorate Government will realize that it has a duty to pursue with vigour those policies calculated to fulfil Britain's mission in her dependencies – to take Uganda to democratic self-government.

I hope that the Government will take this attitude not only in the full confidence that history is on its side, but also with the knowledge that it has the unstinting support of the overwhelming majority of the educated Baganda who will struggle tooth and nail to resist the reimposition of feudal tyranny based on the debasement of the human personality and the vagaries of the so-called customary law.

I should like to warn our reactionary rulers that they are running a great danger of discrediting our traditional institutions, and thus making it impossible for many of us to reform and adapt what is good in them to the conditions of modern life.

I also wish to address a word of warning to the forward-looking, educated Baganda. I think we intellectuals (yes, though some people may laugh at this word) – I think we intellectuals have been much too timid so far. I think we have allowed ourselves the luxury of sleeping in strange beds for too long; I think we have compromised our position much too much; I think it is not too soon for us to declare from the hilltops what we believe in.

Speaking for myself I have crossed the Rubicon. I have set my face firmly against any autocracy whether it be foreign and imperialist or native and feudal. I stake my future and dedicate my life to the realization of democratic principles in my country no matter from which side the obstacles may emanate. This is a declaration of political faith, and I call on other intellectuals to do likewise.

– from *Uganda Argus*, 6 March 1958.

54. 'POPULISM' IN BUGANDA

Statement by some people of Wankulukuku on 'reasons for failure of political parties in Buganda' [no date, late 1950s].

Why do Parties break up now and again in Uganda; so that people do not place their confidence in them, particularly in Buganda? Here in Buganda they have been built on one foundation: that of the foreigners in blood, social behaviour and their origin; together with the sheer lust for power. When they sit at their tables, they consider what they will give to the omukopi [commonman], while the latter merely follows them blindly, so that he is turned into a stepping stone for achieving their aims.

It is God's mercy that we have remained intact as a Nation up to this time. It is because we the abakopi in blood, social behaviour and our origin, have 'Olukiiko'* of the abakopi in our hearts which prevents us from being diverted and removed from our Kabaka. If only the 'olukiiko' which is inside our hearts should be properly organized and brought to the fore during this difficult time surrounding us, so that we can prepare ourselves for the problems that will arise from [the implementation of] the Bill concerning Direct elections, thereby saving ourselves from the wolves which desire to destroy completely our nation as well as its hereditary kingship.

You know very well that we the abakopi are the source of light which has no envy, selfishness, conceit, hatred or lust for power in the country. Even those big men referred to above who are bursting with the ambition to lead the political parties, ought to know first that we abakopi are the voice of the people who will elect only those who have the necessary qualifications for safeguarding our nation and its hereditary kingship.

We, the people of Wankulukuku, have brought up publicly this matter to the people at the appropriate time when it can be understood. Moreover, the right to elect our own representatives is imminent. But you the omukopi what is your attitude? Will you allow yourself to be coerced by the people we have talked about above, the leaders of the political parties; or rather, should not the 'olukiiko' of the omukopi be the one to choose those who ought to lead you? This is not something like a newspaper which you read and simply throw away, but you must establish the proper foundation upon which you will build your nation and your Kabaka – we must weigh and consider carefully among all those people as well as among ourselves so that, in order to get a strong foundation for our nation, we elect leaders who will protect our nation and our hereditary kingship.

> we the undersigned
> G. Musoke; M. Musisi; A. Sembuya; S. Ndege
> On behalf of our friends.
> – from a translation of *Agafa Ebuganda* –
> *Kabaka Yekka* 1961.

Olukiiko: 'spirit of', or 'an understanding' between, the peasantry; a kind of code commonly shared by them, which, the letter implies, seems to be lacking among other social classes in Buganda, particularly the politicians or the 'big' men.

55. BOYCOTT AND THE UGANDA NATIONAL MOVEMENT, 1959

The plan of campaign: the 'Tree of Liberty' meeting, 28 February 1959.

A one-year 'boycott' of non-African shops outside the main towns; and of cigarettes, beer and buses is being planned by the newly formed Uganda National Movement, Mr Augustine Kamya, chairman of the movement, announced at a meeting held under the 'tree of liberty' in Kampala on Saturday.

The motive of the boycott, Mr Kamya explained, was to show by 'positive action' that the people wanted immediate self-determination. The meeting was described as the largest political meeting ever staged in Kampala. It lasted for several hours.

[Mr Kamya said] A new chapter in the history of political development in the country had been started. Confusion, petty differences and hatred had ended and were being replaced by unity, harmony and goodwill among Uganda Africans.

With the formation of UNM the road to self-rule had been paved, Mr Kamya said. The UNM was determined to lead the people to the long desired goal, which was freedom.

[Mr A. D. Lubowa] demanded that Asians 'declare' on what side they were fighting. He said it was no good for them to 'sit on the fence' waiting for the outcome of the African political struggle.

Uganda would get self-government, he said, and added that a difficult future would await the Asians if they did not identify themselves with the Africans.

[Mr Kamya] said the aim was to 'remove Asians from the villages and to bring trade into the hands of Africans'. He said Asians would be 'forced into the big towns' where again they would be subjected to further African pressure.

The meeting ended with singing *kitibwa kya Buganda*, the Buganda anthem, with all the people facing Mengo and their hands raised up.

Mr Kamya said that tribal anthems throughout the protectorate will be sung facing the tribal centre of administration.

E. M. K. Mulira's apologia, 'Why I am in the Uganda National Movement', to his 'English friends', May 1959.

It must have troubled a lot of my English friends to hear that I am in the Uganda National Movement. I am writing not to apologize for it but to try to clear away some misunderstandings.

Perhaps the British with your background of nearly a thousand years without undergoing foreign domination are incapable of appreciating the mental and psychological pressures and stresses and strains subject people experience as a result of colonialism and imperial rule. Therefore, excuse me to paint the following picture which may not please you, but which none the less must be known.

The study of colonial history reveals that you as a nation betray your best friends – the Busia's (I am using Dr Busia of Ghana as an example) of the colonial Empire. Whenever there has been any colonial struggle there have been the Busias, men and women who have tried to uphold the way of life you taught them against the tide of nationalism of their own people. These have been the moderate elements everywhere. What has happened to them? Because the colonial struggle is a national struggle to the nationals, the nationalists speak with one voice which rouses national sentiment. Hence they command a following of the masses. Then they toss you about, and in turn you put them into prison, you deport them but in the end you listen to their demands and you give in to them, and henceforth these nationalists run the country. Then you begin to shower praise on them and to claim them as your best friends. This has been the case from George Washington to Nkrumah and Archbishop Mackarios.

No sooner had agreement been reached between Great Britain and Cyprus than the British Press started showering praises over the Archbishop! The 'Observer' wrote his profile and claimed that there was a possibility of counting upon him as a friend in the Middle East. (I praised him at a public meeting in Kampala on purpose after reading about this praise in your Press).

What about the moderates who advocated the cause you taught them, the Busia's of America, India, Burma, South Africa, Egypt, Gold Coast, Nigeria, Cyprus, etc.? Here I do not mean the stooges or the 'Yes-men' of the colonial Empire, but the people with a moderate Programme.

During your time in the colony you never listen to the demands they make because they lack a following and you only listen to force – and yet the very fact that they pursue a policy that approximates very nearly to your own, they are regarded by their own people as traitors to the cause and, therefore, their enemies. Therefore, after your withdrawal you leave them to suffer an indefinite opposition from their own people. Dr Busia will die in opposition not because Dr Nkrumah is opposed to him but because the majority of the nation do not accept him as one of them. If the Government had listened to the quiet counsels of such people, before it was too late, perhaps they would have commanded a following by sheer example that it paid to be moderate, but under a British Government it never pays to be a moderate. Hence the despair of the Busia's both before and after Independence.

I will come to my own case now. I think no one who has followed my public life during recent years, can accuse me of not having stood for what is right as I know it; of trying to uphold the Christian viewpoint and democracy. I have been a moderate all along, but with what result? – frustration and disappointment at every turn.

After fighting so hard with my friends in the London delegation and in the Namirembe Conference to bring about a peaceful settlement of the Kabaka's crisis, I met Mr Lennox Boyd in Kampala soon after the Namirembe Conference, and told him that we moderates were leading the country at that time, but if they did not allow the Kabaka to return quickly the extremists would throw us out saying that we had failed, and they would assume the leadership.

Weeks passed, then months before any decision was made, and the extremists jumped at us and threw us out. Then the British Government conceded to them demands which we had made with earnestness in the conference but which were denied us. Thus they emerged heroes at the expense of what we had done. Ever since then they have been winning laurel after laurel. On the other hand we have been making in my party suggestion after suggestion for the good of the country, but we have never been listened to, and because our language has been closer to that of the Government and our tactics moderate we have been misunderstood by our own people as pro-British and in Government 'pay', and, therefore, their enemies. As far as we could ascertain we should spend all our days in opposition; and not in an official opposition in Parliament, but in opposition in the wilderness, because the two elections showed that they would not even accord us a seat.

'Ye are the salt of the earth. . . .' Salt is only useful if it mixes with food; salt apart from food is no use (except perhaps as medicine). Therefore, at this juncture we saw that without trying to change our principles why not take a plunge and mix with the masses and try to speak to them from within and speak to Government from a point of mass support which means strength instead of one of isolated moderation which it regards as weakness. Therefore, it was change of tactics and not of principles and it worked. The moment we did this we were accepted, and the masses can now listen to our counsels where before they frowned at and rejected us wholesale.

Here I would like to use the words of Dietrich Bonhoeffer:

'Some seek refuge from the rough-and-tumble of public life in the sanctuary of their own private virtue. . . . Only at the cost of self-deception can they keep themselves pure from the defilement incurred by responsible action. . . . Who stands his ground? Only the man whose ultimate criterion is not in his reason, his principles, his conscience, his freedom or his virtue, but who is ready to sacrifice all these things when he is called to obedient and responsible action in faith and exclusive allegiance to God. The responsible man seeks to make his whole life a response to the question and call of God.'

It is true you read of the Movement of such things as the boycott and what is said at public meetings by individual speakers. What goes on behind the scene is never heard of by the outside world. We may not be listened to every time in the Movement, then we have to abide by the majority vote – that is democracy. And if we must be in opposition it is an opposition that is within and not out in the wilderness, where nobody listened to us.

It is true there is the danger of compromising sometimes, but then one cannot have everything one's way.

Ever since I came back from Caux in Switzerland last year, I have been working to bring about unity in the country by forgetting past differences and showing that the so-called traditionalists and the politicians could work together. We formed the Uganda National Movement to that effect. I publicly forgave all my enemies and showed them willing hands of friendship and I asked for forgiveness myself.

The Movement in its short life has done so much good in the country. It is true mistakes have been made, too, but which Movement has never made mistakes? Criticisms are made of this and that but which Movement has never been criticized from prejudice and ignorance and misunderstanding! But on the whole the Movement can count many things on its credit side:

1. It is a symbol of unity of the country.
2. It is peaceful and orderly – crowds move through the streets of towns without causing damage or obstruction to anybody or to anything.
3. Through the boycott of beer and spirits it has reduced:
   (i) Drunkenness (accidents, etc. on last Easter the police has it were the least ever and they attribute this to reduced drunkenness).
   (ii) Loose living.
   (iii) Highway robbery.
   (iv) House-breaking.
4. African traders are working harder as a result of better prospect of trade.

It is true some people are suffering under it but they needn't have suffered because we made it absolutely clear at the outset what the aim of the boycott was – it was a boycott against political privilege of reserving seats for non-Africans after they had been elected on a common roll with Africans. It was up to the non-Africans to choose privilege or trade. The boycott is prolonged because they have not said anything, which implies that they are bent on privilege.

God's ways are not our ways. In history we often find that His purpose was not fulfilled the way people were expecting it and the Bible is full of instances of this kind. To take one ordinary instance: When Moses was called of God to deliver the children of Israel from Bondage he thought he would step out of the Palace of Pharaoh straight to the job and talk to people in the language of the palace.

That way he failed. God sent him first to the wilderness, and, to my mind, He sent him there for one reason alone – to learn the language of the people and come back and speak to the Pharaoh in that language. In a way I am like Moses: I have been speaking to my people 'your language' (by which I mean that I have been selling to them what I have learnt from you), and they have not listened to me. I now speak to 'you' in their language, and they listen to me. May be that is God's purpose. It wasn't all plain sailing with Moses nor was it unharmful to the Egyptians. I believe God is with me in this as He has been in other things – I have not turned against Him.

> – the first item is from *Uganda Argus*, 2 March 1959; the second from the author's personal papers.

A Memorandum to Her Majesty Queen Elizabeth II submitted by members of the Lukiiko of the Kingdom of Buganda concerning the termination of British protection.

Here below is the resolution passed by the Lukiiko which has called into being this Memorandum:

'The Buganda Lukiiko sitting from the 21st to the 24th September, 1960, has heard the report of the Katikkiro in respect of the talks held in London between His Highness the Kabaka, the Lukiiko Constitutional Committee and the Secretary of State concerning the Buganda Constitutional matters.

In that report the Lukiiko was told that the talks ended in deadlock. In view of this deadlock the Lukiiko has resolved that Buganda is determined to be a Separate autonomous State and consequent upon that Buganda will not be represented in the future Legislative Council.

As Buganda has always stated that while dealing with her constitutional matters it is not her desire to stand in the way of the development of the other parts of Uganda and would like in this connection to be clearly understood that other parts of Uganda are absolutely free to seek the attainment of their autonomy through whatever means they think fit.

The Lukiiko's Memorandum which explains in detail the constitutional plan for an independent Buganda is being prepared and will shortly be forwarded to Her Majesty the Queen of the United Kingdom.'

We intend to divide this Memorandum into three main parts:

    (a) Geographical and Historical background of Buganda;
    (b) Buganda's reasons for going it alone; and
    (c) the Constitutional Plan.

The boundaries of Buganda are defined in Article I of the Agreement of 1900. Within those boundaries, Buganda has an area of 25,390 square miles which is well over a quarter of the size of Uganda whose neighbours are: the Republic of Sudan in the North, Kenya Colony in the East, the Republic of Congo in the West, and Tanganyika in the South. Buganda has a population of approximately two million which is about a third of Uganda's six and a quarter million peoples. Buganda is the wealthiest of the four Provinces into which Uganda is divided, with cotton and coffee as the main cash crops. Buganda contributes nearly sixty per cent to the total revenue of the Uganda Protectorate, which total amounted to more than £26 million in 1957/58. Of this contribution from Buganda, which on that figure amounted to nearly £16 million, Buganda received back only £1⅓ million by way of grants from the Central Government.

Buganda is an ancient Kingdom with a long history and her dynasty exceeds thirty-seven Kings in an unbroken line. The history of Buganda begins with a King, and continues throughout the centuries with Kingship, right up to the present day. There is not a single period in our history when the Baganda had no King ruling over them. The Baganda have a system of clans and by means of royal marriages among women of various clans, and since by custom members of the royal family belong to the clan on their mother's side, a situation has arisen in passage of time, whereby most clans have had a ruling Monarch or an outstanding prince as a member of their clan. This custom has had a profound effect on the Kiganda society. Buganda Kings are unique in that they play two big roles in the tenure of their office as Monarchs, namely that they are rulers as well as being superheads of all heads of Clans in the Kingdom. As a result, the King of Buganda, bears a personal relationship to every single Kiganda family in the Kingdom. In other words it is inconceivable for a Kiganda society to exist without a King.

As far back as imagination can stretch the Baganda have had a system of an organized form of government consisting of The King, a Parliament and a Prime Minister. They also had an army and a navy. When the British first came to the country they found this system of government in operation, whose fundamental concepts they have preserved, enriching it as far as possible with their own democratic principles.

There is a wealth of evidence to be found in the writings of the early travellers and discoverers of what was then known as the 'Dark Continent', and, H. M. Stanley's remarks on Buganda are eloquent enough. Stanley was one of the great Explorers of Africa in the nineteenth century and he speaks of Mutesa I who was ruling Buganda at that time as 'a powerful Emperor, with great influence over his neighbours'. He goes on to say: 'I saw about 3,000 soldiers of Mutesa nearly civilised . . . I saw about a hundred Chiefs who might be classed in the same scale as the men in Zanzibar and Omman, clad in rich robes and armed in the same fashion; and have witnessed with astonishment much order and law as is obtainable in semi-civilized countries.'

Stanley thought Mutesa would 'do more for central Africa than fifty years of gospel teaching, unaided by such authority, could do. I think I saw in him the light that shall lighten the darkness of this benighted region, a Prince well worthy of the most sympathies that Europe can give him.'

It was Mutesa I who requested Stanley to write to the British people in Great Britain that he and his people were like blind men groping in the dark and that he was anxious to invite the British to come and give him the light. This request shall ever stand to all future generations as a sign of greatness of this far-sighted King Mutesa I. As a result of this request the British Missionaries arrived in Buganda in 1877 to be followed by the French Catholic Missionaries in 1879.

This was the period of the 'Scramble for Africa', and, in Buganda, there appeared on the scene the British, the French, the Germans, and the Arabs, each group scrambling for power over the country. The confusion into which the mind of King Mwanga was thrown by this scramble can best be imagined than stated. To make the long story short the Baganda picked on the British as their Protectors and a Treaty of Protection was signed between the Queen's Representative on behalf of the Queen and the King of Buganda, in 1894. In 1897 an incident happened. The British army in Uganda at that time consisted mainly of Nubians under a British Commander. The Nubians mutinied and the British were proposing to ask for troops from India when the Baganda, under the able leadership of Sir Apolo, the then Prime Minister of Buganda, volunteered to fight the Nubians whom he defeated in the battle of Bukaleba in Busoga, thus redeeming the British prestige in Uganda.

Two significant articles stand out in the 1894 Treaty between the Queen and the King of Buganda. The first is Article 2, which reads,

> And whereas Her Britannic Majesty has been graciously pleased to bestow on the said Mwanga, King of Uganda, the Protection which he requested in that Agreement...

This article clearly shows that the Kingdom of Buganda was not conquered or ceded by the British, and that British Protection was requested and so graciously bestowed. The second important article in that Treaty is article 14 which says:

> The foreign relations of Uganda and its dependances are hereby placed unreservedly in the hands of Her Majesty's Representative.

This article indicates that Buganda was a real sovereign state before and at the time the British bestowed their protection.

The Agreement of 1900, which followed the 1894 Treaty has no connection with, and bears no relationship to, the Treaty of 1894, and yet its conclusion was the first move by the British in an attempt to reduce the sovereignty of the Lukiiko, as may be gathered from the official documents between Her Majesty's Representative in Uganda and the Foreign Office in London.

In 1902 an Order-in-Council was passed in the United Kingdom which self-justified the British to rule over Uganda as 'a Colony, and as if it was one of our possessions'. The propriety of this Order-in-Council which changed the status of Buganda without the knowledge or consent of the Baganda will ever be regarded by them as the first classic example of the breach of good intentions on the part of the British. This Order-in-Council, unrelated to the 1894 Treaty, was one of the first major causes of Buganda's misfortunes, and from the time it was launched to the present day the British have been following a policy designed to whittle down Buganda's powers.

The annals of history should never brush aside the important part which the Buganda have played in both administrative and social developments of the Uganda Protectorate. Let it be remembered that it is upon the Kiganda system of government that all tribal governments in the Protectorate have been based; this system has been imported to the other tribes by the Baganda themselves, on request. The same is true in the sphere of education and evangelism.

Since the advent of Pax Britannica, at the end of the last century, Buganda has stood in a special relationship as regards Her Majesty's Government and the rest of Uganda. This relationship is exemplified by the provisions of the Treaty of 1894 and the subsequent Constitutional Agreements 1900–1955. As an illustration, Article 14 of the 1894 Treaty, already referred to above, could only be enacted in relation to a people who had a well organized government run on systematic principles as recognized by Sir Gerald Portal, 'Her Britannic Majesty's Commissioner' in 1894.

By the Treaty of 1894, British protection was subsequently conferred upon the rest of Uganda.

A further illustration of this special relationship is provided by Article 5 of 1900 Agreement which reads:—

'The Laws made for the general governance of Uganda Protectorate by Her Majesty's Government will be equally applicable to the Kingdom of Buganda, except in so far as they may in any particular way conflict with the terms of this Agreement will constitute a special exception in regard to the Kingdom of Buganda.'

Buganda's Treaty and constitutional Agreements have been made between the Kabaka, Chiefs and people of Buganda on the one hand and Her Majesty the Queen on the other. Whereas in the other parts of Uganda similar Agreements have been concluded as between the Protectorate Government on the one hand and any Native Government on the other. The Protectorate Government is subordinate to Her Majesty's Government.

The 1955 Agreement has once again stressed Buganda's position by the fact that part of this Agreement is embodied in an Order-in-Council and forms part of the Laws of Uganda. No such provision obtains in any other Agreements found in the rest of Uganda.

Our ancient institutions of the Kabakaship and the Lukiiko have adopted themselves to change in order to fit themselves into the modern world. Since the 1900 Agreement the tendency of the Lukiiko has been to democratize itself. Today, of the ninety-two members of the Lukiiko sixty are elected by the people, through electral colleges, a method which has so far proved itself as democratic as any other.

By the 1955 Agreement, the Kabaka is a constitutional monarch, who rules the country on the advice of his Ministers. The Lukiiko, the Parliament of Buganda, and the Kabaka's Government, consisting of six Ministers, operate on a Provincial basis whereas in the rest of Uganda all

Native Governments operate on a District level and they are local Government units.

It is that special position which Buganda enjoys now that she wants to maintain even after Uganda's independence. The Baganda believe that they can safeguard their prestige only through the survival in a living and functioning form of the Kabakaship and the Lukiiko. The Kabaka is the spirit and motivating power of political, economic, and social activities and the Lukiiko is the legislative forum of the Baganda. That is why anything, either extrinsic or intrinsic, that tends to weaken our institutions is bound to be resisted in Buganda. One of the extrinsic forces that has tried to weaken our institutions is the Legislative Council which was introduced in Uganda in 1921. This body which was introduced mainly as a forum for the European planters and traders at that time, has never gained popularity in Buganda since its inception because it was regarded as foreign both in origin and composition. Secondly and more significantly, this Council has been viewed with suspicion as a possible agent to sap the strength of the Lukiiko and lower the Baganda's prestige. Part of the 1953 crisis, whereby the Kabaka was exiled by the British Government for two years, revolved round the controversy of Buganda's representation on the Legislative Council. This Council has failed to win the Baganda's confidence.

That is the crucial point. Her Majesty's Government have declared that Buganda shall be represented on the Legislative Council as the only means of Uganda's unity. The Lukiiko and the Kabaka's Government on the other hand have said that before Buganda reconsiders her attitude to the Legislative Council her Treaty and constitutional Agreements must be terminated first and Her Majesty's Government should declare now that at least Buganda will be in a federal relationship vis-à-vis the future Central Government of Uganda. The Lukiiko's Memorandum of 1958 expressing their wish to terminate the Agreements resulted in constitutional talks held between the Lukiiko Constitutional Committee and Her Majesty's Representative since September, 1959 until they ended in deadlock in London this September. The sole purpose of these talks had been for Buganda to receive back the powers exercised by Her Majesty's Representative under the Agreements before Uganda attained independence. The Treaty relationship between Buganda and Britain demanded that Her Majesty's Government could not surrender its powers under the Agreements to a new Government with which Buganda had not concluded an Agreement. Satisfactory conclusion of the constitutional talks would further determine Buganda's federal relationship with the future Central Government.

While these talks were going on, Her Majesty's Government formulated a constitutional plan for the whole of Uganda. This was:

(a) Registration of voters throughout Uganda.
(b) Before the General elections there would be appointed a Rela-

tionships Commission by the Secretary of State for the Colonies to make recommendations as to the form of Government most suitable to Uganda.

(c) General elections early next year for the Legislative Council, 1961.

(d) After the General elections there would be a constitutional Conference, to be held in London in the Summer of 1961, representative of all parts of Uganda, including Buganda, to consider the recommendations of the Commission. This conference would be attended by the elected members of the New Legislative Council.

Although this plan affects Buganda's Constitutional position fundamentally, Buganda's proposals as to how it should apply to their Kingdom have been brushed aside. For example during the recent London talks, the Kabaka's delegation suggested that the Relationships Commission should submit its report before these fundamental changes took place. The Secretary of State rejected this suggestion out of hand but yet declined to answer the relevant question as to what Her Majesty's Government would do should the Relationships Commission recommend a form of government that was contrary to Buganda's desires.

The Secretary of State has declared that he cannot deviate from that plan, whatever Buganda's representations for some modifications, hence the deadlock in the London talks.

Buganda has found it extremely difficult to co-operate in these unnegotiated orders emanating from Whitehall, which orders completely disregard the Kabaka's, his Government's and the Lukiiko's representations. There cannot be any other body of opinion more representative of public opinion in Buganda other than the Kabaka's Government and the Lukiiko. This disregard, on the part of Her Majesty's Government, comes as a great shock to the Lukiiko and the people of Buganda.

The Secretary of State has indicated that public opinion in Buganda and Uganda is that expressed by political leaders in this country. Nothing could be more erroneous and misleading. In Buganda there has been a move to form political parties since the early twenties. But Her Majesty's Government's policy has been to suppress them by either proscribing them or deporting and putting political leaders into prison. The result of this repressive policy has been that political parties have failed to establish themselves firmly and win the confidence of the Baganda whose loyalty has always been towards their Kabaka and the Lukiiko.

It will be recalled that during the 1953–1955 crisis when political party leaders tried to see the Secretary of State, concerning the return of the Kabaka from exile, the Secretary of State said that he could only negotiate with members of the Lukiiko. He did not recognize political party leaders as the right persons to treat with in constitutional matters affecting Buganda.

In these circumstances, it would be asking too much of the Baganda to trust the destiny of their country into the hands of political party leaders whose experience has not been proved by time. This could be extremely risky in the light of recent history which has shown clearly that politicians in emergent countries use parliamentary democracy as a springboard to virtual dictatorship. Buganda has asked Her Majesty's Government to hand back its powers to the Kabaka who under the Treaty and Constitutional Agreements entrusted them to that Government. Her Majesty's Government's refusal to do this and instead preferring political party leaders is not only discourteous in the extreme, but also a complete oversight of the facts.

When the Secretary of State recently said at the opening of the new Legislative Council building that he had firm intention to act vigorously under the law in order to carry out his plan he sounded a warning note that he would use all means to impose the British type of parliamentary democracy which he said the people of Buganda demanded. It is difficult to know what is meant by the 'people of Buganda' in this context. The 'Special Powers Ordinance' hurried through the Legislative Council immediately after the Secretary of State's visit, which Ordinance gives the Police unlimited powers to arrest and detain anyone on suspicion that he may intimidate people who want to register or vote, shows that Her Majesty's Government is determined to introduce the British type of parliamentary democracy even by decree.

If Buganda's legitimate constitutional demands have caused all these most unlikely reactions while the Treaty relations are even still existing between Buganda and Her Majesty's Government, the Lukiiko's apprehensions as to what the future Uganda Government's attitude towards Buganda will be, are greatly intensified. We cannot expect that Government to do much better than Her Majesty's Government as they are going to inherit this form of disguised dictatorship. Public pronouncements made on various occasions by peoples likely to be leaders of a future Uganda are not conducive to unity as Her Majesty's Government envisages it. In order to avoid another 'Katanga' in this country immediately after Uganda's independence, Buganda has decided and is determined to go it alone.

As a result of this decision, Buganda proposes to establish cordial relationship between Her Majesty's Government and herself for a number of reasons: mainly because the British are monarchists like the Baganda and the special relationship that has existed between the two countries has been a paternalistic one, which has been found to be unsatisfactory in the present circumstances. Since neither Britain nor Buganda desire that this superior-inferior relationship should continue beyond what is absolutely necessary, there ought to be a new Anglo–Buganda Cordial Relationship. That proposed relationship should be finalized and put into effect by 31st December, 1960, after which date Buganda will be independent. In the meantime negotiations will be held between representatives of the Lukiiko and Her Majesty's Government with a view to formulating a scheme within which that Anglo–Buganda Cordial Relationship will operate.

Plan for an Independent Buganda

1. Relationship with Great Britain

There shall be established a friendly relationship between an Independent Buganda and Her Majesty's Government on the following lines:

(1) *Defence:* In this connection, Buganda will have her own Army, but she will form a Military Alliance with Britain for a specified period of time which may be revised from time to time.

(2) *Foreign Affairs:* Buganda will establish Foreign Relations by herself where possible, otherwise, in conjunction with Great Britain for a specified period of time.

(3) *Economic Aid:* Buganda will seek economic aid from Britain in her economic and technical development.

A Five-Year Development Plan will be drawn up by Buganda following the attainment of her Independence, so as to give the Kingdom an orderly economic development.

In her economic development, Buganda will encourage free enterprise and make conditions favourable for foreign investment. The Kabaka's Government's Policy as to State Ownership is that such ownership should be restricted to those essential services which cannot be beneficially run by Private Enterprise.

2. Relationship with Neighbouring Countries in East Africa

(a) *Customs.* Buganda will join the Common Customs of East Africa.

(b) *Communications.* (This includes Road, Rail, Water and Air services.) There shall be joint negotiations as to the membership of Buganda on the bodies controlling those services.

(c) *Higher Education.*

(1) All existing institutions of learning will automatically fall under the jurisdiction of Buganda.

(2) This position will however not alter the present status of Makerere University College, nor will it change its legal and administrative position as an Inter-State Institution.

(3) Buganda will have her full share in the management of Makerere, and shall be fully represented on those bodies which control and administer its activities.

(d) *Judicial.* Buganda shall have her own High Court and District Courts. Appeals from the High Court shall lie to the Eastern Africa Court of Appeal and finally to the Privy Council.

(e) *Inter-State Trade in East Africa.*

(i) Any manufacturing and/or secondary industries operating in Buganda will have to be licensed in Buganda, and all Excise Duty will go to the Buganda Kingdom Treasury.

(ii) There will be free movement of trade between Buganda and the States of East Africa.

(f) *Monetary System.* Buganda will remain in the Sterling Area.

(g) *Immigration.* Immigration will be controlled by the Kabaka's Government. This will apply to non-Africans as defined by the existing Uganda Protectorate Ordinance.

Movement of Persons, however, between Buganda and other neighbouring countries in East Africa will be free and unrestricted.

3. *International Relationships*

(i) The fundamental rights of man, and the rule of law as understood in the free world, will be strictly observed.

Thus, there will be freedom of worship, freedom of speech, and freedom of assembly in Buganda regardless of race, colour, or creed.

(ii) On her attainment of Independence, Buganda will be associated with the great family of nations – the Commonwealth, and like any other independent nations in the Commonwealth, Buganda will seek admission to the United Nations General Assembly.

(iii) *Posts and Telecommunication* being services conducted on International level, such services will continue to be run as at present in Buganda. The control of those services in Buganda, will however fall under the Kabaka's Government, and as such, Buganda will make her own postal stamps.

4. *Internal Re-Arrangement of Services*

(a) The Lukiiko will continue to be the Legislative and deliberate body for Buganda.

(b) All powers now exercised by Her Majesty's Representative under the Treaty and constitutional Agreements of Buganda shall vest in the Kabaka and his Government, e.g. all laws and Buganda's Budget shall be effective after the approval of the Kabaka, who is the Supreme Head of Buganda.

(c) Buganda will have an army of which the Kabaka will be the Commander-in-Chief.

(d) Buganda will have her own Police Force for the purposes of maintaining law and order. In this connection, the present Uganda Police Force responsible for the Buganda Province should immediately come under the Kabaka's Government's jurisdiction.

(e) There will be a High Court and District Courts for Buganda with a

Bench of trained, qualified and experienced lawyers. Parties will be legally represented therein.

F. Kampala, Entebbe, Masaka, Mubende, and all Townships and Trading Centres, as well as Entebbe Airport, without prejudice to its international status, will immediately be brought under the jurisdiction of the Kabaka's Government.

G. All lands vested in Her Majesty under the provisions of all Buganda Agreements shall revert to the Kabaka of Buganda for the use and benefit of all.

The Lukiiko is fully conscious of the important fact that in order to realize the scheme as outlined above, Buganda will need technicians, doctors, lawyers and many people trained in various professions and trades. She will need a strong Civil Service. Buganda therefore intends to award as many scholarships as possible for long and short courses here and abroad to candidates who are most likely to make the maximum use of the facilities for the benefit of their country in the long run. In the meantime, Buganda will meet the shortage in personnel by employing expatriates on contract.

As to the financing of the whole scheme as outlined above, Buganda intends to use:– (a) The existing resources which will be greatly increased by the change over from British control and (b) by raising local as well as overseas loan; and (c) by inviting outside capital.

In conclusion, this Lukiiko's decision has been made imperative by Her Majesty's Government's failure to recognize the fact that any possible parliamentary democracy ought to be built on the existing institutions in Buganda, that is to say, the Kabakaship and the Lukiiko. Her Majesty's Government's oversight of the Kabaka's, his Government's, and the Lukiiko's representations to that effect can only result in hard feelings unnecessarily. The only possible way out of these difficulties is for Buganda to go it alone and establish the 'Anglo-Buganda Cordial Relationship' as outlined above.

The Lukiiko would like to stress the fact that it is not opposed to parliamentary democracy as such, but it views with apprehension any induced democracy which is only strengthened by the desire for independence. To the Lukiiko, parliamentary democracy ought to suit the local conditions, because there cannot be such a thing as international parliamentary democracy. Independence should be a means to an end and not an end in itself. Buganda cannot sell all her heritage for the purchase of Uganda's Independence. That heritage is much more precious in the long run. Nor is the Buganda willing to sacrifice everything at the altar of Uganda's unity.

The foregoing does not mean, in the least, that we are not appreciative and actively conscious of the benefits Buganda has derived from Her Majesty's protection for the last seventy years. There cannot be a better

way of expressing that gratitude than the proposed Anglo–Buganda
Cordial Relationship.

> – from The Kabaka's Government,
> *Buganda's Independence*, Kampala,
> 1960, pp. 22–36.

57. DECISION TO CO-OPERATE WITH UGANDA 1961

Kabaka Mutesa II to the Lukiiko, 16 September 1961.

With the agreement of the members of the Buganda Constitutional Committee, I have sent Dr Lumu and Mr C. M. S. Mukasa to bring to you my
personal message [from London] regarding the progress so far made in
the discussions about the kingdom's political future.

As you know, I was invited by Her Majesty's Government to come and
discuss matters concerning Buganda's political position, especially at this
time when the British protection is about to end. It is for the same reason
that the Buganda Constitutional Committee was invited to come and complete the negotiations which had been taking place between the Lukiiko's
delegates and Her Majesty's Representative at Entebbe.

With regard to the talks that we have had since we arrived in London,
it appears that the Colonial Secretary is up to now unable to conclude any
of the outstanding matters; but he has agreed to hold talks with the
Buganda Committee, as requested in the Lukiiko Resolution of 29th
August, 1961. The Colonial Secretary has, however, assured both the
Committee and me that these matters will be finalized. We have accepted
that assurance. But the Colonial Secretary on his part wants Buganda's
representatives to be part of the Conference in which the representatives
of the other parts of Uganda will be taking part and to present our
proposals as to our future relationship with the rest of Uganda. That
Conference opens on 18th September.

The Representatives of Buganda did, however, make it clear that despite the above assurance, they have no mandate to participate in the
Conference unless the Lukiiko, of which they are representatives, has
agreed. The Colonial Secretary saw this point and I have accordingly sent
the aforesaid messengers to you.

Considering the assurances which the Colonial Secretary has given me
and the Committee after detailed and careful discussions and also after

examining what may happen in the future, it appears that Buganda's participation in that Conference will not prejudice Buganda's position at all. Therefore, it seems to us to be advisable that the Lukiiko should permit its representatives to take their places in the Conference; this will also enable Buganda to present its case regarding its future relationship with the rest of Uganda.

Part of the understanding (with the Colonial Secretary) is also the assurance that we shall not lose whatever was already agreed with the Queen's Representative at Entebbe and that outstanding matters will soon be finalized. Any conclusions will, of course, be brought and laid before the Lukiiko, as is the usual practice.

Having regard to the Colonial Secretary's assurances as stated above, and the advice that we have received from our (legal) Advisers, the Committee and I consider it desirable that my aforesaid messengers bring the Lukiiko's endorsement when they return!

I send you all my greetings; my subjects that are here also send you their regards and assure you that they are firm and will not relent or falter.

> – from a translation of a cyclostyled original in
> the editor's possession.

58. POLITICS AND THE KABAKASHIP, 1961

Archbishop Joseph Kiwanuka on 'Constitutional Monarch', November 1961.

... Many Baganda might not understand for what reason the Kabaka was taken out of politics to become a Constitutional Monarch.

I have already explained to you how the form of Government in Buganda went through changes until it allowed representatives to be elected by the people.

When a country with a king reaches the stage where its government is ruled by its people such a country may still want to keep its kings and for that reason it takes its kings out of politics.

When political parties are established in a country, if the king still mixes up in politics the kingship is on the way to digging its own grave. We have the example of other countries to prove that, and therefore Buganda showed clear-sightedness when she decided on Constitutional Monarchy.

Many countries have lost their king, even though the people loved him and took much pride in him. They lost him because he remained in politics after the country had accepted political parties opposing one another. These parties clashed with the king whom they saw blocking the way to their ends, and they overthrew them in such a way that they could never again find supporters. The reason is evident since the country stands on parties in opposition to one another and the king remains involved in politics he himself supporting one of the parties. When a king supports one party he shows himself as being no more the king of all his people, but only of that section of his people of which he says 'These are my men who really care for me, and among whom I am hiding'. Those whom he has chosen in such a way may flatter him as much as they can so that they may pass or reject whatever they want, even if they themselves know that what they are going to do is not right.

As for the people that the king has rejected, their hearts sink into rancour. They still struggle in the political field, and as in politics there are always changes in which there is much friction one day they might overthrow the party that the king has supported and then, as they hold power they will say to the king 'Go with the others, follow your friends'. And then those who were supporting him since they have been over-thrown, they merely look at what is happening, they can no more fight for him even should they wish to do so.

That is why I do not like these slogans of 'Kabaka yekka' (the Kabaka alone) nor the party nor the activities, which they say is 'to be behind the throne' or to 'fight for the throne' or 'support the Lukiko'. Among the parties already established there is not a single one that has done anything on which could be based the accusation 'Now it is evident, that such party wants to destroy the Throne!' Even more, if the Government could prove such a thing, it would be deeply guilty not to take that party to the Court of justice and file a suit against it.

Those 'Kabaka Yekka' and the others who flatter themselves that they are the defenders of the Throne and of the King, are the ones who will spoil our royalty by dragging the king in the back-wash of politics. In fact they are just seeking their own end.

If it was accepted and approved by the Lukiko that the people through-out the counties would elect the candidates who say 'We are behind the Lukiko, we are the defenders of the Kabaka, we fight for the Throne', it is possible that it would succeed. But this would be only temporary and would be most detrimental to the nation, because the opposition of the other candidates who do not support that party would turn against the Kabaka himself and the Lukiko, who would belong to a different party.

Perhaps those who support one side will be angry with me because I brought them to light and exposed them, and because I gave the alarm to the Baganda who still have a sincere love for their country and for the Throne.

However I hope that many who were blindfolded will be grateful to me and will be pleased to see that I have brought to light the snare hidden in the ground which was invisible to them; now if anyone wants to tread on it and is caught in it, everyone will be able to tell him: 'After all, you trod on it while you saw it clearly.' Compete in parties which are known; but for such slogans as 'Kabaka Alone', 'we are behind the Throne', 'we back the Lukiko', keep away from them,

J.K.

– from the Appendix to *Pastoral Letter of the most Rev. Archbishop Joseph Kiwanuka, D.D., Archbishop of Rubaga (Uganda), Church and State, Guiding Principles*, Kisubi, November 1961.

59. THE STAND OF KABAKA YEKKA

Election Pamphlet 1962.

In the booklet embodying the Manifesto of the Democratic Party on pages 30 and 31, regarding Uganda's Head of State, the DP has this to say '. . . The Head of State of Independent Uganda will be chosen by the people of Uganda . . .' They go on to say that what should be understood by everyone, first of all, is the fact that the time is not yet ripe for Uganda to have an African in that position . . . 'we are all agreed that on the attainment of independence we shall remain within the British Commonwealth . . . we of the Democratic Party have already stated that that will be our arrangement unless some inhibitive circumstance prevent us doing so . . .' The DP then ask themselves the following questions:

1. 'Shall we have a Governor-General?'
2. 'Shall we have a President?'
3. 'Shall we have a King [i.e. the Kabaka?]?'
4. 'Shall we have a Council of State made up of certain people as a collective Head of State?'

While elaborating on the idea of a Council of state being the Head of the Country, the DP say '. . . . then complications arise . . .'

On the question of the Kabaka being Uganda's Head of State, the DP say, . . . 'But if the people of Uganda reject the suggestion of having a Governor-General, we shall then either have a King of Uganda or a President . . .'

In short, what the DP are after and in fact what they intend to do is to have a Governor-General. They say, '. . . If we have a Governor-General, appointed on the advice of the Government of Uganda, it will mean that for a long time the problem of who shall be the Head of State of independent Uganda shall have been solved since when we have such a one he will be enough, as is the case with other independent countries . . . Canada for instance . . . who for 93 years to date still have a Governor-General as Head of the country in the name of the Queen . . .'

The above arrangement of the DP will come into effect as from 1st March, 1962, the day on which Mr Benedicto Kiwanuka will become a Prime Minister of the Queen of England and on which date he will assume full responsibility for the Army, the Police and Finance. Study carefully the picture on the opposite pages [not reproduced] which portrays what Uganda will look like if the DP defeats Kabaka Yekka in Buganda.

Finally: The Plan of the DP is supported by Britain; because England (or Britain) is merely changing the white colour for the black, but both the Queen and the Governor retain their positions. The difference is that an African Commoner is to be on top of the Kabaka, the Abakama and the Kyabazinga. That commoner will be called Prime Minister – the Queen's spokesman (Kasajafuba).

What kind of Muganda are you to allow Benedicto Kiwanuka or any other person to 'sit over' the 'Lion', His Highness, the Kabaka of Buganda, as the DP are proposing? . . .

For many years the Kabaka has been struggling to recover his power [or sovereignty] from the British. Now the British want to hand that power over to 'Kasajafuba' [i.e. Benedicto Kiwanuka]; so, if the Kabaka is to regain that power, he must fight both the British and 'Kasajafuba'.

That is why Kabaka Yekka* is opposed both to the British and DP – Nabe.

We of Kabaka Yekka, have stated our major objectives on the third page of our first pamphlet entitled 'What News in Buganda – Kabaka Yekka' as follows:

1. The Kabaka shall not be in an inferior position to anybody on Buganda soil.
2. It is inconceivable that a commoner should ever 'sit over' the Kabaka.

In our second pamphlet published on 28th August, 1961, on page 8 where it reads the Head of State in Uganda, Kabaka Yekka reaffirmed its position as follows: '. . . Nobody can ever have a superior position over the Kabaka on Buganda soil, also in Buganda no one or body of people can ever make laws for the Kabaka's observance, and it is contrary to Buganda's traditions for any person or group of commoners to make a law which the Kabaka is expected to observe.'

As from 1st March, 1962, the seat of Uganda's Prime Minister will be in

Buganda at Entebbe, and the National Assembly of Uganda will also be in Buganda in Kampala. We of Kabaka Yekka cannot hesitate to state that if Uganda is ever to be a prosperous and peaceful country, the Prime Minister of Uganda must always be subordinate to the Kabaka and other hereditary rulers as shown by Kabaka Yekka in the picture opposite.

Kabaka Yekka will use this 'new Atomic Bomb' to destroy the Nabe completely. And we believe that God is on our side.

O God protect the Kabaka

> – from a translation of *Kabaka atta nabbe, atomu bomu ya Kabaka Yekka*, Kampala, 1962.

Kabaka Yekka: the Kabaka alone.
Abakama, Kyabaʒinga: other Ugandan rulers.

60. BELONGING TO UGANDA, 1963

Proposals for a 'fresh political approach in Buganda' by 19 Kabaka Yekka members of the Uganda National Assembly 1963.

Ever since the white man established himself here we in Buganda have been driven by one fear, that is the fear of losing the Nnamulondo* and so losing our own identity. We have persistently resisted anything that tended to detract from our status and we have objected to every suggestion of closer union or federation with other territories in East Africa. When, in 1953, the then Colonial Secretary suggested, at a dinner in London, that some time in the future the territories of East Africa would federate, we in Buganda reacted very sharply to this statement and we know the events that followed that year, resulting in the deportation of the Kabaka. Again we were driven by the fear that a federation would touch on our status and reduce our own standing.

2. Since 1956 the policy in Buganda, which was accepted by all, was to seek a federal status for Buganda, a status which we all believe will preserve the Nnamulondo within the framework of a united Uganda. This we have now achieved, and it was because of the achievement of this status that we chose to co-operate in the building of a strong and peaceful country of Uganda.

3. Since October 9th last year [Uganda's Independence Day 1962] events changed fundamentally. . . . A new Government has been

established in Uganda and we in Buganda agreed, not merely to be under this Government, but to be part of this country, which means that:

(a) We must, in every possible way, give allegience to that Government whether or not we support the particular party holding the reigns of power at a particular time, and

(b) We must do everything possible to uphold the Constitution under which the present system of Government has been set up.

In other words we have agreed to belong to Uganda physically and we must, therefore, even in our thinking and in our spirit, belong to Uganda. We can no longer go to London or appeal to the British, however much we may complain. We can no longer balk at decisions or refuse to co-operate as we used to do under British rule because we are part of the machinery which must from now on, decide the fate of this country. The same attitude is expected of non-Baganda Ugandans towards Buganda. Since the UPC* and KY took office, the responsibilities of both sides became so much greater because we are the parties in power now.

5. However, there are certain developments of an alarming nature in the present circumstances which call for deep thought. Although our National Government is now composed of UPC and KY there are large numbers of us in Kabaka Yekka who do not even seem to appreciate that there is any responsibility devolving upon us to support the Uganda Government and to uphold decisions made by them. . . .

7. It is clear that with the way things are going now in Buganda with constant criticism of the Central Government by some members of the Kabaka's Government and quarrelling between some KY and UPC leaders, it is difficult to establish a stable Government. By 'stable' it does not mean only that there should be no threats to law and order or persistent doubts about safety of property and so on, but also, and most important perhaps, that people should expect the continuation of peaceful Government in the future, and freely act upon that expectation. In the light of the very fundamental requirement of providing stability now as well as to ensure it for the future, it is absolutely necessary that we in this new Nation of Uganda must develop new thinking as well as new attitudes, that will promote that atmosphere which is conducive to stability.

8. There is yet another point. Many of us today talk as if we in Buganda could break off from Uganda and belong to something else. Some people even talk as if everything that is done in Uganda must be conditioned on the wishes of Buganda alone. It must be understood by those who don't know it, and particularly by those who have forgotten, that Buganda is a part of Uganda and so it will remain for ever. In 1960 there was a very strong movement towards secession. A Committee was set up to explore ways and means by which Buganda could secede. A good deal of effort

was wasted on this project and people travelled abroad to seek recognition and support. In the end it was clear that secession was utterly impossible and that Buganda had to get back into the fold of Uganda – and that is where we now belong. If Buganda now attempted to secede the Central Government would be entitled to forcibly keep Buganda in Uganda just as it would be entitled to keep in Uganda any other part of this Nation that threatened to secede. Therefore it should be appreciated that Buganda can never secede, and that being so, therefore, it is our duty to see that we develop new thinking as well as new attitudes best suited to the needs of a Uganda Nation. There is no provision for secession in the Uganda Independence Act, 1962 which establishes Uganda as one united Nation.

9. It is also of little avail to keep saying that Uganda cannot exist without Buganda because it is not as if there are two States dependent on each other. There is just one Nation – one part of which is Buganda. There are no two National Governments but only one. All the others are subordinate to it and it is the subordinate Governments which cannot exist without the National Government of Uganda. For example, it is only the National Government that could defend Buganda against invasion, assure safe conduct of Baganda abroad and guarantee our economic interests in foreign countries. By itself alone Buganda has no standing in any dealing with any Nation. It is important to appreciate this because only by so doing is it possible to understand where the national power and authority lies. If we don't do this we shall always be living under the impression that Buganda is a different country from Uganda and we shall continue to live in the unrealistic isolationistic view that many of us have held up-to-date and which serve only to prejudice Buganda and the Baganda, not only in Uganda but even outside Uganda. It is not incidental that Buganda has rapidly earned herself a bad name outside Uganda in spite of the fact that the Kabaka of Buganda is one of the leading African nationalists who has for years fought against Colonialism.

10. Buganda cannot expect to grow out and flourish unless we realize that we depend for our very existence as a group and for the protection of those very rights and status which we cherish so much on the continued stability and strength of the National Government of Uganda. This is because our Nnamulondo rights and status, are embodied in the Constitution and the Central Government is the supreme protector of this Constitution. The Courts merely interpret it but the Central Government must see to it, by force if necessary, that the Constitution is protected.

14. For one year now we in Kabaka Yekka have never put forward one idea bearing on substantive development of Buganda or Uganda. Every time we meet it is only to quarrel about organizational matters: such as our relations with UPC and even expend time discussing who should sit in the meeting and where, while some faction may storm the meeting in an effort to exclude another faction. We have never sat down to consider

such substantive problems as: How do we develop our economic system? What do we do to promote health in the villages? How are we to avoid the high rates of infant mortality? How can we develop village life so as to attract people to stay there? Until we have got discipline in the organization we can never find time to think about things which matter and until we think about these things it may well be asked whether Kabaka Yekka must be a Party with rules through which discipline can be imposed so that things fall in place and when anybody says anything or does anything disagreeable the machinery is there to deal with him and the rest of us can begin to pay attention to those things that are most pressing and begin to make something of our independence.

15. This idea of Kabaka Yekka being a party brings into discussion a most important question: namely the purpose for which Kabaka Yekka was established. We believe that it was established to safeguard the Nnamulondo and also to see to the preservation of such others of our Buganda traditions as we deem essential to us. This is actually the outline of it but in daily life it really means the carrying out of such services as are required to keep the Nnamulondo and the people together in such a state of existence that the people are happy and therefore do not in desperation seek to disrupt those cherished traditions. If the people are unhappy they will naturally look around to see how they can get out of their unhappiness with the result that they may even undo those things which it was intended to preserve. This may retard economic development and general progress. It has happened in those countries where they have had revolutions.

16. That being so we must begin to question ourselves now whether Kabaka Yekka is primarily fulfilling its function and, if not, what we can do. It is our view that Kabaka Yekka is not fulfilling its functions. It is also our view that Kabaka Yekka is not the best way of fulfilling the function of preserving the Nnamulondo together with such other traditions as we like to observe here in Buganda. . . .

17. In the past years in this country we in Buganda were in the vanguard of political development. Political parties started here; delegations went away from here to Great Britain and elsewhere to discuss the future of this territory. Indeed, we were contributing as much as anybody could to the total growth of political thought in this country. Now, however, we are not. We have established Kabaka Yekka, a working group which to those in Kabaka Yekka, implies keeping out of Buganda every political organization. . . .

20. Here again it is obvious that it is absolutely necessary that we in Kabaka Yekka gear our thinking to new ways so as to bring our whole attitude in line with the requirements of the nationalist ambitions in Uganda. The same appeal is here and now being made to those few UPC supporters who have not yet adjusted their thinking to the new situation which demand that Uganda shall remain one country. We must revive

political strength in us: develop a sense of political direction both in our thinking and in our aims. We, in Buganda, must no longer form a provincial party of parochial people but must look upon ourselves as part of the national group with nationalist aspirations and also contribute in full, as indeed is expected of us, towards the political stature of Uganda both here at home and in international circles. We must also find greater security for the traditions we cherish.

21. What do we do?

(a) A small but very powerful group of people in Buganda have recently suggested that Kabaka Yekka should, in order to protect the traditions of Buganda, quit Government and join the Opposition. Nothing could be more ridiculous! How can we find greater security for the traditions we cherish, which are embodied in the Uganda Constitution, outside the very machinery that would protect them? It is only the wishful thinkers who would imagine that the traditions of Buganda could best be protected by Buganda remaining outside political organizations and the Uganda Government. If such people are not wishful thinkers or ignorant, then they are not genuine lovers of Buganda and Uganda. The mere crossing of the floor by Buganda members of Parliament would not automatically overthrow the Government nor would it destroy the political organizations generally associated with Parliamentary democracy. On the contrary, if such a thing took place political parties would gang themselves against Buganda and the winner would be obvious! This was exactly the position before UPC entered into an alliance with Buganda. Are the interests of Buganda to secure her cherished traditions and the desire of the Baganda to make a contribution towards the building of the Nation of Uganda best satisfied by Buganda remaining in the Opposition?

(b) The vast majority of the people of Buganda, because they lack the knowledge of how parliamentary democracy works, and because they have never been made aware of the true constitutional position of Buganda in Uganda and are, therefore, ignorant of the proper sources of power over all matters affecting them, have suggested that the Baganda should let things take their course in Uganda and that the Baganda should concentrate on Buganda affairs alone! Let it be known from now on that all major legislation in Parliament affects the entire Nation of Uganda of which Buganda is a part. Whatever the Uganda Government does is done in the name of Uganda as a whole. There is no need to enumerate such important issues as the federation of East Africa, the Unity of Africa, or even the representation at the United Nations Organization, and, of course, many others.

(c) There are even some people in Buganda who have suggested that if, as time goes on, Buganda finds herself utterly dissatisfied with the course of things in Uganda, she would secede! It has already been sufficiently indicated elsewhere that there is no provision for secession in the Uganda Constitution. The best that Buganda can hope for is the state of affairs of which Katanga provides the best example. The events in the Congo have already sufficiently indicated beyond doubt who the winner would be.

22. We believe that there is only one solution and that is that the Kabaka Yekka should merge with the UPC...

25. We therefore urge all those who love Buganda, and in the interests of Buganda and Uganda, to make the only realistic decision of merging with UPC...

27. The fact is that since Kabaka Yekka is a provincial party it has little or no bearing on the development of a central national party, and *ipso facto* has no bearing on the formulation of national policies which, it should be realized, are formulated for the whole of Uganda including Buganda. If Kabaka Yekka stubbornly stood out alone and went into the Opposition, the DP and UPC could merge into a single national party entirely ignoring Kabaka Yekka. There we would have a one-party system which would run the National Government and the existence of the Kabaka Yekka party in Buganda would not have the slightest effect on that party's projection of Uganda in international organizations or in national representations with foreign countries. Therefore the question of whether the merger would precipitate the development of one central party or not is of no consequence in the present consideration.

28. But when we merge there will be great advantages in promoting the development of the Nation and these are of the greatest weight. Added to this is the great point, often overlooked by us, of putting the primary responsibility of preserving the Nnamulondo of Buganda on the Central Government where it belongs and who have the primary duty of preserving the Constitution in this country. If we think that the preservation of the Nnamulondo is the exclusive duty of the Buganda Government we thereby grossly misunderstand the Constitution as well as the spirit in which it was made. ....

> – from a pamphlet circulated by 19 Baganda Members of the Uganda National Assembly, *Fresh Political Approach in Buganda. Basis of the M.P.s Recommendation for KY–UPC Merger*, 1963.

Nnamulondo: the Kabaka's throne.
UPC: the Uganda People's Congress.

61. THE SUSPENSION OF THE CONSTITUTION, 1966

Annexure to the Appeal by Kabaka Mutesa II to the Secretary-General of the United Nations, 11 March 1966.

... 2. Uganda, a former British Protectorate, is a confederation of as many as 37 tribes ranging from 1,500 Teuso in Karamoja to about 1,000,000 Baganda in the Kingdom of Buganda. These tribes speak different dialects and languages. The main ethnical dividing line being the Bantu Group in the South and the Nilotics roughly in the North of Uganda. English is the official language of the country, but this is a common language only to the educated few as education is neither free nor compulsory; only those who can afford it, get it. The cohesive forces in operation today, after independence, is accentuated more by way of tribalism than nationalism. This is mainly because although Uganda is about the size of the British Isles (91,134 square miles), road and railways communications are developing, but not yet fully developed. The country is mainly agricultural with cotton and coffee being the main cash crops, which form the economic basis of the country. The existing industries are not big enough to make the mobility of population a substantial factor to talk about. Trade unions are certainly a force, but not to the extent of putting tribalism in the shade. The first loyalty therefore, is to the tribe. This loyalty becomes undiluted when a group of persons live off the land in virtual isolation from their immediate neighbours whose language may be different from their own. The forces which break these barriers are yet to come, they are not here...

4. The last population census was carried out in Uganda in 1959 and it was then 6·5 million. Today, seven years after, the population is estimated at 7·5 million. Roughly, of the 6·5 million, 2·7 million are non-Bantu, the remainder belong to the Bantu Group. One of the most important characteristics of the Bantu Group is that since time immemorial the Bantu people have had viable and centralized political and social institutions which are non-existent in the North. For instance, among the Lango, one of the Nilotic tribes in the North, before 1914, when the British imposed the conception of a centralized Government, the political organization there used to be essentially military. Over each village was a 'jago' or leader of a company and above him was a 'rwot' or leader of a column. The office of a 'jago' was not necessarily hereditary nor was that of a 'rwot'. Their prestige in the community depended on their success and prowess in war. The 'rwot' was the nearest approach to a chief who ruled over from three to ten villages. This would roughly mean from 150 to 7,500 people under one chief in comparison with over a million people, for example, under the Kabaka of Buganda.

5. The centralized institutions, among the Bantu, helped to unify them by bringing them under one recognized authority to whom everyone owed allegiance. The bringing together of these two different groups of peoples, with different backgrounds cannot be an easy task. The monarchists and the republicans must necessarily differ on the fundamentals that go to make society tick.

6. During their seventy years of overrule, the British did not seek to minimize those differences, instead they maintained them. Units of local governments were carved out throughout the country along the main tribal lines. The District Councils and the Buganda Lukiiko (Parliament) which we have today, all over Uganda, follow those lines. Of those only Buganda is on a provincial level, the other thirteen are divided among the remaining three Provinces or Regions namely Acholi, Karamoja, Lango, Madi and West Nile in the North: Bugisu, Bukedi, Busoga, Sebei and Teso in the East and Ankole, Bunyoro, Kigezi and Toro in the West. Sebei is the smallest single tribe with a District status; its population is 24,000 souls. Despite its size it has got all the trappings of any other District, e.g. of Lango, which has a population of 265,000. It has got its own Constitutional Head, called the Kingoo of Sebei, who for the purposes of presidential elections, is at par with the Kabaka who now rules over two million people, and yet Sebei became a District only in September 1960. The position of the District is entrenched in the Constitution of Uganda. This pattern repeats itself in varying degrees throughout the country. The identities are sharper at the tribal level and the nation is still a hazy concept, which cannot be brought into clear focus by any magic wand at once. The present Constitution has been a serious attempt to create a nation.

7. The long and revered traditions of the Kingdom, e.g. of Buganda which has had its own centralized political institutions for centuries back are vehemently guarded by the Baganda. Their argument being that the stability of the whole country – the nation – largely depends on the continued existence of their traditional institutions, upon which the new and foreign national institutions must be built; loyalty to the nation is only forming, whereas tribal loyalty is an accomplished and ingrained fact. It is therefore much easier to start with the existing tribal loyalty towards the bigger concept. This argument led Buganda to insisting on a federal form of government which would take into account all the political, cultural, social and other differences of the different tribes in the country and which would allow for unity in diversity. Upon that basis, Buganda's apprehensions as to what would happen to her institutions in independent Uganda were put to rest. Would Buganda be identified in the bigger independent unit?

8. That question of identity looms very large in the politics of Uganda. The Prime Minister of Uganda, Dr Milton Obote, clearly recognized this in 1961 just before independence when he sympathized with Buganda's cause, which he supported at the London Constitutional Conference. At

222

that Conference, Buganda received more or less what it wanted and in recognition of Dr Obote's support, he was then in the Opposition, Buganda decided to have all its 21 representative members of the National Assembly in alliance with Dr Obote's party, the Uganda People's Congress (UPC). When independence came in October 1962, members of Kabaka Yekka (KY) Buganda's main party together with UPC formed a government with Dr Obote as Prime Minister.

9. Dr Obote comes from Lango, he belongs to the Nilotic Group. The Baganda supported him, nevertheless, because he seemed to them to appreciate their anxieties better than the first, and disappointing Prime Minister of Uganda, Mr Benedicto Kiwanuka, leader of the Democratic Party (DP) who is himself a Muganda. This choice was further made simpler by the fact that it appeared to most Baganda that DP did not draw a clear line between politics and religion. The opponents of DP alleged that its politics emanated from pulpits. The party did not effectively refute this accusation which particularly said that DP and the Roman Catholic Church were identical.

10. Buganda, under the leadership of Dr Obote, for the first time took an effective role in the Central Government, and this was a very welcome sign because it meant, to a very great extent, real national unity before independence. Before 1962 Buganda was playing shy of the Central Councils because it felt that this would mean the demise of its own institutions. With the federal Constitution as an assurance, Buganda was determined to go with the rest of the country.

11. Unfortunately, the alliance was doomed, the honeymoon lasted for only two years and on 24th August, 1964, Dr Obote declared the UPC/KY alliance dissolved. Uganda's unity had that shock. In November 1964 while Buganda was intending to withstand that blow Dr Obote decided to implement section 26 of the Uganda (Independence) Order in Council 1962, which provided that at least two years after independence the thorny question of the 'Lost Counties'* would be resolved. There was no time limit after the minimum number of years but Dr Obote insisted that he had to carry out the provisions of the Constitution no matter what the feelings of the Baganda were. The referendum was carried out, while the area was still under curfew, and Buganda lost. The immediate reaction of the Baganda was to pass a vote of no confidence in the Kabaka's Government of the time, which resigned forthwith. The Baganda further thought that Dr Obote was no longer interested in the unity and Buganda's friendship; they accused him of deliberate attempts to create a breach between Buganda and the rest of Uganda; he did not need Buganda's support anymore. As far as the referendum was concerned, Dr Obote could not accept the accusation; his ready answer was that he was merely carrying out the Constitution which was the supreme law of the land. . . .

[The Kabaka however had been elected President of Uganda.]

14. The Baganda were rather pleased with this move as they thought

that the election of the Kabaka was the most appropriate one for many reasons. Some of these are:

The seat of Government is in Buganda; and the capital of Uganda, Kampala, is in Buganda.

The Kabaka, who remains King of his people, has got the most tremendous popular support in his own Kingdom. He rules over the most populous and the largest single political entity in Uganda. He was educated at Makerere and Cambridge, and is a Colonel of the Grenadier Guards. Buganda has got the greatest number of the educated elite; this is due to fact that the per capita income is highest in Buganda. Thus in 1959, cash income per head per annum in Buganda was $57; $30 in the Eastern Province and only $15 in the West and Northern Provinces.

The total African money income for the same period was $49,672,00 for the rest of Uganda and $106,322,000 for Buganda. This is mainly due to the fact that 92% of coffee which in 1963 formed 53% of Uganda's exports is produced in Buganda. With all these factors and a lot more, it was wise to have elected the Kabaka as President.

The Baganda showed their appreciation of this foresight by their undoubted support of Dr Obote. That support was temporarily received and later on rejected as we have seen. A miscalculation had been made. The stability or otherwise in Uganda greatly depends on the political climate in Buganda which has been called the heart of Uganda.

15. Against this rather sketchy backdrop we can now proceed with the events which have so far culminated in the temporary suspension of the Constitution by the Prime Minister on 24th February, 1966. . . .

35. On 22nd February, 1966, out of the clear blue came the following bolt. The Prime Minister made a 130 word public statement saying:

'In the interest of national stability and public security and tranquility, I have today – the 22nd day of February 1966, taken over all powers of the Government of Uganda. . . .'

41. On 24th February, 1966, the Prime Minister suspended the Constitution with effect from 7 p.m. on that day. . . .

50. In the early evening of 3rd March, 1966, Dr Obote made a nation-wide TV and Radio broadcast. He accused the President, Sir Edward Mutesa, of [various] misdemeanors in justification of the suspension of the Constitution and the abolition of the offices of the President and the Vice-President. . . .

53. On 4th March, 1966, the President broke silence and published [a] letter he had written to the Prime Minister on 3rd March, 1966.

P.M.

Your endeavours to introduce a totalitarian regime in this country, in complete violation of the Constitution of Uganda, which endeavours culminated in your announcement last night, have got no support of the people of this country. You must be aware of this yourself.

Your intentions are now clear, they are not motivated by the sense of service to one's own country. You would otherwise realize that the happiness and prosperity of Uganda are being jeopardized by your unconstitutional actions, which you have been pursuing single-handed since the 22nd February, 1966. The public in this country and abroad that believes in representative democracy will never recognize the fact of your usurpation of the powers which the Constitution clearly vests in the President whose election is by Parliament and by nobody else. I myself cannot be a party to your present illegal exercise. I would like to add this further point – that your current conduct is very harmful to the cause of our brothers in the rest of Africa where every wrong step we take out here adds to their already unbearable burden. The existing tensions in the whole world today demand that we do our utmost best to reduce them instead of adding to them in any manner.

I should be failing in my duty if I left you in the slightest doubt that the people of this country would ever accept these, your unconstitutional measures.

There are far too many warnings elsewhere already for anybody to think that our people can ever acquiesce in this insult of their intelligence.

Please read this letter alongside mine of 28th February.

(Sgd.) Mutesa
President

– from *Sir Edward's Appeal to the Secretary General of the UNO – Uganda's Constitutional Crisis of* 1966.

Lost Counties: counties held by Buganda between 1895 and 1964, previously and subsequently part of neighbouring Bunyoro.

62. PAST AND FUTURE, 1966

*Erisa Kironde,** 'Uganda, Buganda and Elections'*, The People, *17 December 1966.*

Over the last three weeks, *The People* has carried headlines that have disturbed many, particularly in view of previous statements by members of Government.

For those with short memories, the headlines have been: 'Elections are not needed', followed by 'Government will Use its Power in a Revolutionary manner', and last week *The People* screamed: 'Scrap Parliamentary Democracy.'

As a Muganda member of the UPC who will not deny either, I would like to express a dissenting view by insisting on an essential corollary of power.

Politically, Buganda went bankrupt. Buganda had been, as a matter of fact, living on its political overdraft for much too long and it was purely a matter of time before her establishment, not the people, led her into liquidation.

A tiny, tiny tribe trying to hold to ransom a small, land-locked country in the middle of Africa could live in the world of political fantasy under a benign, alien imperial power with extensive global resources.

Under a national government with very limited resources this just could not be sustained and it is not as if we were not warned. During the period of threatened secession in 1961, David Apter wrote, in his *The Political Kingdom of Uganda*:

> Perhaps the greatest danger is that the Buganda Government will retreat from its ultimatum [which it did do] in favour of temporarily joining with the other people of Uganda [do you remember the UPC/-KY Alliance?] in constitutional negotiations [London 1961, October] that will lead the entire country to independence. [9 October 1962]. Biding her time until the last link is severed and the Agreement dissolved by the official ending of the tie with Britain, Buganda can then either attempt to dominate the entire country, putting the Kabaka forward as king of Uganda, or, failing that, declare her independence from Uganda at some future time, even at the risk of civil war. [1966] [... the brackets are mine].

Ironically, in the preface Apter writes 'Although he disagrees with many of my conclusions, I am heavily indebted to Mr A. Kalule Sempa. ...' Obviously our evil genius was already at work if such a highly placed official of the Buganda establishment could ignore such explicit warnings.

First intimations of political bankruptcy was when, in spite of promises to the contrary from the establishment, two of Buganda's counties passed democratically to Bunyoro in 1964. Ordinary Baganda were disillusioned and Kintu's government collapsed.

The second and final disillusionment has been this year. If only the Buganda establishment had heeded the moral of Aesop's fable of the frog who, hearing of an animal much larger than himself, the cow, puffed himself up until he burst.

We are not, after all, a small nation like the Welsh. No, only much smaller.

If, as the M.P. for West Nile and Madi says elections are not needed the reason must not be because of the more urgent need in the eradication of disease, ignorance and poverty.

The non-urgency might be because of the present emergency in Buganda but why should this affect elections in Bugisu, Karamoja or West Nile? Some of us who participated, however humbly, in the independence struggle on the platform of democracy must have serious misgivings when the Minister of Defence and, more importantly, the Acting Secretary-General of our party states that we must scrap Parliamentary Democracy.

How can we then expect to retain the moral platform of our attack on Smith in Rhodesia or Vorster in South Africa?

Anil Clerk, a Hindoo Ugandan is quoted as advocating that feudal monarchies must be abolished.

I admit that the machinations of the Mengo establishment did get Uganda on the verge of civil war, but what makes the kingdoms of Bunyoro, Ankole and Toro feudal, or how have they interfered with the orderly progress of Uganda.

The President has stated that Uganda has no quarrel with these kingdoms and, more important, the UPC constitution, on which the government was returned nationally, states in its Aims and Objects 3 (ii) that the UPC will 'uphold the dignity and prestige of the hereditary rulers and other heads of the African Governments'.

Scrapping for scrapping's sake can easily result in the scrapping of churches and Hindoo temples and I am certain this would not please my friend Clerk.

A historical figure who has had some influence on human thought and progress over the years is reputed as having said that 'Man shall not live by bread alone' and neither can Uganda live entirely by the eradication of ignorance, poverty and disease.

In my view what is needed is an urgent revamping of Buganda's institutions just to the extent at which Buganda can never blackmail Uganda again.

The system has been unfair if scholarships and chieftainships could only go to bona fide Baganda whereas many counties have more non-Baganda taxpayers than Baganda.

Many of these people have been settled in Buganda for generations and must get a fairer share of the purchase of their taxes.

Unfortunately we, the public, are confused by the seemingly ad hoc reorganization of the Buganda administration.

That Mengo Ministers' salaries have been stopped but their personal drivers are still being paid will serve to illustrate.

Any reorganization must assume the Presidential undertaking implicit in the new Constitution, that the Kabakaship must be restored.

Some, many shed tears at the destruction of the Lubiri.* The Lubiri has never been the Kabakaship and used to change locations frequently.

Anyway, palaces were notoriously inflammable in the past, when they were made of clusters of reed huts which often caught fire burning down much of the paraphernalia of office.

From the time of Kabaka Ndaula when the divine (Juma Katebe) and political offices (the Kabakas) were separated, Kabakas too were changed if the incumbent went politically bankrupt.

New paraphernalia of office were hastily made and given the traditions they were supposed to embody.

As it is, the most important symbol of office, the Mujaguzo, was never kept in the Lubiri but in a village in Bulemezi where it is today.

All this leads me back to the second headline which stated that Government will use its powers in a revolutionary manner.

Excellent idea if the intention is to recreate institutions which are more in line with the centrally identified requirements of the country as a whole.

At no date in the future should a single unit, I repeat, be in a position to hold the whole of Uganda to ransom.

This was the main fault, in my view, of the green book which was rightly abolished this year.

There must be a supreme authority responsible for the country as a whole. And responsible to the country as a whole. This is why I disagree that Democracy must be scrapped or that elections are not needed. The supreme authority is Parliament. But Parliament too, for its own sake and health, must have a check in the mandate of the people. Us.

It would be fatal for Uganda if we, the people, abdicated our right to question statements made by our parliamentarians.

I therefore humbly suggest that as soon as security permits we must have elections, that while Government must use its powers in a revolutionary manner, government itself is a tool of Parliament which in turn must remain a tool of us, the people.

– from *The People*, 17 September, 1966.

Lubiri: the Court of the Kabaka.

INDEX